ON TARGET: THE BOOK ON MARKETING PLANS

How to develop *and implement*
a successful marketing plan.

By:

Tim Berry

and

Doug Wilson

Palo Alto Software, Inc., Second Edition, March, 2001

Second Printing April, 2004

Publisher:

Palo Alto Software, Inc.
144 E. 14th Ave.
Eugene, OR 97401
USA
Fax: (541) 683-6250
Email: info@paloalto.com
Website: www.paloalto.com

Library of Congress Catalog Number: 00-108434

ISBN 0-9664891-3-6

Book layout by Teri A. Epperly and Steve Lange

Acknowledgments

Thanks very much to Teri Epperly and Steve Lange for putting up with us during this book's journey through its different stages of development.

---*Tim Berry*

I am honored to be able to work with Tim Berry on this effort. His insight and enthusiasm made for an incredible experience. The work of Steve Lange and Teri Epperly enhanced it further.

To Judy, Beth and Layne, thank you for all that you have given me and for tolerating my periodic confusion of priorities. You are more important to me than life itself.

---*Doug Wilson*

Sample Business Plans

This book includes three complete sample marketing plans.

- AMT is a computer store that is actually a composite of several computer reseller businesses that Tim Berry consulted with during the early 1990s.

- Franklin & Moore LLC is based on a marketing plan for a CPA firm Doug Wilson consulted with as they faced increased competition and further defined their areas of specialty.

- All4Sports is a nonprofit organization that offers a wide spectrum of sports programs for school-age children, after public school programs had been eliminated due to budget cuts. It is also based on a marketing plan written for one of Wilson's clients.

All were published using *Marketing Plan Pro*®, published by Palo Alto Software, Inc.

Palo Alto Software online

You can find many additonal business and marketing resources on Palo Alto's website network:

www.mplans.com

www.bplans.com

www.sampleplans.com

For information on all Palo Alto Software's business planning products visit our home website at:

www.paloalto.com

Table of Contents

Part 3: Situation Analysis 79

An accurate assessment of your market, your environment and your competitors will add reality and practicality to your marketing plan.

Part 4: Strategy 97

Establishing your product position will allow you to take your strategy from concept to implementation.

Part 5: Tactics 121

The tactical decisions you make should directly complement your marketing strategy in a manner that is practical and can be implemented.

The process of developing a sales forecast begins with gathering data, continues with making informed guesses, and then follows up by testing those guesses against reality.

This page intentionally blank.

Part 1:

INTRODUCTION

Introduction

The right tools will enable you to create a marketing plan that will effectively use your resources to attain your marketing goals and objectives.

CHAPTER 1:

ABOUT THIS BOOK

Our goal is to give you what you need to develop a successful marketing plan.

It's About the Plan

So you're looking to develop a marketing plan. You might be a business owner or business manager. You might be a marketing expert, beginner, or pragmatic do-it-yourself person. Either way, our goal is to help you get that plan built in a logical, orderly way, and accomplish your goals.

If you're already a marketing expert, we think we can still help you develop a plan. You probably already know all we have to offer about marketing strategy and tactics, but we can help you through the planning process, give you the step-by-step guide, and suggest a methodology for channeling what you know into a logically sequenced, orderly plan that you'll be able to implement. You know as well as anybody that marketing plans are not as generally accepted and defined as business plans, so the framework itself can help you get the job done.

If you're not a marketing expert, then look at this book as a practical guide to the basics and a part of the process of developing a plan. We've tried to give you all you really need to know, from a practical point of view, to develop a marketing plan. This book includes details on how to develop your strategy, how to focus on key elements, analyze and research your market, develop strategy and tactics, project your sales and build your budget, so you can create a plan that you can implement.

Regardless of your background or experience, you want your marketing plan to be a useful document that describes your current situation, states your strategy, and outlines a pragmatic approach to accomplish your desired results.

This Began as a Web Book

This publication was originally written as an online Internet book for people who use the World Wide Web, with the added benefits of links and Web browsing, as they develop their plan. It has been converted to print format, covering the same ground as the Web presentation. You can view the book in Portable Document Format (pdf) at:

www.mplans.com/to/

There are website references (called "hyperlinks") throughout the book. We have highlighted each link so you can readily access this information the next time you sit down at your computer and connect to the Internet. For example, the Palo Alto Software, Inc. website is:

www.paloalto.com

We suggest you bookmark those pages with links that are most interesting or relevant to you and your plan.

And here's a warning: if you don't want to use the Internet for research, you won't like this book. We no longer believe you can do good, time-relevant planning anymore with library research. We're not going to back up all the research recommendations with additional information for people who want to go to the library instead. Many references will be Web-based only.

About the Authors

Tim Berry and Doug Wilson are also authors of Marketing Plan Pro software, published in 1999 by Palo Alto Software, Inc. Both have MBA degrees, both have run their own companies, and both teach entrepreneurship while running a business.

Tim Berry

Tim Berry is president of Palo Alto Software, Inc. and the principal author of its software products, *Business Plan Pro* and *Marketing Plan Pro*. He is also the author of several other software products, six published books, and numerous magazine articles. He has given seminars on business planning, for large and small companies, in more than a dozen countries. His most recent book, **Hurdle: The Book on Business Planning**, is a step-by-step guide to practical business planning. First published in 1998 by Palo Alto Software, it has been republished as the manual for the latest version of *Business Plan Pro*. Also in 1998, he finished **CPA's Guide to Business Planning**, published by Harcourt Brace Professional Publishing, now in its fourth edition.

Tim has been a successful business consultant and entrepreneur, a cofounder of one of the largest companies in software, and consultant to high-growth computer companies. After graduating magna cum laude from the University of Notre Dame and receiving an MA with honors from the University of Oregon, Tim was a journalist based in Mexico City during most of the 1970s. He was a correspondent for United Press International, Business Week, Business International, and other publications.

He became head of Mexico-based business consulting and research for Business International, and left Mexico in 1979 to enroll in the Graduate School of Business at Stanford University. While studying for an MBA degree, he was a full-time consultant to Creative Strategies, where he became Vice President for software research after graduating in 1981.

In 1983 he founded Infoplan, which later became Palo Alto Software. During the 1980s and early 1990s he consulted in business planning and marketing planning to companies including Apple Computer, Hewlett Packard, and IBM. Apple Latin America grew from $4 million annual sales to more than $30 million during the four years he did its business planning as a consultant, and Apple Japan grew from less than $200 million per year to $1.5 billion in sales during the four years he worked with that organization as a consultant. In 1983 he was a cofounder, and one of four members of the board of directors, of Borland International. He resigned that position in 1986 when Borland successfully launched an initial public offering (IPO).

As president of Palo Alto Software, he has taken the company to a position of market leadership, over 35 employees, and more than $5 million in annual sales, without outside investment.

Tim is an adjunct professor at the Lundquist School of Business at the University of Oregon and teaches a 400-level course titled "Introduction to Entrepreneurship."

Doug Wilson

Doug Wilson is vice president of sales and marketing at Palo Alto Software, Inc. He has extensive marketing experience, including marketing management with AT&T and US West Communications, as well as working with several high-tech entrepreneuring companies. He is also the founder of the consulting firm Strategic Advantage, which has worked with a range of large and small business.

With Strategic Advantage, he developed a focus on the business of professional services, including CPAs, attorneys, physicians, consultants, and professional sports organizations. The marketing challenges of selling "intangible products" require unique approaches to optimize client revenues. Doug developed a one-day seminar entitled "Client Development Strategies" that assisted hundreds of people in better understanding and developing customized programs to enhance their client revenues.

Doug has created business plans and marketing plans for a variety of firms, including nonprofit organizations.

Doug has an MBA degree from the University of Oregon. He is also an adjunct professor at the Lundquist School of Business at the University of Oregon. He teaches a 400-level course titled "Introduction to Entrepreneurship" and has also taught courses on marketing strategy and marketing channels.

CHAPTER 2:

MARKETING PLANS

The exact nature of your plan, and your marketing situation, dictates its contents. You add or subtract detail to suit your needs. However, there are some absolutely essential standard components that your plan ought to contain.

The Essential Contents of a Marketing Plan

Every marketing plan has to fit the need and the situation. Even so, there are standard components you just can't do without. A marketing plan should always have a situation analysis, marketing strategy, sales forecast, and expense budget.

- **Situation Analysis:** Normally this will include a market analysis, a SWOT analysis (strengths, weaknesses, opportunities, and threats), and a competitive analysis. The market analysis will include market forecast, segmentation, customer information, and market needs analysis.

- **Marketing Strategy:** This should include at least a mission statement, objectives, and focused strategy including market segment focus and product positioning.

- **Sales Forecast:** This would include enough detail to track sales month by month and follow up on plan-vs.-actual analysis. Normally a plan will also include specific sales by product, region, or market segment, by channels, manager responsibilities, and other elements. The forecast alone is a bare minimum.

- **Expense Budget:** This ought to include enough detail to track expenses month by month and follow up on plan-vs.-actual analysis. Normally a plan will also include specific sales tactics, programs by management responsibilities, promotion, and other elements. The expense budget is also a bare minimum.

Are They Enough?

These essentials are not the ideal, just the minimum. In most cases, you'll begin a marketing plan with an Executive Summary, and you'll also follow those essentials just described with a review of organizational impact, risks and contingencies, and pending issues.

Include a Specific Action Plan

You should also remember that planning is about the results, not the plan itself. A marketing plan must be measured by the results it produces. The implementation of your plan is more important than its brilliant ideas or massive market research. You can influence implementation by building a plan full of specific, measurable, and concrete plans that can be tracked and followed up. Plan-vs.-actual analysis is critical to the eventual results, and you should build it into your plan.

Marketing Plan Text Outline

In the real world you'll want to customize your plan's text outline according to whether you are selling products or services, to businesses or individual consumers, or you're a nonprofit organization. Although the outline does change in some respects as a result, the following sample outline is a good standard for a basic marketing plan. You can add detail or take it away to suit your needs.

Text Outline Example

1.0 Executive Summary

2.0 Situation Analysis
  2.1 Market Summary
    2.1.1 Market Demographics
    2.1.2 Market Needs
    2.1.3 Market Trends
    2.1.4 Market Growth
  2.2 SWOT Analysis
    2.2.1 Strengths
    2.2.2 Weaknesses
    2.2.3 Opportunities
    2.2.4 Threats
  2.3 Competition
  2.4 Services
  2.5 Keys to Success
  2.6 Critical Issues
  2.7 Channels
  2.8 Macroenvironment

3.0 Marketing Strategies
  3.1 Mission
  3.2 Marketing Objectives
  3.3 Financial Objectives
  3.4 Target Marketing
  3.5 Positioning
  3.6 Strategy Pyramids

3.7 Marketing Mix
  3.7.1 Services and Service Marketing
  3.7.2 Pricing
  3.7.3 Promotion
  3.7.4 Service
  3.7.5 Channels of Distribution
3.8 Marketing Research

4.0 Financials, Budgets, and Forecasts
  4.1 Break-even Analysis
  4.2 Sales Forecast
    4.2.1 Sales Breakdown 1
    4.2.2 Sales Breakdown 2
    4.2.3 Sales Breakdown 3
  4.3 Expense Forecast
    4.3.1 Expense Breakdown 1
    4.3.2 Expense Breakdown 2
    4.3.3 Expense Breakdown 3
  4.4 Linking Sales and Expenses to Strategy
  4.5 Contribution Margin

5.0 Controls
  5.1 Implementation Milestones
  5.2 Marketing Organization
  5.3 Contingency Planning

Essential Tables

Even though we agree that marketing plans will vary depending on the exact nature of your plan, it is hard to imagine a plan that doesn't contain, at the very least, these four essential tables: market forecast, sales forecast, expense budget, and milestones, as shown in the following illustrations. Usually you'll have these plus several others:

Illustration 2-1: Market Forecast

Target Market Forecast Potential Customers	Growth	2000	2001	2002	2003	2004	CAGR
US High Tech	10%	5,000	5,500	6,050	6,655	7,321	10.00%
European High Tech	15%	1,000	1,150	1,323	1,521	1,749	15.00%
Latin America	35%	250	338	456	616	832	35.07%
Other	2%	10,000	10,200	10,404	10,612	10,824	2.00%
Total	6.27%	16,250	17,188	18,233	19,404	20,726	6.27%

*Analyze your market by segments and project market growth for five years. Look for the details in **Chapter 23: Market Forecast**.*

Illustration 2-2: Sales Forecast

Sales Forecast Sales	Plan Jan	Feb	Mar	Nov	Dec	2000	2001	2002	2003	2004
Retainer Consulting	$10,000	$10,000	$10,000	$20,000	$20,000	$200,000	$350,000	$425,000	$500,000	$550,000
Project Consulting	$0	$0	$10,000	$50,000	$15,000	$270,000	$325,000	$350,000	$400,000	$450,000
Market Research	$0	$0	$0	$20,000	$20,000	$122,000	$150,000	$200,000	$250,000	$300,000
Strategic Reports	$0	$0	$0	$0	$0	$0	$50,000	$125,000	$250,000	$375,000
Other	$0	$0	$0	$0	$0	$0	$25,000	$50,000	$100,000	$150,000
Total Sales	$10,000	$10,000	$20,000	$90,000	$55,000	$592,000	$900,000	$1,150,000	$1,500,000	$1,825,000
Direct Cost of Sales	Jan	Feb	Mar	Nov	Dec	2000	2001	2002	2003	2004
Retainer Consulting	$2,500	$2,500	$2,500	$2,500	$2,500	$30,000	$20,000	$15,000	$10,000	$10,000
Project Consulting	$0	$0	$1,500	$8,500	$2,500	$45,000	$20,000	$15,000	$10,000	$10,000
Market Research	$0	$0	$0	$14,000	$14,000	$84,000	$86,000	$88,000	$90,000	$92,000
Strategic Reports	$0	$0	$0	$0	$0	$0	$20,000	$25,000	$32,500	$40,000
Other	$0	$0	$0	$0	$0	$0	$10,000	$10,000	$10,000	$10,000
Subtotal Cost of Sales	$2,500	$2,500	$4,000	$25,000	$19,000	$159,000	$156,000	$153,000	$152,500	$162,000

*Forecast your sales by product or service. The mathematics are simple, but important. You can't do a marketing plan without a sales forecast. This is covered in **Chapter 6: Business Forecasting** and **Chapter 22: Sales Forecast**.*

Illustration 2-3: Expense Budget

Marketing Expense Budget	Jan	Feb	Mar	Nov	Dec	2000	2001	2002	2003	2004
Advertising	$3,000	$3,000	$3,000	$10,000	$0	$57,000	$65,000	$75,000	$90,000	$100,000
Graphics and Printing	$4,000	$4,000	$1,000	$0	$0	$10,500	$15,000	$20,000	$25,000	$30,000
Public Relations	$2,500	$2,500	$2,500	$2,500	$0	$40,000	$50,000	$55,000	$60,000	$65,000
Travel	$0	$0	$2,000	$10,000	$1,000	$45,000	$55,000	$60,000	$75,000	$100,000
Websites	$2,000	$10,000	$10,000	$2,000	$2,000	$51,000	$65,000	$75,000	$100,000	$125,000
Miscellaneous	$1,000	$1,000	$1,000	$1,000	$1,000	$12,000	$25,000	$40,000	$50,000	$60,000
Total Sales and Marketing Expenses	$12,500	$20,500	$19,500	$25,500	$4,000	$215,500	$275,000	$325,000	$400,000	$480,000
Percent of Sales	125.00%	205.00%	97.50%	28.33%	7.27%	36.40%	30.56%	28.26%	26.67%	26.30%
Contribution Margin	($5,500)	($13,500)	($4,000)	$39,000	$31,500	$211,500	$457,000	$647,000	$912,500	$1,133,000
Contribution Margin / Sales	-55.00%	-135.00%	-20.00%	43.33%	57.27%	35.73%	50.78%	56.26%	60.83%	62.08%

The budget is another absolute essential. How much are you going to spend? On what? How does your spending relate to strategy? Look for this topic discussion in **Chapter 24: Expense Budget**.

Illustration 2-4: Milestones

Milestones Milestone	Plan Start Date	End Date	Budget	Manager	Department
Corporate Identity Revisions	1/15/00	3/1/00	$8,000	Tracy	All
PR Development Quotes	2/1/00	10/15/00	$18,000	Leslie	All
Website Online	1/1/00	2/28/00	$12,000	Tracy	All
Standard Page Brochure	2/15/00	4/30/00	$2,500	Tracy	All
PR: Speaking Campaign	4/20/00	11/15/00	$6,000	Leslie	All
Targeted Advertising	7/15/00	9/30/00	$2,500	Tracy	Europe
Latin American Advertising	7/15/00	9/30/00	$1,000	Kelly	Latin America
US Advertising	6/1/00	11/30/00	$20,000	Tracy	US
Press Release 1	9/15/00	9/15/00	$5,000	Kelly	All
Press Release 2	11/15/00	11/15/00	$5,000	Kelly	All
Totals			$80,000		

This is perhaps the most important table in the whole plan: concrete milestones to make it real, with managers, deadlines, and budgets. We discuss plan implementation in **Chapter 26: Keep It Alive**.

Illustrate Numbers With Charts

Marketing is visual. A marketing plan should include text, tables, and charts.

The following pages show samples of the key basic marketing charts that ought to be in a marketing plan:

Illustration 2-5: Target Markets Chart

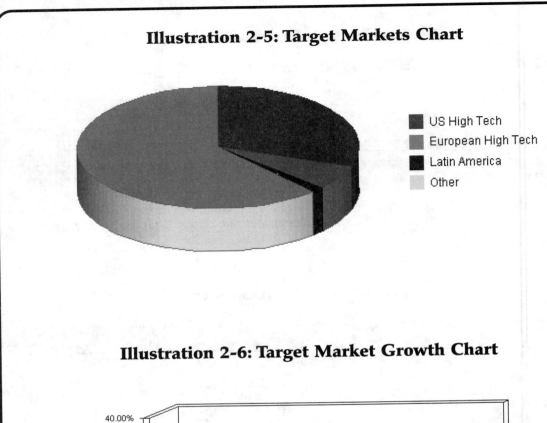

- US High Tech
- European High Tech
- Latin America
- Other

Illustration 2-6: Target Market Growth Chart

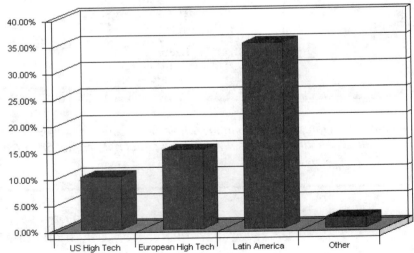

Illustration 2-7: Annual Market Forecast Chart

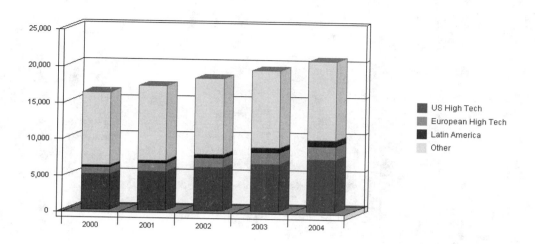

Illustration 2-8: Annual Sales Forecast Chart

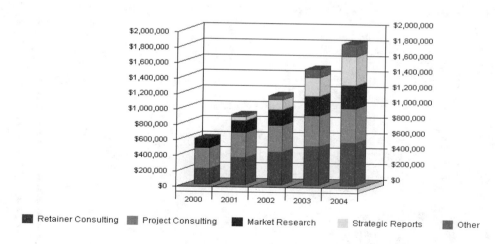

Illustration 2-9: Monthly Sales Forecast Chart

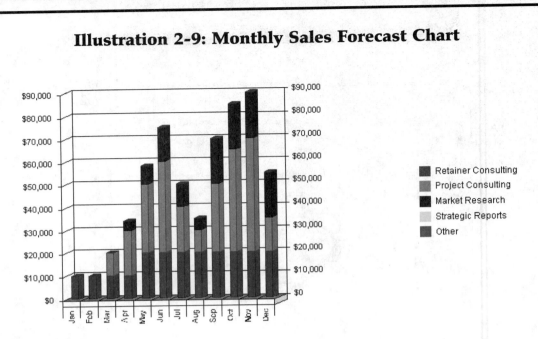

Legend:
- Retainer Consulting
- Project Consulting
- Market Research
- Strategic Reports
- Other

Illustration 2-10: Monthly Expense Budget Chart

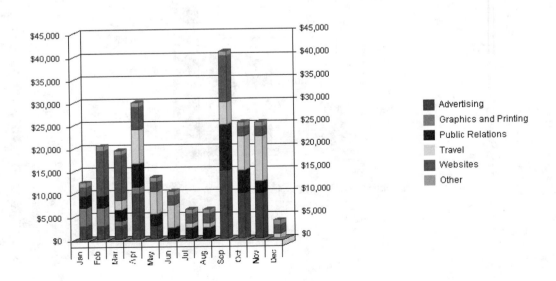

Legend:
- Advertising
- Graphics and Printing
- Public Relations
- Travel
- Websites
- Other

Illustration 2-11: Annual Expense Budget Chart

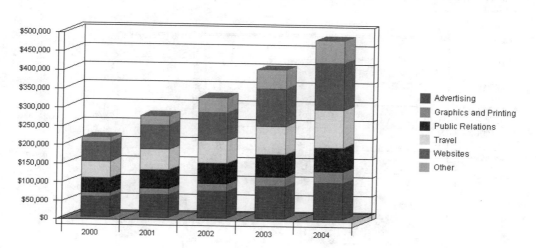

Illustration 2-12: Break-even Analysis Chart

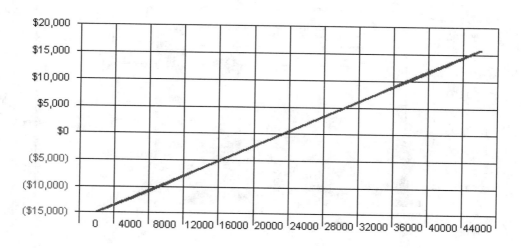

Illustration 2-13: Monthly Sales vs. Expenses Chart

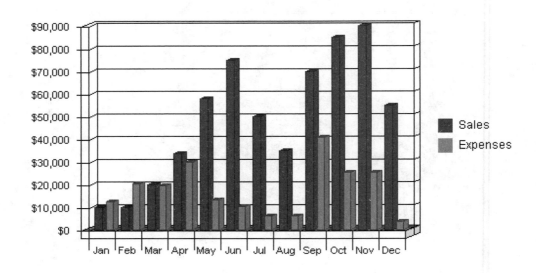

Illustration 2-14: Annual Sales vs. Expenses Chart

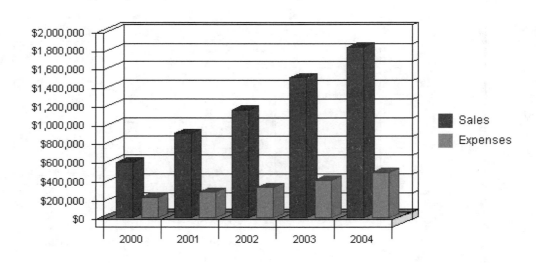

Illustration 2-15: Milestones Chart

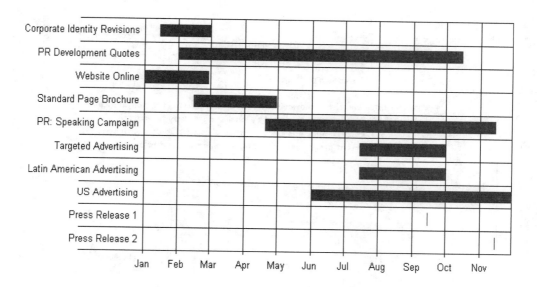

Bring it Together in a Printed Document

If you can, keep the tables and charts together with the related text discussions so that your readers can refer to them while they read. With the computer tools available, you should be able to produce a good looking plan document with text, tables, and charts merged into a design that's easy to read and easy to follow.

Illustration 2-16, on the next page, shows a sample page created using *Marketing Plan Pro* that combines text, a table and a chart.

Illustration 2-16: Sample Page-Marketing Plan

Acme Consulting

4.3.1 Expense Breakdown by Partner

As the table and chart shows -- with more information in the appendices --
most of our expenses are managed by marketing, not by the partners
themselves. Each partner has some expense allocation to deal with specific
client development programs, marketing of expertise, and related projects.

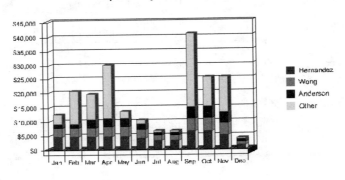

Expenses by Partner Monthly

Table 4.3.1: Expenses by Partner

Expenses by Partner					
Expenses	2000	2001	2002	2003	2004
Hernandez	$52,300	$44,000	$48,000	$53,000	$58,000
Wong	$37,400	$24,000	$26,000	$29,000	$32,000
Anderson	$29,000	$24,000	$26,000	$29,000	$32,000
Other	$96,800	$183,000	$225,000	$289,000	$358,000
Total	$215,500	$275,000	$325,000	$400,000	$480,000
Average	$53,875	$68,750	$81,250	$100,000	$120,000

Page 1

This sample page shows a combination of text, table, and chart.

CHAPTER 3:

GLOSSARY OF TERMS

The following is a list of common marketing terms and their definitions.

A

Acquisition costs

The incremental costs involved in obtaining a new customer.

Advertising opportunity

A product or service may generate additional revenue through advertising if there is benefit from creating additional awareness, communicating differentiating attributes, hidden qualities or benefits. Optimizing the opportunity may involve leveraging emotional buying motives and potential benefits.

Agent

A business entity that negotiates, purchases, and/or sells, but does not take title to the goods.

B

Brand
A name, term, sign, symbol, design, or a combination of all used to uniquely identify a producer's goods and services and differentiate them from competitors.

Brand equity
The added value a brand name identity brings to a product or service beyond the functional benefits provided.

Brand extension strategy
The practice of using a current brand name to enter a new or different product class.

Brand identity
Positions customer's relative perceptions of one brand to other competitive alternatives.

Break-even analysis
The unit or dollar sales volume where an organization's revenues equal expenses and results in neither profit nor loss.

Broker
An independent intermediary that serves as a go-between for the buyer or seller.

Bundling
The practice of marketing two or more product or service items in a single package with one price.

Business mission
A brief description of an organization's purpose with reference to its customers, products or services, markets, philosophy, and technology.

c

CAGR

Compound average growth rate; commonly used to calculate past, or project future growth rates.

Cannibalization

The undesirable trade-off where sales of a new product or service decrease sales from existing products or services and detract from the increased potential revenue contribution of the organization.

Channel conflicts

A situation where one or more channel members believe another channel member is engaged in behavior that is preventing it from achieving its goals. Channel conflict most often relates to pricing issues.

Channels of distribution

The system where customers are provided access to an organization's products or services.

Co-branding

The pairing of two manufacturer's brand names on a single product or service.

Commission

The compensation paid to the person or entity based on the sale of a product; commonly calculated on a percentage basis.

Competitive advantage

The strategic development where customers will choose a firm's product or service over its competitors based on significantly more favorable perceptions or offerings.

Competitive analysis

Analyzing and assessing the comparative strengths and weaknesses of competitors; may include their current and potential product and service development and marketing strategies.

Concentrated target marketing

> A process that occurs when a single target market segment is pursued.

Contribution

> The difference between total sales revenue and total variable costs, or, on a per-unit basis, the difference between unit selling and the unit variable cost and may be expressed in percentage terms (contribution margin) or dollar terms (contribution per unit).

Contribution margin

> Gross margin less sales and marketing expenses.

Core marketing strategy

> A statement that communicates the predominant reason to buy, to a specific target market.

Cost of goods sold

> Expenses associated with materials, labor, and factory overhead applied directly to production.

Cross elasticity of demand

> The change in the quantity demanded of one product or service impacting the change in demand for another product or service.

D

Deep brand

> A name, term, trademark, logo, symbol, or design that successfully communicates a broad range of meaning about a product and its attributes.

Differentiated target marketing

> A process that occurs when an organization simultaneously pursues several different market segments, usually with a different strategy for each.

Differentiation	An approach to create a competitive advantage based on obtaining a significant value difference that customers will appreciate and be willing to pay for, and which, ideally, will increase their loyalty as a result.
Direct mail marketing	A form of direct marketing that involves sending information through a mail process, physical or electronic, to potential customers.
Direct marketing	Any method of distribution that gives the customer access to an organization's products and services without intermediaries; also, any communication from the producer that communicates with a target market to generate a revenue producing response.
Distinctive competency	An organization's strengths or qualities including skills, technologies, or resources that distinguish it from competitors to provide superior and unique customer value and, hopefully, is difficult to imitate.
Diversification	A product-market strategy involving the development or acquisition of offerings new to the organization and/or the introduction of those offerings to the target markets not previously served by the organization.
Dual distribution	The practice of simultaneously distributing products or services through two or more marketing channels that may or may not compete for similar buyers.

E

Early adopters	A type of adopter in Everett Rogers' diffusion of innovations framework that describes buyers that follow "innovators" rather than be the first to purchase.

Early majority	A type of adopter in Everett Rogers' diffusion of innovations framework that describes those interested in new technology who wait to purchase until these innovations are proven to perform to the expected standard.
Economies of scale	The benefit that larger production volumes allow fixed costs to be spread over more units lowering the average unit costs and offering a competitive price and margin advantage.
Effective demand	When prospective buyers have the willingness and ability to purchase an organization's offerings.
Exclusive distribution	A distribution strategy whereby a producer sells its products or services in only one retail outlet in a specific geographical area.
Experience curve	A visual representation, often based on a function of time, from the initial exposure to a process that offers greater information and results in enhanced efficiency and/or operations advantage.

F

Fighting brand strategy	Adding a new brand to confront competitive brands in an established product category.
Fixed cost	Static expenses that do not fluctuate with output volume and become progressively smaller per unit of output as volume increases.

Focus group

Groups of people representing target audiences, usually between 9 and 12 in number, brought together to discuss a topic that will offer insight for product development, service, or marketing efforts.

Full-cost price strategies

A process that considers both variable and fixed costs (total costs) in determining the price point of a product or service.

Frequency marketing

Activities which encourage repeat purchasing through a formal program enrollment process to develop loyalty and commitment. Frequency marketing is also referred to as loyalty programs.

G

Gross margin

The difference between total sales revenue and total cost of goods sold, or, on a per unit basis, the difference between unit selling price and unit cost of goods sold. Gross margin can be expressed in dollar or percentage terms.

H

Harvesting

Selling a business or product line.

I

Idea adoption

The process of accepting a new concept to address a need or solve a problem and is often discussed in the context of the rate or speed of that acceptance.

Innovators   A type of adopter in Everett Rogers' diffusion of innovations framework describing the first group to purchase a new product or service.

Integrated marketing communications

The practice of blending different elements of the communication mix in mutually reinforcing ways.

Intensive distribution   A distribution strategy whereby a producer attempts to sell its products or services in as many retail outlets as possible within a geographical area without exclusivity.

J

Jobber   An intermediary that buys from producers to sell to retailers and offers various services with that function.

L

Laggards   A type of adopter in Everett Rogers' diffusion of innovations framework describing the risk adverse group that follows the late majority, generally not interested in new technology and are the last group of customers to make a purchase decision.

Life cycle   A model depicting the sales volume cycle of a single product, brand, service or a class of products or services over time described in terms of the four phases of introduction, growth, maturity and decline.

Loyalty programs

Activities designed to encourage repeat purchasing through a formal program enrollment process and the distribution of benefits. Loyalty programs may also be referred to as frequency marketing.

M

Manufacturer's agent

An agent who typically operates on an extended contractual basis, often sells in an exclusive territory, offers non-competing but related lines of goods, and has defined authority regarding prices and terms of sale.

Market

Prospective buyers, individuals or organizations, willing and able to purchase the organization's potential offering.

Market development funds

The monetary resources a company invests to assist channel members increase volume sales of their products or services. Referred to by the acronym MDF.

Market-development strategy

A product-market strategy whereby an organization introduces its offerings to markets other than those it is currently serving. In international marketing, this strategy can be implemented through exportation licensing, joint ventures, or direct investment.

Market evolution

Incremental changes in primary demand for a product class and changes in technology.

Market-penetration strategy

A product market strategy whereby an organization seeks to gain greater dominance in a market in which it already has an offering. This strategy often focuses on capturing a larger share of an existing market.

Market redefinition

Changes in the offering demanded by buyers or promoted by competitors to enhance its perception and associated sales.

Market sales potential

The maximum level of sales that might be available to all organizations serving a defined market in a specific time period.

Market segmentation

The categorization of potential buyers into groups based on common characteristics such as age, gender, income, and geography or other attributes relating to purchase or consumption behavior.

Market share

The total sales of an organization divided by the sales of the market they serve.

Marketing

The set of planned activities designed to positively influence the perceptions and purchase choices of individuals and organizations.

Marketing audit

A comprehensive and systematic examination of a company's or business unit's marketing environment, objectives, strategies, and activities, with a view of identifying and understanding problem areas and opportunities, and recommending a plan of action to improve the company's marketing performance.

Marketing-cost analysis   Assigning or allocating costs to a specific marketing activity or entity in a manner that accurately captures the financial contribution of activities or entities to the organization.

Marketing mix   The controllable activities that include the product, service, or idea offered, the manner in which the offering will be communicated to customers, the method for distributing the offering, the price to be charged for the offering, and the services provided before and after the sale.

Marketing plan   A written document containing description and guidelines for an organization's or a product's marketing strategies, tactics, and programs for offering their products and services over the defined planning period, often one year.

Mission statement   A statement that captures an organization's purpose, customer orientation and business philosophy.

Multiple-channel system   A channel of distribution that uses a combination of direct and indirect channels where the channel members serve different segments.

N

New-brand strategy   The development of a new brand and often a new offering for a product class that has not been previously served by the organizations.

Net profit margin before taxes

The remainder after cost of goods sold, other variable costs revenue, or simply, total revenue minus total cost. Net profit margin can be expressed in actual monetary values or percentage terms.

O

Offering

The total benefits or satisfaction provided to target markets by an organization. Consists of a tangible product or service plus related services such as installation, repair, warranties or guarantees, packaging, technical support, field support, and other services.

Offering mix or portfolio

The complete array of an organization's offerings including all products and services.

Operating leverage

The extent which fixed costs and variable costs are used in the production and marketing of products and services.

Operations control

The practice of assessing how well an organization performs marketing activities as it seeks to achieve planned outcomes.

Opportunity analysis

Identifying and exploring revenue enhancement or expense reduction options to better position the organization to realize increased profitability, efficiencies, market potential, or other desirable objectives.

Opportunity cost

Resource-use options that are forfeited as a result of pursuing one activity among several possibilities. This can also be described as the potential benefits foregone as a result of choosing another course of action.

Original equipment manufacturer (OEM)

The process that is facilitated through licensing or other financial arrangements where the initial producer of a product or service enters into an agreement to allow another entity to include, remanufacture, or label products or services under their own name and sell through their distribution channels. This approach typically results in a "higher volume, lower margin" relationship for the original producer, and offers access to a broader range of products and services the buyer can offer their consumers at more attractive costs.

Outsourcing

Purchasing a service from an outside vendor to replace accomplishing the task within an organization's internal operations.

P

Payback period

The amount of time required for an organization to recapture an initial investment. This may apply to an entire business operation or an individual project.

Penetration pricing strategy

Setting a relatively low initial price for a new product or service to generate increased sales volumes, resulting in greater market share.

Perceptual map

A market research based two- or three-dimensional illustration of customer perceptions of competing products and comparisons of select key attributes that influence purchase decisions.

Perceived risk

The extent to which a customer or client is uncertain about the consequences of an action, often relating to purchase decisions.

Personal selling

The use of face-to-face communication between the seller and buyer.

Point of purchase (POP) advertising

A retail in-store presentation that displays product and communicates information to consumers at the place of purchase.

Positioning

Orchestrating an organization's offering and image to occupy a unique and valued place in the customer's mind relative to competitive offerings. A product or service can be positioned on the basis of an attribute or benefit, use or application, user, class, price or level of quality.

Premiums

A product-oriented promotion that offers a free or reduced-price item based on the purchase of an advertised product or service.

Price elasticity of demand

The change in demand relative to a change in price for a product or service.

Price inelastic — The low influence that a price change has on the buyer's decision to purchase a product or service. An appendectomy is an exaggerated example of a price inelastic purchase.

Product definition — A stage in a new product development process in which concepts are translated into actual products for additional testing based on interactions with customers.

Product development strategy — A product-market strategy whereby an organization creates new offerings for existing markets innovation, product augmentation, or product line extensions.

Product life cycle (PLC) — The phases of the sales projections or history of a product or service category over time used to assist with marketing mix decisions and strategic options available. The four stages of the product life cycle include introduction, growth, maturity, and decline, and typically follow a predictable pattern based on sales volume over time.

Product line — A group of closely related products with similar attributes or target markets offered by one firm.

Pro forma income statement — An income statement containing projected revenues, budgeted fixed and variable expenses, and estimated net profit, product, or service during a specific planning period, usually a year.

Product-line pricing

The setting of prices for all items in a product line involving the lowest-priced product price, the highest price product, and price differentials for all other products in the line.

Public relations

Communications through the "press," often in the form of news distributed in a non-personal form which may include newspaper, magazine, radio, television, Internet or other form of media for which the sponsoring organization does not pay a fee.

Pull communication strategy

The practice of creating interest among potential buyers, who then demand the offering from intermediaries, ultimately "pulling" the offering through the distribution channel.

Push communication strategy

The practice of "pushing" an offering through a marketing channel in a sequential fashion, with each channel focusing on a distinct target market. The principal emphasis is on personal selling and trade promotions directed toward wholesalers and retailers.

R

Regional marketing

The practice of using different marketing mixes to accommodate unique preferences and competitive conditions in different geographical areas.

Relevant cost

Expenditures that are expected to occur in the future as a result of a specific marketing action and differ among other potential marketing alternatives.

Repositioning	The process of strategically changing consumer perceptions surrounding a product or service.
Rogers, Everett	Author who studied and published work on the diffusion of innovation.

S

Sales forecast	The level of sales a single organization expects to achieve based on a chosen marketing strategy and assumed competitive environment.
Scrambled merchandising	The practice by wholesalers and retailers that carry an increasingly wider assortment of merchandise.
Selective distribution	A strategy where a producer sells their products or services in a few select retail outlets in a specific geographical area.
Situation analysis	The assessment of operations to determine the reasons for the gap between what was or is expected, and what has happened or what will happen.
Skimming pricing strategy	Setting a relatively high initial price for a new product or service when there is a strong price-perceived quality relationship that targets early adopters that are price insensitive. This strategy may include lowering the price over time.
Slotting allowances	Payments to retail stores for acquiring and maintaining shelf space.

Strategic control   The practice of assessing the direction of the organization as evidenced by its implicit or explicit goals, objectives, strategies, and capacity to perform in the context of changing environmental and competitive actions.

Strategic marketing management

The planned process of defining the organization's business, mission, and goals; identifying and framing organizational opportunities; formulating product-market strategies, budgeting marketing, financial, and production resources; developing reformulation and recovery strategies.

Success requirements   The basic tasks that must be performed by an organization in a market or industry to compete successfully. These are sometimes categorized as "key success factors."

Sunk cost   Past expenditures for a given activity that are typically irrelevant in whole or in part to future decisions. The "sunk cost fallacy" is an attempt to recoup spent dollars by spending still more dollars in the future.

SWOT analysis   A formal framework of identifying and framing organizational growth opportunities. SWOT is an acronym for an organization's internal Strengths and Weaknesses and external Opportunities and Threats.

T

Tactics   A collection of tools, activities and business decisions required to implement a strategy.

Target market

A defined segment of the market that possesses common characteristics and a relative high propensity to purchase a particular product or service.

Target marketing

The process of marketing to a specific market segment or multiple segments. Differentiated target marketing occurs when an organization simultaneously pursues several different market segments, usually with a different strategy for each. Concentrated target marketing occurs when a single market segment is pursued.

Telemarketing

A form of direct marketing that uses the telephone to reach potential customers.

Trade margin

The difference between unit sales price and unit cost and each level of a marketing channel usually expressed as a percent.

Trading down

The process of reducing the number of features or the quality of an offering to realize a lower purchase price.

Trading up

The practice of improving an offering by adding new features and higher quality materials or adding products or services to increase the purchase price.

V

Value

The ratio of perceived benefits compared to price for a product or service.

Variable cost

Costs that fluctuate in direct proportion to the volume of units produced.

Variance	A calculation of the difference between plan and actual results, used by analysts to manage and track the impact of planning and budgeting.

W

Wholesaler	A channel member that purchases from the producer and supplies to the retailer and primarily performs the function of physical distribution and stocking inventory for rapid delivery.
Working capital	The accessible resources needed to support the day-to-day operations of an organization; commonly in the form of cash and short-term assets, and includes accounts receivable, prepaid expenses, short-term accounts payable, and current unpaid income taxes.

Part 2:

FUNDAMENTALS

Fundamentals

Developing a marketing strategy with focus sets the foundation for your marketing plan.

CHAPTER 4:

STRATEGY IS FOCUS

Strategy is focus. You have too much to do with too few resources. You therefore focus on specific target markets, on your most important products or services, and on your most productive sales and marketing activities.

Introduction to Marketing Strategy

Much like the artist squinting to improve his vision, you need to see the high points and main priorities only, or the important points get lost in the details. Strategies that aren't focused won't work. When people have more than three or four priorities to deal with, the priorities get lost. When you have 20 strategic objectives in a plan, you won't accomplish any.

Developing Your Strategy

- Focus on selected target markets.

- Focus on selected target market needs and selected product or service offerings.

- Focus on your company's strengths. Play toward your strengths and away from your weaknesses and take advantage of the opportunities ahead.

When to say no

"I don't know the secret to success, but the secret to failure is trying to please everybody." *--Bill Cosby*

"Management is knowing when to say no." *--Hector Saldana*

Notice how strategy fits into this general description. For example, our next diagram, taken from **Chapter 15: Market Segmentation**, selects target segments and rules out others:

Illustration 4-1:
Simple Market Segmentation

	Networking	Accounting	Productivity
Home Office			
Small Business	✓		
Large Business			✓
Government & Education			

Our next example of product positioning, found in more detail in **Chapter 12: Positioning**, is also a matter of focusing on certain portions of the possibilities and ruling out others.

Illustration 4-2:
Initial Product Positioning

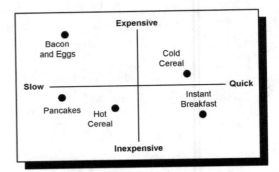

Your Value Proposition

State your business in terms of its underlying value proposition. A value proposition defines the benefit offered, the target market group, and the relative pricing.

- What are the main benefits you offer?

- To what target customers?

- At what relative price?

Some Sample Value Propositions

These examples are personal interpretations, used without permission, of the underlying value propositions.

- **Michelin Tires**: Offers safety-conscious parents greater security in tires, at a price premium.

- **McDonald's Restaurants**: Offers convenience-oriented eaters fast meals at competitive prices.

- **QuickBooks**: Offers user friendly, dynamic accounting software at an affordable price point for small businesses.

Value Propositions and Marketing Plans

When you are comfortable with the underlying value proposition, you can use it to develop and implement a marketing plan:

1. First, **understand the value proposition** in all three parts: the benefit, the target customer, and the pricing.

2. Second, **communicate the value proposition**. Using all the means you have, from advertising, positioning, public relations, packaging, or whatever other tools you have available, communicate that value proposition to your target market.

For example, the importance of communicating a value proposition is obvious in the advertising message. However, it goes much deeper. With a retail location, the layout and design of the store are communicating a value proposition. Consider the difference between an expensive clothing boutique and a discount merchandiser. A computer retailer wanting to communicate service and reliability might have a large service counter prominently displayed. Long ago, auto dealerships learned the value of putting service representatives into white coats.

3. Third, **fulfill the promise**. If you're offering greater reliability at a price premium, for example, make sure you deliver. If you're stressing customer service, then deliver on that promise. Review all elements of the business in terms of how they affect your value proposition.

Keys to Success

The idea of keys to success is based on the need for focus. You can't focus efforts on a few priorities unless you limit the number of priorities. In practice, lists of more than three or four priorities are usually less effective. The more the priorities (beyond three or four), the less chance of implementation.

Virtually every marketing plan has different keys to success. These are a few key factors that make the difference between success and failure. This depends on who you are and what services you offer. In a manufacturing business, for example, quality control and manufacturing resources might be keys to success for one strategy, and economy of scale for another. In another example, the keys might include low cost of assembly, or assembly technology in packaging kits. The channels of distribution are often critical to manufacturers. You might also depend on the brand or the franchise.

Think about the keys to success for your marketing plan. This is a good topic for a discussion with your management team. What elements are most important? This discussion will help you focus on priorities and improve your business plan.

Your Competitive Edge

What is your competitive edge? How is your company different from all others? In what way does it stand out? Is there sustainable value that you can maintain and develop over time?

The most classic of the competitive edges are those based on proprietary technology and protected by patents. A patent, an algorithm, even deeply entrenched know-how, can be a solid competitive edge. In services, however, the edge can be as simple as having the phone number 1 (800) SOFTWARE, which is an actual case. A successful company was built around that phone number.

Sometimes market share and brand acceptance are just as important. Know-how does not have to be protected by patent to offer a competitive edge.

For example, for years Apple Computer used its proprietary operating system as a competitive edge, while Microsoft used its market share and market dominance to overcome Apple's earlier advantage. Several manufacturers used proprietary compression to enhance video and photographic software, looking for a competitive edge.

The competitive edge might be different for any given company, even between one company and another in the same industry. You don't have to have a competitive edge to run a successful business - hard work, integrity, and customer satisfaction can substitute for it, to name just a few examples - but an edge will certainly give you a head start if you need to bring in new investment. Maybe it's your customer base, as in the case with Hewlett-Packard's traditional relationship with engineers and technicians, or it's image and awareness, such as with Compaq. Maybe your competitive edge is quality control and consistency like that of IBM.

This page is intentionally blank.

CHAPTER 5:

FOCUS ON CUSTOMER BENEFITS

Good marketing first identifies a market need and then fills that need. Too often we focus on what we have to sell and who we can sell it to.

Focus on Market Needs from the Beginning

Do it right from the beginning! The most successful planning process begins with a customer need. Your whole marketing strategy, from the product development stage on, is based on fulfilling that need better than any competitor.

Illustration 5-1:
Marketing Focus

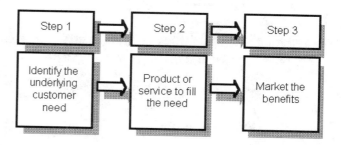

Scene 1: Business Lobby

It's a sunny late-spring day in 1987, in an office park setting in suburban California. Sitting in the lobby of a large office building, a young woman waits for her next appointment. There's a reception desk, couches, potted plants, and a telephone. Some magazines are on a coffee table in front of the main couch.

The young woman caught waiting for her appointment is early. She expects she has at least 10 or 15 minutes to wait. She opens her briefcase and starts browsing through a small leather notebook containing appointments, names and phone numbers. She'd like to make a quick phone call but can't find the right number. She flips the pages of her little leather book. Did she file it under his name, or his company? Small notes fall out of the book, post-it notes from an office, receipts from business lunches, and business cards. She gathers them up off the floor. As she does, she looks at each one of them, hoping she might find the number she wants.

She's visibly frustrated. She can't find the number she needs. She stashes her notebook back in her briefcase, and stares dejectedly at the old magazines on the coffee table, deciding what she'll read to kill the waiting time.

As you imagine that scene, think about the underlying market need. Ask yourself:

- What is the underlying market need?

- Who (what kind of person) has such a need?

- How could this need be filled? What sorts of products or services would solve this woman's problem?

Scene 2: Brainstorming

It's 1993. The scene is a meeting room in a 12-story modern office building overlooking the Olympic Park in Tokyo, Japan. Eight people of different nationalities sit around a conference table, and a ninth is standing with a marker in his hand, writing on a white board. The notes on the board indicate the ideas they've been through. Top executives might use this thing, perhaps in their limos as they travel between appointments. Of course it's expensive, so only a select few would really be interested. Maybe it would be used for some special applications, like meter readers, or airline maintenance.

They're struggling. The task at hand is a marketing strategy for a Personal Digital Assistant (PDA) that weighs more than a pound, is about as big as a running shoe, and costs $850. They've spent several hours in the room and they're frustrated. Whose needs are solved by this product?

"This is not working!" one of them announces. "Look at what we're doing. Isn't this the worst kind of marketing planning? We're not looking at market needs and how to fill them; we've got a product already built, and we're trying to figure out how to sell it, and who to sell it to." Everybody in the group agrees. They went out to lunch together, complained about the product and the project, then went back to their meeting. Eventually they had a marketing plan. The product failed.

Scene 3: A Need Filled

It's 1999. A line of people stand waiting for tables at the breakfast restaurant in a packed downtown hotel. Most of them are dressed for business, and visibly unhappy with the 10 to 20 minute wait for a table. They have appointments and schedules. Several of them peer into their palm-sized personal digital assistants that are about as big as a deck of cards. If you watch closely, you'll see them get telephone numbers out of the PDAs and dial the numbers on their cell phones. Some are reading downloaded news items on the PDAs while another is playing chess. The

PDA became a product only after it served a real market need, at the right price. The people who made money with the PDA planned it correctly -- or so it seems -- based on customer needs. The process, apparently, was the right one, and included these simplified steps:

1. Identify the market need.

2. Build the product to fill it.

3. Market it by putting it where customers can find it, and telling them where it is.

Start with Customer Needs

Don't get caught with a marketing process that begins with what you have to sell, then wonder who are you going to sell it to, and where to sell it. Start with the customer need and then design a solution to fill the need.

Features and Benefits Statements

Features and benefits statements are classics of standard marketing. For every product and every service you sell, develop your features and benefits statements. First, understand the difference between features and benefits.

The following example, describes features and benefits of a hypothetical automobile:

Features

- Six cylinders
- Four cup holders
- Stereo system
- Leather seats
- Cell phone
- 25 cubic foot trunk
- Reclining seats
- On-board GPS system

Benefits

- Prestige
- Reliability
- Safety
- Comfort
- Transportation
- Storage
- Sex appeal
- Convenience

Now consider the distinctions. Features are characteristics of the product or service, while benefits are positive values to the purchaser. The features serve as a vehicle to offer the customer benefit. Usually people buy benefits more than features. The auto's power, its aerodynamic smoothness, and its reclining seats are features while the purchaser's gain in power and prestige are benefits. Product designers create features, but people buy benefits.

Good marketers understand features, but emphasize benefits. They use features to explain and develop benefits. There are exceptions to the general rule. Some markets and even some industries are feature-driven. For some buyers computers and personal electronics have this tendency. Sometimes the features and benefits merge together.

When communicating features and benefits, always emphasize benefits. Generally the benefits sell your product (or service), not the features. Engineers and product development teams love features, as do gadget-oriented buyers, but benefits sell while features really just deliver benefits.

In the automotive industry, for example, advertising often sells different features and benefits. As you look at the automobile comparison, think about automobile advertising. Some ads push benefits, some push features. Think about ads you know and how they suggest benefits and specifically inform about features.

Benefits Marketing Example

Our first example below is **Climate Insulating Products**.

This one sells you on the benefits of the windows advertised. Normally stressing benefits is a better way to take your message to market.

Illustration 5-2: Benefits Marketing

AN AUTHORIZED 3M DEALER

CLIMATE INSULATING PRODUCTS
Professional Window Tinting

HOME · ABOUT US · STAFF · COMMERCIAL · RESIDENTIAL · CONTACT US · F.A.Q.

Commercial Window Film Features and Benefits

3M Scotchtint Plus All Season Window Film Improves Your Building.

More information can be found by clicking the links below

- Enhances the <u>value and appearance</u> of your building.
- Improves the <u>comfort inside</u> your building.
- Makes your building <u>less expensive</u> to heat and cool.
- Can improve the <u>safety and security</u> of your building.
- Reduces damage caused <u>by fading</u>.
- Read customer <u>testimonials</u> about the product.

For more information, visit this website at: http://www.climatepro.com/commerci.htm.

Features Marketing Example

The second example shows a website marketing technique that lets you click a link button, which is part of the graphic image, to display information about the feature. This may be appropriate for a feature-driven market.

Illustration 5-3: Features Marketing

To learn more about features and benefits provided, you can click on a displayed feature on the handset and a description will appear.

Numeric paging

Digital Data

Real-Time Network Clock

Multi-Party Calling

Calendar event reminder

Phone Book

Voice Mail

E-mail

Profile settings

Caller ID

Infrared

Combination Marketing Example

Intel Corporation uses a classic approach of putting features and benefits side by side, relating the features to the benefits they create.

Illustration 5-4: Combination Marketing

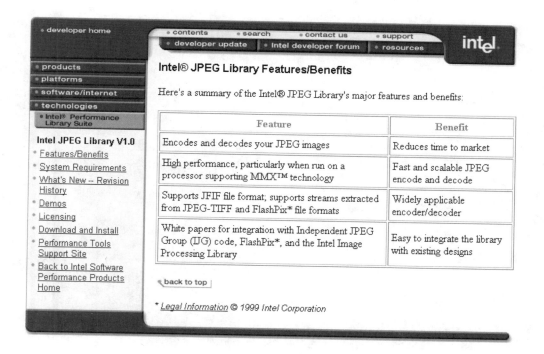

For more information, visit this website at: http://developer.intel.com/vtune/perflibst/ijl/ijlfeat.htm.

Academic Marketing Exercise

This website demonstrates an academic exercise developed by Dr. Linda Laduc, used to teach marketing:

http://www.umass.edu/buscomm/fnb.html

CHAPTER 6:

BUSINESS FORECASTING

Business forecasting is not a pure science. It is more likely to be a matter of common sense, patience, research, and educated guessing than statistical analysis or higher mathematics.

More Art Than Science

Consider the weather forecast: it's one of the best forecasts available anywhere. Meteorologists study wind patterns, satellite pictures, air pressure, and years of past trends. Each forecast is based on careful analysis of what's going on, why it's going on, and why it might lead to something else tomorrow. If a storm is over the ocean and is headed toward the coast, then the probability of rain or sunshine is a professional guess, based on a wealth of knowledge, some good judgment, and common sense. Computers, satellites, and other tools increase the store of knowledge, but they can't do it all alone.

The same general idea applies to many other good forecasts. Market researchers, stock brokers, and even political analysts base their guesses on huge volumes of carefully analyzed information. They might use computerized econometric or simulation models or complicated trends analysis. But even the most sophisticated computerized forecasting models do little more than pull equations out of the past and spread them into the future. This is a good way of considering alternatives and a valuable check on the thinking process. But there is still no substitute for consideration of trends and alternatives: the famous "what if" we hear so much about.

There are no magic forecasting methods that always work, let alone a computer program that will forecast by itself. The heart of forecasting is good guessing and the best guess is an educated guess. So use common sense, judgment and as much information as possible. Look at as many angles as you can and consider past trends, new developments, anticipated cycles, and anything else that gives you a hint of what is to come.

Respect Your Own Educated Guess

Insufficient information isn't sufficient reason for not making an educated guess. You have no choice. You're in business. The only thing worse than guessing is not guessing at all. Many people think they aren't qualified to forecast because they don't understand statistics or advanced mathematics. Relax, you can do it. More

than mathematics and statistics, you need patience and a little bit of confidence mixed together with common sense.

With that in mind, let's look at some concerns about forecasting. These have also come up and been discussed in our **Ask the Experts** feature on Palo Alto Software's business resource website:

www.bplans.com

How can I forecast a new product without past history?

There may not be history on your new widget, but there is a lot of history on introduction of new products in general. There is the standard *product life cycle*, the sociological research on *idea adoption*, and you could even use a *diffusion model* that compares the spread of new products to the spread of disease. All three of these topics are discussed in detail in **Chapter 23: Market Forecast**.

You can also look at descriptions of existing products and make reasonable guesses. Most new businesses fall into the pattern of the product life cycle. Growth is slow at first as the product is accepted by the innovators, accelerates as it penetrates the larger market, and then slows when it becomes an older product selling replacements only.

How can I forecast when I can't get demographic information?

This is a common problem. Lots of business forecasters don't have the luxury of starting with good data. Take a look at our section on *Web links for getting market data* in **Chapter 23: Market Forecast**. There may be some data that you just haven't found yet. There are excellent sources for basic demographic data referred to in this chapter.

Even so, you can still be looking at markets that don't have basic demographic data. In this case look for a way to estimate what you don't know from what you do. Here are some examples:

- You can't find data on private schools for the Mexican state of Sinaloa. But you can find private school attendance for the entire country, and you can find student age population for Sinaloa, and student age population for the whole country. Then you can estimate that the private school pupils in Sinaloa will be the same percentage of the total population as they are for the country.

- You need to know how many CPAs use Microsoft Excel. You can't get this data from Microsoft, but you can find out how many CPAs there are in the United States, you can find out how many copies of Microsoft Excel are sold, and you can make an estimate. You could also call different CPAs and ask them what they think the percentage might be. Then you could check with the American Institute of CPAs and see if they have statistics or educated guesses.

- You need to know the Mexico market for business plan software. You can't get any statistics on actual sales, but you can get government statistics on PC purchases, on small business and new business start-ups. If you know the market in the U.S., then you can estimate the market in Mexico as a percentage of the one in the U.S., using the small business statistics to determine the percentage.

How can I forecast when I can't get the government statistics I need?

Look for data elements that are available as a way to estimate the figures you can't find. If you can't find statistics on farms, look for statistics on tractors and estimate. If you can't find statistics on lung cancer, look for statistics on sales of cigarettes. If you can't find statistics on product sales, look for import and export statistics and estimate.

Remember, the one thing harder than forecasting is running a business without a forecast.

Calculate Average Growth Rates

There is a standard way to calculate average growth rates from your forecast or market data. It is normally called Compound Average Growth Rate (CAGR). You can use it to calculate monthly or annual growth rates from forecast numbers.

As an example, say I want to project the market for eating and drinking establishments in Lane County, Oregon. I market restaurant equipment in Lane County, so the eating and drinking establishments are my potential market. I can go to the U.S. Census website and view their "County Business Patterns" database:

http://tier2.census.gov/cbp/cbp_sts.htm

The database shows that Lane County had 611 eating and drinking establishments in 1993 and 639 in 1996. The following illustration shows those numbers in a simple spreadsheet.

Illustration 6-1:
Collect Prior Year Data

Potential Customers	1993	1996
Eating and drinking places	611	639

I don't particularly like the fact that these numbers are several years old, but they are the latest available and they are also better than any other numbers I can find. So, I accept the latest available census data.

To take these two numbers and use them to calculate the intervening growth, the standard formula is:

(last number/first number)^(1/periods)-1

You can see that formula at work in the next illustration.

Illustration 6-2:
Calculate Average Growth Rate

B12	=	=(D12/C12)^(1/3)-1	
Potential Customers	Growth	1993	1996
Eating and drinking places	1.505%	611	639

In the spreadsheet, the formula (shown in the edit bar) is located in cell B12 (column B/row 12). The formula identifies the last year as D12, and the first year as C12. The growth rate calculation produces the CAGR number showing in B12, 1.505%.

In Illustration 6-3, we take the growth rate forward in time. The formula in cell E12 (the next year) applies the growth rate in B12 to the last year's data in D12. You add 1 to the growth rate, then multiply it to the previous year to get the next year's calculated amount.

Illustration 6-3:
Calculate Future Growth Rate

E12	▼	= =D12*(1+$B12)			
Potential Customers		Growth	1993	1996	1997
Eating and drinking places		1.505%	611	639	649

NOTE: The $ symbol ($B12) means the formula applies to the B column, even when copied to other columns.

To convert this into a market forecast for a current marketing plan, we continue the same growth rate into the year 2000.

Now we have the numbers to put into a market forecast table, as shown in Illustration 6-4. The growth rate is calculated and applied to the future. This example was produced using *Marketing Plan Pro*™ software.

Illustration 6-4: Market Forecast in a Marketing Plan

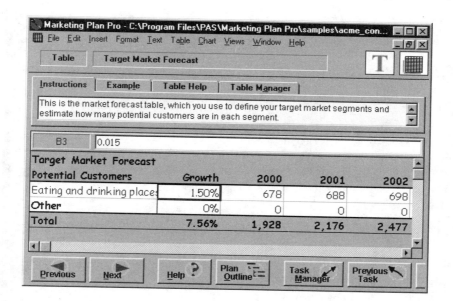

Build on Past Data When You Can

When you have past data to call on, use it. Compare your forecast to past results, and look to the past as a reality check. Understand what's changing, why, and what may remain the same. A forecast-to-past comparison is quick, practical, and very powerful. Illustration 6-5 shows furniture unit sales for 1998 and 1999, as actual past results.

Illustration 6-5:
Prior Year Sales by Month

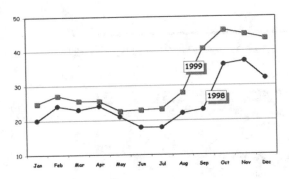

Now compare the two hypothetical forecasts in Illustrations 6-6 and 6-7. Each of them shows projected future unit sales compared to monthly unit sales from the recent past. Ask yourself which is a better forecast?

In Sample 1, the forecast for unit sales in Year 2000 seems unrealistic. Why are sales so high early in the year, when they haven't been like that in the past?

Why would sales go down toward the end of the year? You would want to ask the forecaster what causes these radical changes.

Illustration 6-6:
Monthly Sales Forecast - Sample 1

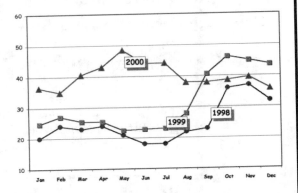

Illustration 6-7:
Sales Forecast by Month - Sample 2

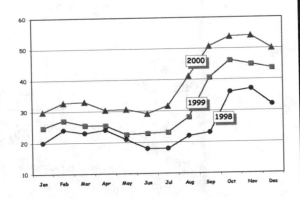

In Sample 2, the Year 2000 forecast seems immediately more logical. Notice how closely it follows the previous years' results. This is an obvious application of common sense in forecasting.

Use past history where possible to help you forecast your future sales. But don't let the lack of history keep you from making your best guess.

Graphics as Forecasting Tools

Business charts are more than just pretty pictures; they are an excellent tool for understanding and estimating numbers. Most people can see numbers better in charts because they sense the relative size of shapes better than they sense numbers. In the monthly sales forecast chart shown in Illustration 6-8, you can immediately see the ebb and flow of sales during the year.

Illustration 6-8: Monthly Sales Forecast Chart

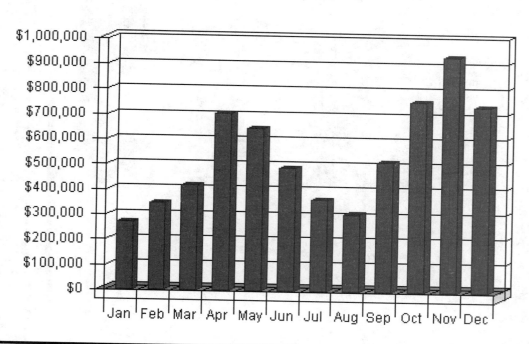

Total Sales by Month in Year 1

For another example, all you have to do is take a quick look at the way we used graphics to explain concepts in the previous section on using past data. Ask yourself whether that pattern is correct. Is that really the pattern your sales follow?

In our final example, Illustration 6-9 compares annual sales over three years. You'd probably still want to know more detail about the assumptions behind this forecast, but you'd have a very good initial sense of the numbers already from this chart.

Illustration 6-9: Annual Sales Forecast Chart

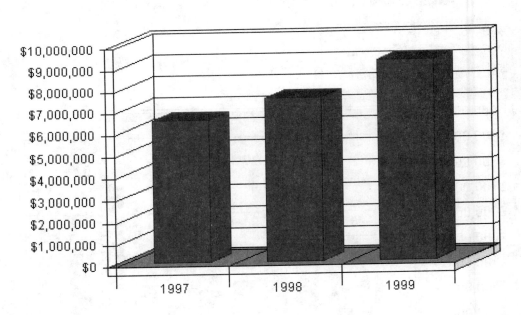

CHAPTER 7:

MARKET RESEARCH

Most every organization will benefit from even the most elementary market research. If it does not provide new information, it will confirm what is known.

Market research is the process of gaining information about your market. Preferably, this is specific information about your target market and the key factors that influence their buying decisions. Market research can be casual and limited in scope and, although it may not be "statistically significant" research, it can still be valuable. The value and "degree of fit" may be based on the quality, cost, or the amount of time to acquire the information using these practical market research tools.

Determine what form of market research is going to work best for you. Make that decision based on the value you will receive, versus the time and other resources you need to invest to gain access to that information.

Market research is often confused with an elaborate process conducted by a third party that takes a tremendous amount of time and money. It may be important to take a different perspective on what market research is and how it is conducted.

Primary Market Research

Primary market research is research that you conduct yourself, rather than information that you find already published.

Primary market research may result from you having direct contact with your customers or the public. This may be through the following types of information gathering.

- Focus groups
  A focus group gathers a small group of people together for a discussion with an assigned leader.

- Customer surveys
  · Existing customers
  · Potential customers

- Your competition
  · Solutions
  · Technologies
  · Niches

Secondary Market Research

Market research may also come from secondary sources. This is information others have acquired and already published which you may find relevant. Access to this secondary market research data may be yours for the asking and cost you only an email, letter, phone call, or perhaps a nominal fee for copying and postage. Much of it is entirely free.

- Trade associations

- Government information
  · Federal, state and local government reports
  · Small Business Administration - SBA, Small Business Development Center - SBDC and Service Corp Of Retired Executives - SCORE
  · U.S. Bureau of Census

- Educational resources

- Chambers of Commerce

- Market research firms
  · General market profiles
  · Specific information

Most of the sources listed here have their information available to search on the Internet.

Finding Information on Competitors

You can find an amazing wealth of market data on the Internet, much of it free. The hard part becomes sorting through it and determining what information to use and what to discard.

Your access to competitive information will vary, depending a lot on where you are and who the competition is. Competitors that are publicly traded may have a significant amount of information available, as regular financial reporting is a requirement of every serious stock market in the world. Wherever your target is listed for public trading, it has to report data each year.

Competitive information may be limited when your competitors are privately held. If possible, you may want to take on the task of playing the role of a potential customer and gain information from that perspective.

Industry associations, industry publications, media coverage, information from the financial community, and their own marketing materials and websites may be good resources to identify these factors and "rate" the performance of each competitor.

Where to Find Information on the Internet

The next few sections will present many websites sponsored by a variety of organizations that can provide you with almost all the business information you'll need for your marketing plan. These provide a beginning, a jump off place for more in-depth research. We'll refer to these sources in several chapters in this book, so we suggest you bookmark this page right now for easy future reference.

Market Data for the United States

Here are sites that provide excellent data within the United States:

* U.S. Census Cendata:

  http://www.census.gov/econ/www/index.html

  This page has a menu of available reports that include reports on different manufacturing industries, county-specific economic surveys, and others. You can even get 1996 business patterns for a specific zip code. Each of those includes detailed numbers and sizes of business of every type.

- Dow Jones Business Directory:

  http://dowjones.com/index_aboutdow.htm

  Factiva, is a DowJones pay site. If you're looking at one of the industries that this directory includes, you're in luck. It will give you excellent information on that industry, including good listings of websites for companies, associations, and publications.

- IMarketInc:

  http://ww.b2bsalesandmarketing.com

  Now part of D&B, this site offers very good industry data reports, sorted by Standard Industrial Classification code, with a powerful SIC code searcher. The industry-specific (based on SIC code) reports tell you how many companies there are, average sales, and employees. There are also breakdowns by company size and location.

  You have to register with an email and password before you get the industry data, but it's free.

- CEOExpress:

  http://www.ceoexpress.com

  This site provides an excellent compilation of additional sites you might want to try.

Market Data for Other Countries

As the power of the Internet spreads throughout the world, demographic and economic statistics are becoming more available. If you're working on market data for your own country, check with your local business development agencies, business schools, and industry trade associations for help in finding the information you need. These Web links might also help:

- Web links for international economics:

  http://rfe.wustl.edu/

  This site has a good list of statistical availability for several countries.

- Statistical data locators:

  http://www.ntu.edu.sg/library/home

  This is another good collection of statistical and economic sources from different countries and regions.

- United Nations Statistics Division:

  http://unstats.un.org/Depts/unsd/

  This site also has a list of national sources within different countries.

  http://unstats.un.org/unsd/methods/inter-natlinks/refs3.htm

U.S. Websites for Market Data on Other Countries

Although you should always check locally first, there are some U.S.-oriented sites that offer data for other countries and other markets.

- U.S. Census:

  http://www.census.gov/foreign-trade/www/

  Their Cendata site includes an international trade report on U.S. trade with different countries.

- Department of Commerce

  http://www.ita.doc.gov/

  This international information site has a collection of data sources, including the country business reports.

- Yahoo.com

  http://dir.yahoo.com/
  Business_and_Economy/
  Trade/Statistics/

  A list of international trade data available within the U.S. can be found here.

Web Links for Fundamental Demographic Data

There seems to be no way to keep up and catalog the ever-growing abundance of marketing information on the World Wide Web.

Your first quest in market research is for your fundamental demographics. That means the basic numbers. How many is very important. At what growth rate?

Fundamental Demographics for the United States

If you are operating in the United States, your first stop should be the U.S. Census Bureau:

http://www.census.gov/

Here are some specific search examples that can help you find your way:

NOTE: All website addresses were tested at the time of printing, but websites change often. If any of the links described don't work, please send an email to: authors@paloalto.com.

Illustration 7-1: U.S. Census Main Page

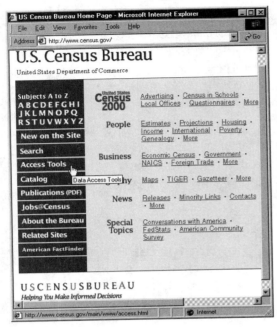

Illustration 7-2: U.S. Census Data Access Tools Page

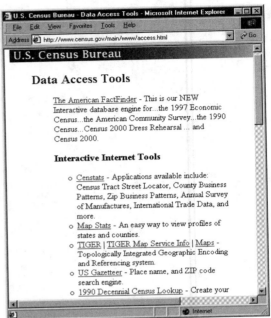

State and County Demographic Profiles Search

- From the main page, click the Data Access Tools link, as shown in Illustration 7-1.

- That brings you to the Data Access Tools page, shown in Illustration 7-2. From the Interactive Internet Tools section, click on the Map Stats link.

- This takes you to the demographic profiles page, which shows a map of the United States, seen in Illustration 7-3.

- Click on your state on the map, and then on your county within the state. You'll end up with a selection of specific data reports for your specific county.

Statistical Reports Search

- From the Census main page, click on the Data Access Tools link, shown in Illustration 7-1.

- From the Data Access Tools page shown in Illustration 7-2, click on the Censtats link.

Illustration 7-3: U.S. Census Map Statistics

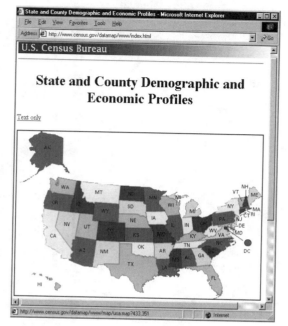

Illustration 7-4: U.S. Census Censtats Page

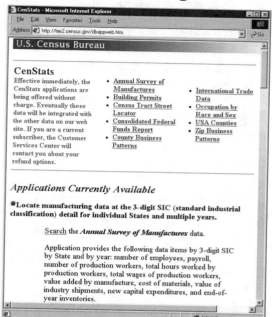

- The link takes you to the Censtats page, shown in Illustration 7-4. It includes a menu of reports on manufacturing industries, economic surveys by county, and others. You can even get 1996 business patterns for a specific ZIP code.

U.S. Census data will be extensive, comprehensive, and somewhat out of date. Frankly, this data doesn't change fast enough to make the Census dates a problem for standard demographic information. Growth rates are low, and industries are accustomed to turning to Census data whenever it is available.

Fundamental Demographics for Other Countries

Demographic and economic statistics are becoming more available throughout the world, as the power of the Internet spreads. If you're working on market data for your own country, please don't assume you can't get statistics where you are. Check with your local business development agencies, business schools, and industry trade associations for help in finding the information you need. The following are additional websites which might also be helpful:

- Resources for Economists:

    http://rfe.wustl.edu/Data/World/index.html

    This site includes Web links for international economics and has a good list of statistical availability for several countries.

- Statistical Data Locators:

    http://www.ntu.edu.sg/Library/Collections/Databases/

    This site is another good collection of statistical and economic sources from different countries and regions.

- United Nations Statistics Division:

    http://unstats.un.org/Depts/unsd/

    This site has a U.N. collection of statistics and sources, and also a good list of national sources within different countries.

    Although you should always check locally first, there are some U.S.-oriented sites that offer data for other countries and other markets.

- U.S. Census/International Trade Report:

    http://www.census.gov/foreign-trade/www/

    This report outlines U.S. trade with different countries.

- Yahoo.com Trade Statistics Search:

    http://dir.yahoo.com/Business_and_Economy/Trade/Statistics/

    This search list includes statistics from the National Trade Data Bank, U.S. Imports and Exports History, International Trade Statistics, and other trade-related information within the U.S.

- U.S. Department of Commerce International Trade Administration:

    http://www.ita.doc.gov/

    This site has a collection of data sources, including the country business reports.

Information from Trade and Industry Associations

Many industries are blessed with an active trade association that serves as a vital source of industry-specific information. Such associations regularly publish directories for their members, and the better ones publish statistical information that track industry sales, profits, ratios, economic trends, and other valuable data. If you don't know which trade associations apply to your industry, find out.

Look for Associations on the Internet:

- Yahoo.com list of trade associations:

http://dir.yahoo.com/
Business_and_Economy/Organizations/
Trade_Associations/

This is an amazing list of hundreds of trade and industry associations, starting with Air Movement & Control Association and ending with World Wide Pet Supply Association.

- Encyclopedia of Associations:

http://www.galegroup.com

This is probably the most established, respected source on associations. These cost several hundred dollars each and are normally available at reference libraries. This organization also offers the more updated Associations Unlimited online database of more than 400,000 organizations.

- The Internet Public Library has a large list of associations on the Web:

http://www.ipl.org/ref/AON/

- The Training Forum has an associations database on the Web listing more than 10,000 associations:

http://www.trainingforum.com/assoc.html

- "Action Without Borders" initiative lists thousands of not-for-profit organizations:

http://www.idealist.org/

The ultimate goal is information. Most of these associations have industry statistics, market statistics, guides, annual references, and other industry-specific information. Many provide business ratios by region or by comparable business size. As you find possible associations, contact them or visit their websites to see what information they have available. Most have directories of industry participants. When in doubt, call or email the industry association offices and communicate with the managers. Associations are often led by elected officers or a board of directors but managed on a day-to-day basis by professional employees.

Information from Magazines and Publications

Industry-specific magazines offer a wealth of information on your business and your market.

Business magazines are an important source of business information. Aside from the major general-interest business publications (*Business Week, Wall Street Journal,* etc.), there are many specialty publications that look at specific industries.

Specialization is an important trend in the publishing and Internet businesses. Dingbats and Widgets may be boring to the general public, but they are exciting to Dingbat and Widget manufacturers who read about them regularly in their specialized magazines. The magazines are an important medium for industry-specific advertising, which is important to readers as well as advertisers. The editorial staffs of these magazines have to fill the space between the ads. They do that by publishing as much industry-specific information as they can find, including statistics, forecasts, and industry profiles. Paging through one of these magazines or visiting a website can sometimes produce a great deal of business and market forecasting, and economic information.

Finding the Right Publications

If you don't already know what magazines focus on your business area, then the best place to start looking is on the Internet:

- Yahoo.com listing of magazines:

  http://dir.yahoo.com/News_and_Media/Magazines/

- Ulrich's International Periodicals Directory:

  http://www.ulrichsweb.com/ulrichsweb/

An R.R. Bowker website, this is probably the most established and respected source on associations and one of the largest listings of magazines. It is also available in hard copy (ask your library reference section, because it's expensive) as well as online.

- Audit Bureau of Circulation:

  http://www.accessabc.com/

This is another source you can look for in library reference. If you have any association with an advertising agency, ask them to loan it to you for a few hours.

For traditional printed directories, several good reference sources list magazines, journals, and other publications. They also offer indexes to published articles which you can use to search for the exact references you need. These will be kept in the reference section of most libraries.

- Readers Guide to Periodical Literature:

http://www.hwwilson.com

Published by H.W. Wilson of New York, this guide indexes popular magazines. It is also available in most library reference sections.

- Business Periodicals Index:

Also published by H.W. Wilson of New York, this is an index of business magazines and journals only.

Getting the Information

Once you've identified the right magazines, contact the editorial departments using their website, fax or phone number and published contact information. Many industry-specific magazines publish statistical editions and market reviews at regular intervals.

Another good idea is to contact the magazine staff. Start with the managing editor, who is normally the highest journalist in the publication. Find a convenient time to ask him or her for a few minutes of expert advice. The journalists who cover your industry are frequently very knowledgeable.

Use the indexes to identify published information that might help your marketing plan. When you find an index listing for an article that forecasts your industry or talks about industry economics or trends, jot down basic information on the publication and ask the library for a copy of the publication.

This page is intentionally blank.

CHAPTER 8:

TARGET MARKETING

Everybody talks about target markets and taking aim, but not everybody does it. Target marketing is the only effective way to optimize marketing resources.

Target Marketing is a Better Use of Resources

Your marketing budget is going to be most effective when it reaches your selected target market. When we look at the big picture and sort through the marketing jargon, the benefit of target marketing is simple -- efficiency. Solid target marketing is a method to more efficiently reach your customers. Target marketing is a better use of your most valuable resources, i.e. time and money, to generate additional revenue. It is as straightforward as that. Now, let's talk more about how to get there.

Your goal is to get to know as much information as you can about your existing or prospective customers. The more you know about your customers, the better you will be able to make decisions that will enhance your ability to communicate and connect with them.

Who do you consider will benefit the most from your products and services? Think of the people and their most common characteristics and attributes. One of the best ways to identify your target market is to look at your existing customer base. Who are your ideal clients? What do they have in common? If you do not have an existing customer base, or if you are targeting a completely new audience, speculate on who they might be, based on their needs and the benefits they will receive. Investigate competitors or similar businesses in other markets to gain insight.

Four Ways to Identify Target Markets

Use these four category areas as you collect information to identify and define your target market:

1. **Geographics**

   The location, size of the area, density, and climate zone of your customers.

2. **Demographics**

   The age, gender, income, family composition and size, occupation, and education of your customers.

3. **Psychographics**

   The general personality, behavior, life-style, rate of use, repetition of need, benefits sought, and loyalty characteristics of your customers.

4. **Behaviors**

   The needs they seek to fulfill, the level of knowledge, information sources, attitude, use or response to a product of your customers.

Focus on Benefits

One of our marketing fundamentals is focusing on benefits, addressed in **Chapter 5: Focus on Customer Benefits**. This perspective is critical to target marketing.

Pay close attention to the needs section of the market behaviors. Establishing an intimate understanding about the needs of your target market is critical. How will your customer profit or otherwise gain from using your products or services? Meeting this need is one of the most convincing points for sales to be made, cash to flow, and profits to result.

You must seek to quantify the value of offering a solution to this need. You may be able to do this by asking these questions about your products and services:

1. How much can it save your customer?

2. How much can it earn for your customer?

3. What intangible benefits might customers realize, and is it possible to quantify these benefits?

What is your customer really buying? People purchase products and services to realize one or more of the following benefits:

1. **To Save:**
   - Money
   - Time
   - Effort
   - Resources

2. **To Increase:**
   - Income
   - Investments
   - Future
   - Personal relationships

3. **To Reduce:**
   - Expenses
   - Taxes
   - Liabilities
   - Trouble

4. **To Improve:**
   - Productivity
   - Abilities
   - Confidence
   - Appearance
   - Peace of mind

The Target Market Profile

The target market process allows us to break down these groups of people so we can better understand how to reach them. One way to do this is to create a target market profile.

Here is an example of a target market profile:

Geographics:

- Lives within the ZIP codes 97401, 97402 and 97405.

Demographics:

- Married.

- Between the ages of 21-35.

- At least one child.

- Condominium or home owner.

- Education experiences beyond high school.

- Earning a combined annual family income of $50,000 or greater.

Psychographics:

- Values time and considers it their single most limited resource.

- Excited about accepting and using innovative ideas and products.

- Consistent Web users. Prefer the Internet over magazines and newspapers for information they trust.

- Increasing resources invested into safety and security issues.

- Beginning to plan for their future.

Behaviors:

- They are leaders in product selection and respond to the opinions of the "industry experts" when making purchase decisions. This group will first look to the Internet to acquire this information. They defend these decisions under most any circumstance and will adamantly "sell" those that ask why they use the product or service and why they made the choice they did. This group can be a powerful, unpaid sales force resulting from the referral network they build and use.

The more detail you know about your "ideal" customers and clients, the better you will be able to make them aware of your products and services, and how to purchase them through you.

Target marketing allows you to reach, create awareness in, and ultimately influence, that group of people most likely to select your products and services as a solution to their needs, while using fewer resources and generating greater returns.

Part 3:

SITUATION ANALYSIS

Ch 9:   Market Analysis

Ch 10: SWOT Analysis

Ch 11: Competitive Analysis

Situation Analysis

An accurate assessment of your market, your environment and your competitors will all reality and practicality to your marketing plan.

Chapter 9:

MARKET ANALYSIS

Market analysis is the foundation of the marketing plan. Every marketing plan should include a clear explanation of the market segmentation, target market focus, and a market forecast.

Essential Market Analysis

To develop an effective plan based on your customers' needs and nature, you should be able to answer these questions:

- Who are they?

- Where are they?

- What do they need?

- How do they make their buying decisions?

- Where do they buy?

- How do you reach them with your marketing and sales messages?

Knowing the answers to these questions is critical no matter who your potential customers may be. This is also true when a nonprofit organization goes into a market looking for funding, in-kind contributions and volunteer participation.

The specific research related to this market analysis begins with statistics that provide total numbers of households, classrooms, businesses, and workers in a market. These are your basic demographics. What you need depends on whether you're looking at businesses, households, or individuals as your main target groups. When possible, you should be able to segment households by income level, businesses by size, and workers by job type, education, and other factors. Employment statistics can add information about types of workers and their education and background. You can also divide your target customers into groups according to psychographics. This is your strategic market segmentation, a core element of your marketing strategy as we will see in **Chapter 15: Segmentation**.

Build Your Assumptions

While estimating the total potential market, you must make some wide-reaching basic assumptions. You have to assume a price level for the new product, a relationship to substitutes, and certain economic justifications. You have to assume that the total market potential is a stable concept, not changing annually. This assumption allows you to project a gradual increase in penetration.

Use a market segment spreadsheet as you make your strategic selections to develop your target segment analysis. Illustration 9-1 below is a simple spreadsheet to keep your market numbers organized. It helps you track the basic numbers of potential customers by segment, with columns to estimate growth rates and the projected future numbers.

Illustration 9-1: Target Market Illustration

Target Market Forecast Potential Customers	Growth	2000	2001	2002	2003	2004	CAGR
US High Tech	10%	5,000	5,500	6,050	6,655	7,321	10.00%
European High Tech	15%	1,000	1,150	1,323	1,521	1,749	15.00%
Latin America	35%	250	338	456	616	832	35.07%
Other	2%	10,000	10,200	10,404	10,612	10,824	2.00%
Total	6.27%	16,250	17,188	18,233	19,404	20,726	6.27%

Research, Explore, Explain

For each of your market segments, the market analysis should explain as much as possible about the target customers included in that group. That normally includes the segment description, needs and requirements, distribution channels, competitive forces, communications, and keys to success. Each of these might be a topic in the plan:

Segment Description

You need a basic description of each target segment that includes attributes that characterize the segment, such as number of potential customers, annual growth rate, annual spending, and market value. The more detail you include, the better.

Needs and Requirements

The best marketing always focuses on customer needs. Why do they need your product or service? What is going to make them buy? Don't get trapped into merely marketing what you have when you should be identifying a customer need and working toward fulfilling it.

Distribution Channels

What are the standard channels of distribution for this customer segment? How are they different from other segments? This is especially important for product businesses marketing through channels, but in all cases you need to know where your customers go to satisfy the needs and requirements you've identified.

Competitive Forces

Know the buying process for these target customers. What are the key decision factors? For example, some customers are more sensitive to price than others, some segments are more concerned about quality than price, and some care most about availability and convenience. In each case, those customers are willing to pay to realize the desired benefits.

Communications

Where do members of this segment go for information? What kinds of information will be most effective? Know where to send marketing communications, such as advertising and press releases, so that the right customers will find them. Know how to create those messages so that they will generate the right response.

Keys to Success

What factors make the most difference to success or failure with this market segment? Key factors will vary between segments, and may include price, value, availability, image, features, financing, upgrade or return policies, and customer service. List the three or four most important factors.

Getting Market Information

A great deal of market information is readily available. Look to the Internet first. This information is accessible, current, and much of it is free. Most of the sources listed should have websites, or publish information through search sites, in addition to more traditional methods of publication. Market research firms and industry experts publish much of their information in trade and business magazines. Reference works index these magazines and libraries stock them. Again, trade associations publish many listings and statistics. Public stock laws require detailed reporting of financial results, and stock market information sources compile industry statistics from financial reports. You can probably find everything you need at a local library. If not, you can turn to computerized database services, professional information brokers, United States' and other nations' government-supported publications.

Know Your Customers

Unless you are a new business without a customer base at all, your market research should begin with learning as much as possible about your present customers.

- Who are they?

- How did they find you?

- What do they like about you?

- What don't they like?

Use customer surveys, random interviews, feedback sheets, and a lot of common sense to acquire this information.

Start by classifying your customers into useful groups, or segments. Market segmentation, presented further in **Chapter 15: Segmentation**, can lead you to better marketing. Classifying customers can help you understand their needs, channels, and differences.

More is not necessarily better when it comes to customer data. If your company sells three products a year, the crucial data will come from these key customers. After collecting some demographic information, your company will be able to focus on the best way to get customer feedback. For example, if your company sells home and garden tools, your best target might presumably be the married, dual income, weekend shopper. As soon you have qualified the customer, move on to the surveys and complaint responses to build on this information.

Look at complaints and problems as a valuable source of customer market information. Studies show that 2-4% of dissatisfied customers complain, which leaves 96-98% unaccounted for. Can you identify these other unhappy customers? By contacting them you may learn of a product problem, discover a solution to a problem, and/or repair and save customer relationship. Remember, if they are not talking to you, they may be complaining to your next potential customer.

User Satisfaction Surveys

Consider using customer survey information to find out more about your customers. The obvious information includes general characteristics that help divide the customers into segments. Do your customers divide into groups by age, income, or gender? By profession or educational level? By type of company or industry? This information can be extremely useful. However, you may need to filter information from questions that might encourage customers to give incorrect answers, such as questions about age, income level, and intent to buy.

The following material is taken from the book **Inc.'s How to Really Deliver Superior Customer Service**, *published by Inc. Magazine:*

After systematically gathering targeted expectation data, consider using the following information to design a quantitative survey. Here are some guidelines for that survey. These were provided by Tom Carnes, of PDQ Printing in Las Vegas, NV:

1. *Obtain inside agreement as to the purpose of the survey. Too many have eight purposes, none of which is served very well by a short survey. Firms need to ask all critical stakeholders: How do you think we should use the satisfaction data? Then consensus should be reached before the survey is designed.*

2. *Keep the survey fairly short. The response rate drops significantly when a survey starts to take more than 10 to 15 minutes to complete. At 10 or 15 minutes, though, you can achieve an average response of 65% to 75%.*

3. *Send the survey to more than one contact within the account. If this is not done, you run the risk of getting high levels of satisfaction and then having the relationship ended by a dissatisfied and unsurveyed account contact.*

4. *All responses need to be confidential. The rule of research is that unless confidentiality is guaranteed, you are probably not going to get the whole truth.*

5. *Use the appropriate scale to generate actionable data: account-prioritized improvement areas. A comparison of performance data with expectations provides comparison of the most robust improvement data.*

Focus Groups

Consider using focus groups to find out more about your customers and what they think of your products and services. Most people know the focus-group technique, where customers are brought together and asked their opinion by a professional facilitator. In initial business-to-business satisfaction focus groups, we usually ask key account contacts a number of pointed questions about their expectations and how well the supplier is meeting them.

Focus groups may take more time and effort than surveys, but the interaction with the group may provide clearer feedback.

Many companies use focus groups to look at new products, or focus on identifying solutions to problems. Software publisher Intuit used focus groups to assemble people who hadn't purchased its software but were considered potential customers. It asked them why they weren't customers, what problems they had in related areas, how software could help them.

This case study was included in Inc.'s **"How to Really Deliver Superior Customer Service."** *The following is an excerpt from that case study:*

Phelps County Bank of Rolla, Missouri, whose case is included in the same Inc. book, turned to focus groups to ask senior citizens what they liked and didn't like about the bank. The bank invited 80 seniors from among its customers, and was surprised when 60 people, instead of the 20 it expected, showed up for a discussion. The facilitators broke the group into three separate groups, and ran three focus groups. Among the important discoveries was that seniors wanted special treatment, but didn't like most existing programs in competing banks. Eventually the bank created a seniors group, called "PC-Bees," that became very successful.

At PDQ Printing from Las Vegas, NV, focus group discussions with customers are videotaped and used for several related purposes. With the tapes, there is an edited record of customer responses whose uses are limited only by the firm's creativity. Such tapes can be used to:

1. *Tighten and align the questions on satisfaction surveys.*

2. *Bring the "voice of the customer" into internal training programs.*

3. *Help determine which internal delivery systems are out of alignment with customer expectations.*

4. *Develop quicker employee buy-in for any process or system improvement.*

Video focus groups are among the most powerful ways to create a sense of urgency about service quality. Employees tend to listen to customers more than they listen to their own supervisors. At the same time, video focus groups are a powerful way to capture targeted customer expectations systematically. There's no better way to leverage a research investment.

Web Links for Fundamental Data

In **Chapter 7: Market Research** we introduced many websites, along with their URLs, where you could search for the data necessary to write and implement an effective marketing plan. Those sites will help you find the data for this topic as well.

This page intentionally blank.

CHAPTER 10:

SWOT ANALYSIS

A SWOT analysis stands for Strengths, Weaknesses, Opportunities, and Threats, and is a simple and powerful way to analyze your company's present marketing situation.

Developing Your SWOT Analysis

As you can see from the following illustration, the SWOT analysis is conceptually simple. As simple as it is, SWOT can be a useful tool for looking at the present situation.

Illustration 10-1: The Standard SWOT Format

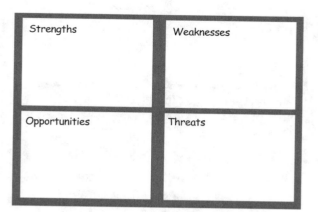

| Strengths | Weaknesses |
| Opportunities | Threats |

Use the SWOT analysis to evaluate your company's marketing situation.

A SWOT Example

This real-life SWOT analysis is taken from the sample marketing plan AMT, Inc., a computer store threatened by growing competition from national office store chains. The complete sample plan can be viewed in the appendices:

AMT is a computer store in a medium-sized market in the United States. Lately it has suffered through a steady business decline caused mainly by increasing competition from larger office products stores with national brand names. The following is the SWOT analysis included in its marketing plan.

Illustration 10-2: A SWOT Analysis Example

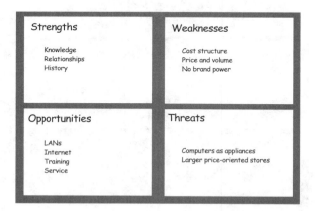

Strengths
- Knowledge
- Relationships
- History

Weaknesses
- Cost structure
- Price and volume
- No brand power

Opportunities
- LANs
- Internet
- Training
- Service

Threats
- Computers as appliances
- Larger price-oriented stores

Strengths

1. *Knowledge. Our competitors are retailers, pushing boxes. We know systems, networks, connectivity, programming, all the VARs, and data management.*

2. *Relationship selling. We get to know our customers, one by one. Our direct sales force maintains a relationship.*

3. *History. We've been in our town forever. We have loyalty of customers and vendors. We are local.*

Weaknesses

1. *Costs. The chain stores have better economics. Their per-unit costs of selling are quite low. They aren't offering what we offer in terms of knowledgeable selling, but their cost per square foot and per dollar of sales are much lower.*

2. *Price and volume. The major stores pushing boxes can afford to sell for less. Their component costs are less and they have volume buying with the main vendors.*

3. *Brand power. Take one look at their full page advertising, in color, in the Sunday paper. We can't match that. We don't have the national name that flows into national advertising.*

Opportunities

1. *Local Area Networks. LANs are becoming commonplace in small business, and even in home offices. Businesses today assume LANs as part of normal office work. This is an opportunity for us because LANs are much more knowledge and service intensive than the standard off-the-shelf PC.*

2. *The Internet. The increasing opportunities of the Internet offer us another area of strength in comparison to the box-on-the-shelf major chain stores. Our customers want more help with the Internet, and we are in a better position to give it to them.*

3. *Training. The major stores don't provide training, but as systems become more complicated, with LAN and Internet usage, training is more in demand. This is particularly true of our main target markets.*

4. *Service. As our target market needs more service, our competitors are less likely that ever to provide it. Their business model doesn't include service, just selling the boxes.*

Threats

1. *The computer as an appliance. Volume buying and selling of computers as products in boxes, supposedly not needing support, training, connectivity services, etc. As people think of the computer in those terms, they think they need our service orientation less.*

2. *The larger price-oriented store. When we have huge advertisements of low prices in the newspaper, our customers think we are not giving them good value.*

This page is intentionally blank.

CHAPTER 11:

COMPETITIVE ANALYSIS

Who competes with you for your customers' time and money? Are they selling directly competitive products and services, substitutes, or possible substitutes? What are their strengths and weaknesses? How are they positioned in the market?

Your Competitive Analysis

A good competitive analysis varies according to what industry you're in and your specific marketing plan and situation. A comprehensive competitive analysis does have some common themes.

Begin by explaining the general nature of competition in your type of business, and how customers seem to choose one provider over another. What might make customers decide? Price or billing rates, reputation, or image and visibility? Are brand names important? How influential is word of mouth in providing long-term satisfied customers?

For example, competition in the restaurant business, might depend on reputation and trends in one part of the market and on location and parking in another. For the Internet and Internet service providers, busy signals for dial-up customers might be important. A purchase decision for an automobile may be based on style, or speed, or reputation for reliability.

For many professional service practices, the nature of competition depends on word of mouth because advertising is not completely accepted and therefore not as influential. Is there price competition between accountants, doctors, and lawyers?

How do people choose travel agencies or florists for weddings? Why does someone hire one landscape architect over another? Why would a customer choose Starbucks, a national brand, over the local coffee house? Why select a Dell computer instead of one from Compaq or Gateway? What factors make the most difference for your business? Why? This type of information is invaluable in understanding the nature of competition.

Compare your product or service in the light of those factors of competition. How do you stack up against the others? For example:

- As a travel agent your agency might offer better airline ticketing than others, or perhaps it is located next to a major university and caters to student traffic. Other travel agents might offer better service, better selection, or better computer connections.

- The computer you sell is faster and better, or perhaps comes in fruity colors. Other computers offer better price or service.

- Your graphic design business might be mid-range in price, but well known for proficiency in creative technical skills.

- Your automobile is safer, or faster, or more economical.

- Your management consulting business is a one-person home office business, but enjoys excellent relationships with major personal computer manufacturers who call on you for work in a vertical market in which you specialize.

In other words, in this topic you should discuss how you are positioned in the market. Why do people buy your products or services instead of the others offered in the same general categories? What benefits do you offer at what price, to whom, and how does your mix compare to others? Think about specific kinds of benefits, features, and market groups, comparing where you think you can show the difference.

Describe each of your major competitors in terms of those same factors. This may include their size, the market share they command, their comparative product quality, their growth, available capital and resources, image, marketing strategy, target markets, or whatever else you consider important.

Make sure you specifically describe the strengths and weaknesses of each competitor, and compare them to your own. Consider their service, pricing, reputation, management, financial position, brand awareness, business development, technology, or other factors that you feel are important. In what segments of the market do they operate? What seems to be their strategy? How much do they impact your business, and what threats and opportunities do they represent?

Finding Information on Competitors

Again, you can find an amazing wealth of market data on the Internet. The hard part, of course, is sorting through it and knowing what to stress.

Your access to competitive information will vary, depending on where you are and who the competition is. As we pointed out in **Chapter 7: Market Research**, competitors that are publicly traded may have a significant amount of information available, as regular financial reporting is a requirement of every serious stock market in the world. Wherever your target is listed for public trading, it has to report data. Competitive information may be limited in situations where your competitors are privately held. Industry associations, industry publications, media coverage, information from the financial community, and their own marketing materials and websites may be good resources to identify these factors and "rate" the performance and position of each competitor.

Website Links for Fundamental Data

In **Chapter 7: Market Research** we introduced many websites, along with their URLs, where you can search for the data necessary to write and implement an effective marketing plan. Those sites will help you find the data for this topic as well.

This page is intentionally blank.

Part 4:

STRATEGY

Strategy

Establishing your product position will allow you to take your strategy from concept to implementation.

CHAPTER 12:

POSITIONING

Product positioning is another important way to enforce strategic focus. Position your product properly in the market where it will stand strongest.

Product Positioning

Product positioning is closely related to market segment focus. Product positioning involves creating a unique, consistent, and recognized customer perception about a firm's offering and image. A product or service may be positioned on the basis of an attitude or benefit, use or application, user, class, price, or level of quality. It targets a product for specific market segments and product needs at specific prices. The same product can be positioned in many different ways. The illustration below is taken from Philip Kotler's book, **Marketing Management** published by Prentice Hall. This two-dimensional perception map shows how Kotler analyses the positioning of an instant breakfast drink relative to variables of the price of the product and the speed of preparation.

Another common framework for product positioning is taken from a series of questions. You can position a product using a positioning statement that answers these important questions:

Illustration 12-1: Product Positioning

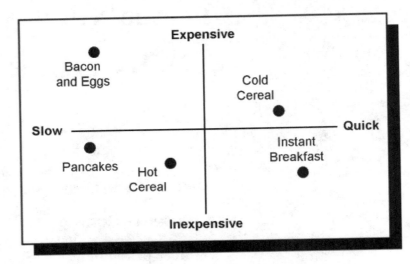

Visit http://www.prenhall.com/kotler/ for more information.

- For whom is the product designed?

- What kind of product is it?

- What is the single most important benefit it offers?

- Who is its most important competitor?

- How is your product different from that competitor?

- What is the significant customer benefit of that difference?

For example, the following are positioning statements used by Palo Alto Software to focus marketing of two new products introduced in late 1994:

Business Plan Pro

"For the businessperson who is starting a new company, launching new products, or seeking funding or partners, Business Plan Pro is software that produces professional business plans quickly and easily. Unlike (deleted), Business Plan Pro is a stand-alone product, and requires no other programs to buy or learn."

Marketing Plan Pro

"For business owners and managers who oversee their company's marketing programs, Marketing Plan Pro is software that creates and helps manage professional marketing plans. Unlike

our most aggressive competitor, Marketing Plan Pro provides a system for scheduling and tracking the entire marketing process from plan to action."

Some positioning strategies work better than others. The best positioning plays to your company's strengths and the product's strengths, and away from weaknesses. Position your product to reach the buyers whose profiles most closely match the needs you serve, in the channels you can reach, at prices you set.

Product Positioning Web Links

Product positioning is another important way to enforce strategic focus. Position your product properly in the market where it will stand strongest. The following are product positioning examples:

- Illustration 12-2 shows an article on brand positioning called **"How to be a better client advertiser,"** from the Strategic Ad College website. It is well written and worth reading.

Illustration 12-2: Strategic Ad College Brand Positioning

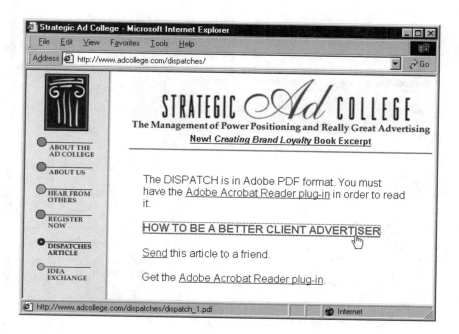

Visit http://www.adcollege.com/dispatches for more information.
Note that websites change their look and content regularly to stay fresh and contemporary.

- Illustration 12-3 is taken from the Widecom Group Inc. website, which includes an example of detailed positioning in the real world. This is part of an information piece from a copier company.

- Illustration 12-4 is a website page from Positioning Strategies of Cupertino, CA called Attributes of Great Positioning. This is a good summary and includes links to good explanations (and some sales pitches).

Illustration 12-3: Widecom - Detailed Positioning

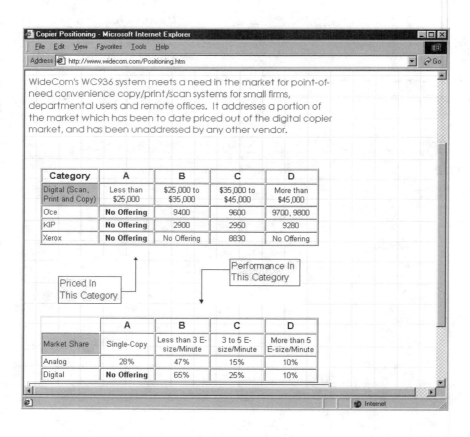

Visit http://www.widecom.com/Positioning.htm for more information.

Illustration 12-4: Positioning Strategies
Attributes of Great Positioning

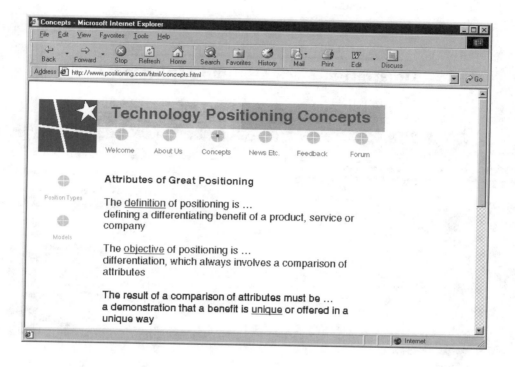

Visit http://www.positioning.com/models.htm for more information.

You can get lost in some of these conceptual models, but if you like conceptual frameworks, then take a look at their Technology Positioning Concept:

http://www.positioning.com/
methodology.htm

For the record we've never done business with Positioning Strategies and have no direct references from their clients, although the list is impressive.

Illustration 12-5 shows positioning as the art of creating "mental shelf space," posted by Dolphin Multimedia, based outside of San Francisco.

We do know these people, worked with them years ago, and found them to be reliable and professional.

Illustration 12-5: Dolphin Multimedia

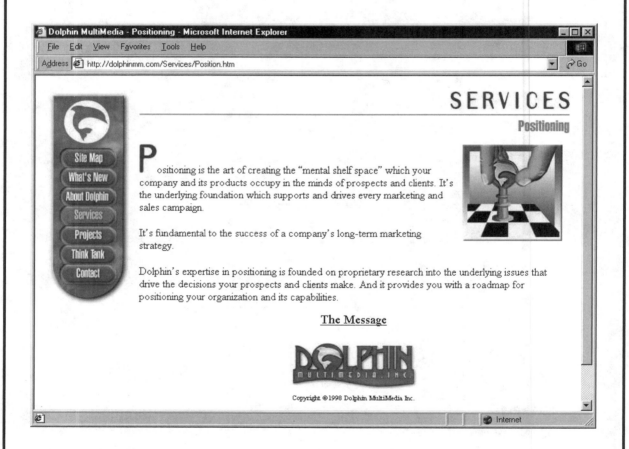

Visit http://dolphinmm.com/capabilities/identity.htm for more information.
Note that websites change their look and content regularly to stay fresh and contemporary.

Illustration 12-6 shows a page from <u>Positioning</u>, a presentation posted by Dr. Carl Mela of Duke University, formerly at the University of Notre Dame.

This presentation is now available as a PowerPoint presentation at the link in the caption below. This would be much better with Dr. Mela's commentary. Few presentations really stand alone.

Illustration 12-6: Dr. C. Mela - Formerly at University of Notre Dame

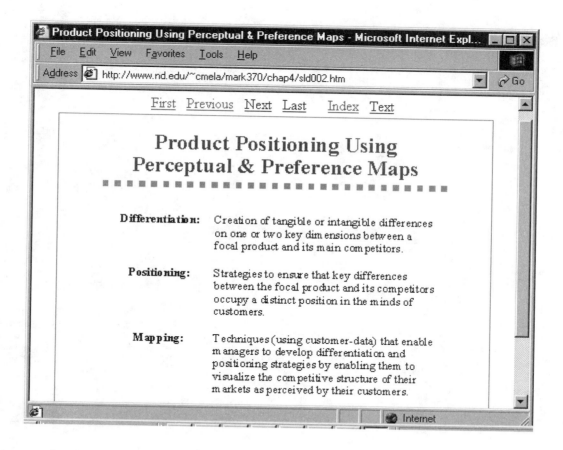

Visit http://www.dsrgroup.co.kr/upload/3_file.PPT for the PowerPoint presentation.

This page is intentionally blank.

CHAPTER 13:

STRATEGY PYRAMID

The Strategy Pyramid places strategy at the top, supported by tactics in the middle, and programs at the base. Strategy means nothing without tactics and programs to make it real.

Illustration 13-1:
The Strategy Pyramid

The graphic shows a basic Strategy Pyramid for marketing plans.

The Strategy Pyramid emphasizes the practical importance of building a solid marketing plan structure. Most marketing plans are developed from the top-level strategy first.

Strategy, at the top of the pyramid, is a matter of focusing on specific markets, market needs, and product or service offerings. Tactics follow and set the marketing message and the way it should be transmitted. Programs, at the base of the pyramid, provide the specifics of implementation. Programs include specific milestone dates, expense budgets, and projected sales results.

Strategy Pyramid and Strategic Alignment

Strategic alignment is essentially matching up your strategy to your tactics and specific programs, or business activities. The strategy pyramid is a visual tool to help you act on what your plan says you're going to accomplish.

Strategic alignment sounds simple: bring your activities and spending into logical harmony with your strategy. However, things frequently go wrong. It's easy to think strategically for a while, and hard to consistently implement all the time. For example, blue-sky strategy is easier than day-to-day implementation.

- Your key management team has gone away from the office for a day or two to develop strategy. Most groups enjoy that, and most are good at it too. They enjoy the experience and are excited about their accomplishments.

- They return to the office. The phone's ringing, emails have gone unanswered, problems come up, opportunities appear. Are they still implementing strategy or do they forget it as soon as they restart their daily routine?

As you develop your strategy with the strategy pyramid, you design the tactics and implementation programs you'll need to make it real. You develop those specific programs within your milestones so you can track implementation by assigning each program to a manager, with a budget and milestone dates.

It is important to track and measure the expense of the programs for each tactic. Does the emphasis in spending match the emphasis in strategy? If your emphasis is on one tactic, are you spending to match? This process increases the likelihood of implementation.

Illustration 13-3 shows one of the AMT sample marketing plan's (Appendix A, page 259) two Strategy Pyramids, each containing three tactics.

Illustration 13-2: AMT, Inc. - Monthly Expenses by Tactic

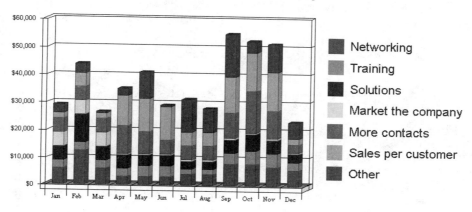

Expenses by Tactic Monthly

The Illustration 13-2 chart shows how expenses were broken down into the tactics of each pyramid. Managers assigned their budgets for program activities to one of the six tactics.

People do what they like to do. Often they twist their job descriptions around to do what they like doing. This isn't a bad thing, really, because people are good at what they like; however, it can foil your efforts to create and implement strategy. Use milestones, with dates, budgets, and manager responsibilities, to make sure your daily activities follow your strategic guidelines.

Unfortunately, strategic alignment isn't easy. Companies frequently talk about one strategy and implement another. For example, in the middle 1980s Apple Computer's strategy was focused on developing desktop publishing as a competitive advantage. The Macintosh was the first computer to integrate laser printing and page layout at popular prices, and Apple had a huge advantage. However, it took several years to make people understand what desktop publishing was, and by the time the message was clear, Apple's managers were tired of it. So while the strategy was desktop publishing, the managers focused on multimedia and personal digital assistants instead. Budgeted marketing activities didn't focus as much on desktop publishing as the strategy dictated.

That was a lack of strategic alignment that failed to support and implement the desired strategy.

Illustration 13-3: AMT, Inc. Strategy Pyramid Example

3.6.1 Focus on Service and Support

Our first pyramid, shown in the illustration, is under the main strategy point of focusing on service and support instead of brand names and computers. We must differentiate ourselves from the box pushers. We need to establish our business offering as a clear and viable alternative, for our target market, to the price-only kind of buying. We do this by promoting our value added resources.

As the illustration shows, our first tactic under that strategy is related to networking expertise. The Internet is booming and LANs are everywhere in our target market. Major retailers simply can't match us for going to our customers' locations and solving their networking problems. This is an excellent example of something we can give that our competitors can't, and our customers want. Our specific programs for this tactic include our service training, our regular mailers to our customers, and our revised price list. Our second tactic is to develop training as a line of business. Programs include train the trainer and developing of sales and marketing programs intended to sell training as a line of business. This includes more mailers, a new training price list, and special sales promotions related to training.Finally, the third tactic is custom solutions. This generally links to our growing experience with databases and SQL server applications. Our only specific sales and marketing program for this is the VAR remarketing program, but we do have an active product development budget related to custom solutions.

Chapter 14:

MISSION AND OBJECTIVES

A marketing strategy often begins with a mission statement. A good mission statement normally focuses on the benefits you offer to your customers, and links to your corporate mission.

Develop Your Mission Statement

To develop your marketing mission statement, start by reading your corporate mission statement. If you don't have a corporate mission statement, it's time to develop one.

A good marketing mission statement will focus on the underlying market needs and customer benefits which are critical to good marketing. This is normally a subset of the corporate mission, which establishes fundamental goals for the quality of your business offering, customer benefits, customer satisfaction, employee welfare, and compensation to owners. A good corporate mission statement can be a critical element in defining your business and communicating to employees, vendors, and customers, as well as owners, partners, or shareholders.

The corporate mission statement is an excellent opportunity to define what business you are in. This can be critical to understanding your keys to success. For example, many experts say railroads suffered badly in the 1930-1960 period because they thought they were in the business of trains when they were really in the business of transporting goods and people. As a result, competition from highway transportation and the emerging airline industry was brutal. The U.S. railroad industry has never recovered.

In a similar way, an accounting practice is probably in the business of offering peace of mind as much as it is tax reporting and financial statements. A medical office is concerned about preserving health as much as treating sickness. A graphic artist is in the business of communication and marketing, not drawing and painting.

Value-based marketing experts recommend a mission statement that includes what they call a "value proposition," which we first discussed in **Chapter 4: Strategy is Focus**, summarizes what benefits you offer, to whom, and at what relative price. Using this reasoning, a tire company might be selling the benefit of highway safety to safety-minded consumers (especially parents) at a price premium. A luxury car might actually be selling the benefit of prestige to status-conscious consumers at a price premium; or the benefit of reliability to value-conscious consumers at a price premium.

Mission Statement Websites

If you use the Internet to search for mission statements, you'll likely find a lot more than you want. Here are some related links:

- **How to Create a Mission Statement**, by Jack Deal:

    http://www.bplans.com/qa/article.cfm/363

    This is a good short treatment of how to create the main corporate mission statement.

- Search HotBot for the phrase "Mission Statement":

    http://www.hotbot.com/

    You'll end up with hundreds of mission statement examples. As I read through them, I found relatively few that stress customer benefits.

- Dilbert's Mission Statement generator:

    http://www.dilbert.com/comics/dilbert/
    career/bin/ms2.cgi

This is a must. First, it's funny; and second, it illustrates what's wrong with most mission statements.

Set Marketing Objectives

A good marketing plan sets specific marketing objectives. Think about sales, market share, market positioning, image, awareness, and related objectives.

Remember to make all your objectives concrete and measurable. Develop your plan to be implemented, not just read. Objectives that can't be measured, tracked, and followed up, are less likely to lead to implementation. The capability of plan-vs.-actual analysis and the discipline to use it, is essential.

Marketing objectives are likely to be based on sales revenues and market share. They may also include related marketing objectives such as presentations, seminars, ad placements, review coverage, or proposals.

Sales are easy to track and measure. Market share is harder because it depends on market research. There are other marketing goals that are less tangible and harder to measure, such as positioning or image and awareness. Remember, as you develop the objectives, it is much better to include the measurement system within the objective itself. This is especially true when those measurements aren't obvious.

Set Financial Objectives

State your financial objectives as clearly as you can. Marketing involves sales, costs of sales, and sales and marketing expenses, all of which affect profitability and cash flow.

Financial objectives are very different from marketing objectives and generally easier to measure. A financial objective might be to increase 1999 profits by 10%, or sales by 10%, or contribution margin by 5%, or gross margin by 10%. Financial objectives might also be stated to hold spending to a specific level, as a percent of sales.

Contribution Margin

One of the most common financial measurements for marketing is the contribution margin. To calculate your contribution margin:

1. **Gross margin** is sales less cost of sales. If you sell one computer system per month for $10,000 each and they cost you $2,500 each, then your monthly gross margin is $7,500.

2. **Contribution margin** is gross margin less sales and marketing expenses. If you spend $6,000 per month on advertising and sales salaries, then your contribution margin is $1,500.

CHAPTER 15:

SEGMENTATION

Research your market to know how many potential customers you have, what their needs are, and how to reach them. Then divide them into segments based on their common characteristics.

Segmentation is Strategic -- Divide to Conquer

Segmentation divides a market into workable groups or divisions. Divide a market by age, income, product needs, geography, buying patterns, eating patterns, family make-up, or other classifications. Good marketing plans rarely address the full range of possible target markets. They almost always select segments of the market. The selection allows a marketing plan to focus more effectively, to define specific messages, and to send those messages through specific channels.

The following illustration shows an example of segmentation and focus. In this example, the theoretical total market for computer systems is divided into four kinds of buyer companies and three kinds of usage, a total of 12 segments. The hypothetical marketing plan focuses on two of those 12 segments.

Illustration 15-1: Identifying Market Segments

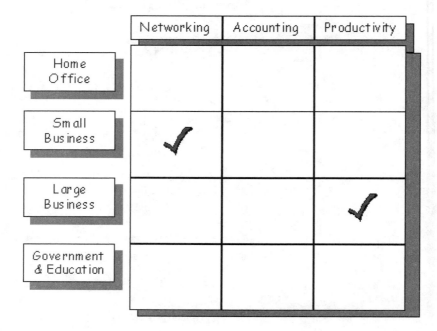

The illustration shows the general idea of market segmentation.

The segment focus leads to a series of related strategic decisions. Defining the target market quickly leads to a series of important questions, such as: What product or service offerings are most appropriate to the needs of the target segment? What prices are appropriate?

Few companies have the power to address all possible market segments. It is a better use of marketing resources to focus on key segments. Market segmentation is critical to marketing. A good segmentation analysis can be the creative foundation of an excellent plan. For example, consider how many different ways you can divide personal computer users. Does it help to focus on home offices vs. home entertainment? Classroom education vs. home education? Multimedia video development vs. arcade game users? Windows vs. Macintosh? Personal productivity vs. data management? Consumer vs. business to business? Home vs. education vs. small business vs. medium business?

Segmentation Options -- You Make the Call

You can segment a market several different ways: demographic, geographic, psychographic, ethnic, or a combination. Use the segmentation that works best for your marketing strategy:

Demographic

These segmentations are classic. Divide your market into groups based on age, income level, and gender. Some marketing plans focus mainly on demographics because they work for strategy development. For example, video games tend to sell best to adolescent males, dolls sell mainly to preadolescent females. Cadillac automobiles generally sell to older adults, while mini-vans sell to adults, with families, between the ages of 30 and 50.

Business demographics may also be valuable. Government statistics tend to divide businesses by size (in sales or number of employees) and type of industry (using industry classification systems like SIC, the Standard Industrial Classification). If you're going to be selling to businesses, then you're likely to want to segment using types of business. For example, you might want to sell to optical stores, CPA firms, or auto repair shops. Or you might have something of interest only to companies with more than 500 employees.

Geographic

This is another classic method of segmentation. This divides people or businesses into groups according to location. It's very important for retail businesses, restaurants, and services addressing their local surroundings only. In those cases, you'd want to divide your market into geographic categories such as by city, ZIP code, county, state, or region. International companies frequently divide their markets by country or region.

Psychographic

This system divides customers into cultural groups, value groups, social sets, motivator sets, or other interesting categories that might be useful for segmentation purposes. For example, in literature intended for potential retailers, First Colony Mall of Sugarland, Texas, describes its local area psychographics as including "25% Kid & Cul-de-Sacs (upscale suburban families, affluent), 5.4% winner's circle (suburban executives, wealthy), 19.2% boomers and babies (young white-collar suburban, upper middle income), and 7% country squires (elite ex-urban, wealthy)."Going into more detail, it calls the Kids & Cul-de-Sacs group "a noisy medley of bikes, dogs, carpools, rock music and sports." The winners circle customers are "well-educated, mobile, executives and professionals with teenaged families. Big producers, prolific spenders, and global travelers." The country squires are "where the wealthy have escaped urban stress to live in rustic luxury. No. 4 in affluence, big bucks in the boondocks."

Stanford Research Institute (SRI) provides another example. Its VALS (Values and Lifestyles) service offers information on U.S. customers classified according to value sets including Fulfilleds, Makers, Believers, Achievers, Experiencers, and others.

The VALS segment profiles includes an interesting graphic map of the different psychographic profiles, as shown in Illustration 15-2:

Illustration 15-2: SRI Values and Lifestyles Segmentation

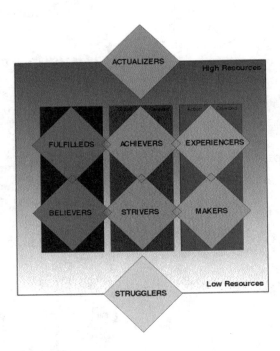

Visit http://www.sric-bi.com/VALS/types.shtml for more information.

Another interesting psychographic segmentation divides marketers themselves into psychographic groups. This analysis by Strategic Directions ends up with five kinds of marketing executives: Sophisticates, Direct Answers, Mass Marketers, Constrained, and Networkers. It is an interesting study based on understanding the various attitudes and motivations of each group. Illustration 15-3 shows a view from their old website. Their new website was under construction at the time of this printing.

Ethnic

This type of segmentation is somewhat uncomfortable for those of us living in a country with a history of ethnic-based discrimination. Still, the segmentation by ethnic group is a powerful tool for better marketing. For example, Spanish-speaking television programming became a very powerful medium in the United States in the 1990s, and Chinese and Japanese stations appeared in the major metropolitan areas.

Illustration 15-3: Strategic Directions -- Old Website

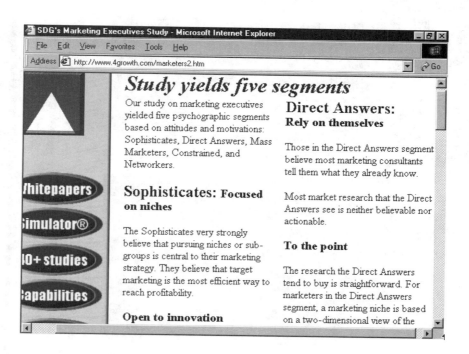

Visit www.attitudebase.com to preview Strategic Directions' founders' latest studies. Note that websites change their look and content regularly to stay fresh and contemporary.

Combination

Combining different segmentation methods are also quite common. You frequently see demographic and geographic segmentations combined -- population groups or business types in a specific area are an obvious example, or ethnic groups in a certain city, or "boomers with babies" within reach of a shopping center. These are all combinations of factors. For example, Apple Computer has used a combination of business and general demographics by region, segmenting the market into households, schools, small business, large business, and government. Each of those groups was further divided into countries and regional groups of countries.

How do you decide which segmentation to use? Look at your customers and look at your business. Think about what factors will give you the most marketing power. The goal is guiding decisions, gaining insight into which media, which messages, and how to market. Divide your customers up in a way that makes it easy to develop marketing strategy and implementation.

Segmentation Website Link

Abbott Wool's segmentation resource locator offers links to segment-specific Web resources for marketers:

http://www.awool.com

Part 5:
TACTICS

Tactics

The tactical decisions you make should directly complement your marketing strategy in a manner that is practical and implementable.

CHAPTER 16:

PRICING

Before you talk about pricing as strategy or positioning, take a good hard look at your real business situation. Not all businesses have the luxury of setting their own prices.

Understand Your Pricing Choices

There are businesses that can't set their own prices as easily as others.

Businesses that are regulated by government agencies, or insurance companies, don't always have much price leeway. Some dentists and doctors set their own prices, and some, based on their relationships with HMOs and insurance programs can not. Some public agencies and utilities require government approval in order to change prices.

Businesses that sell standard commodities also may have price limitations. For example, the service station by a highway exit that has three visible competitors is going to have trouble charging more or less than the others. Movie theaters tend to make certain they have competitive prices. Video rentals have to stay within a certain range to keep volume up.

There is a direct relationship between businesses selling commodities and businesses bound by competition. Gas stations and video stores have trouble raising prices when they have nearby competition. When they get into rural areas where distance is a factor, they have more options. Sometimes a local supplier can charge a higher price than the more distant competitors.

In most businesses there are some upper constraints based on competition. Look at most products and you'll see established price points based on competition, positioning, etc. As this is written, a cup of coffee costs about a dollar, a four-door, four-cylinder car costs $12,000-$16,000, a mid- to high-performance computer system costs about $3,000. You really can't go way over these standard prices without offering some serious additional benefits.

Even in these examples, however, despite the pricing constraints there are still ways you can influence pricing through adding value. A gas station can have promotions on oil changes, or offer hot coffee. A video store may charge less for its older items than new releases, allow five day rentals instead of one, have a larger inventory, or include video games for rent to increase its average price.

Pricing for Product Positioning

Positioning is very important, and pricing is your most powerful tool for product positioning, as we discussed in **Chapter 12: Positioning**. The best way to price your product is as part of your marketing strategy.

Your pricing sends a message. Some businesses have been extremely successful with very high pricing and matching positioning. For example, some cars with similar specifications sell for much more than others (think of the luxury cars such as Mercedes, Jaguar, and Lexus). Many businesses would sell less, not more, if their prices were lower (luxury shopping stores such as Nordstrom, fine restaurants, and hotels). In addition to offering higher margins, high prices are an important part of the benefits they sell. These higher price points offer prestige and exclusivity and make these products more desirable.

People don't always want the least expensive product. The original Pillsbury cake mix failed commercially at $0.10 a package (in the early 1950s) and then became an instant success just a year later when it was introduced at $0.25 per package. The initial home hair coloring products experienced the same. When the product was very inexpensive, people didn't believe it offered value.

As you work with pricing, refer back to your positioning statements often. If you believe that your product or service is as good as it is, then consider pricing it above the competition. If, on the other hand, your business model calls for low prices and discounting, then pull your prices down to match your positioning.

Price Point Determination

Understanding your costs is a critical component in establishing the price for your product or service. Determining the cost "floor" for your product is an important step toward establishing the range of where your price should be. This will help you understand where you can exercise pricing discretion to set your price point.

Know Your Price Floor

Pricing at the floor means that you are not making any money, or margin, on the products you sell. Therefore, the price of your product or service must be greater than your total costs. This may seem like common sense, but many business failures have occurred from not fully understanding the total costs they incur to produce the product or provide the service to their customers. When the price of your product or service is not contributing to your bottom line, you don't have the opportunity to "make it up in volume."

Understanding your total costs requires you to conduct an accurate assessment of your variable costs and your fixed costs. Your variable costs are those associated with each product you create. Raw materials and the labor expenses required to create products are examples of variable costs. Fixed costs are those costs that remain constant, regardless of the volume of product that you produce. Rent and utilities are examples of fixed costs.

Fixed costs may be more challenging to assess. Fixed costs may be allocated based on a prorated factor based on the time associated with creating the product or providing the service. This is more complex when multiple products or services are being produced simultaneously or have dramatically different production cycles.

Calculate these costs as accurately as you can to find the price floor. This exercise will make certain that you don't price your product too low and prevent you from making revenue from each unit sale of your product.

As mentioned before another consideration in pricing too low is the risk of having a low price associated with low quality. This will be based on the customer's perceived value and its correlation to the price that they will pay to benefit from their purchase. Some products are considered to be price inelastic. Consumers continue to purchase the product regardless of its price. An appendectomy is one example, but we also see examples of this in consumer products from hair coloring to software.

In addition to the cost structure, the price point may be determined by these factors:

- Level of demand.

- Degree of competitive threat.

- Impact of government regulation.

- Presence of substitute products.

- Product positioning.

- Production and distribution capabilities.

- Overall marketing strategy.

You may choose a "skimming price strategy" that will result in higher margins, and usually low sales volumes. A "penetration pricing strategy" often results in a lower contribution margin for each product sold complemented by increased sales volumes.

Illustration 16-1 demonstrates the process of determining the highest and lowest price limits and how these prices may be seen by the customer.

Illustration 16-1: Price Point Determination

Customer's Perceived Value		
Price Ceiling		
Highest Price Point		Skimming Strategy
Strategic Price Point		Pricing Discretion
Lowest Price Point		Penetration Strategy
Price Floor		
Total Costs		

Before you can chose a price point, you must research the top price possible and compute your lowest price possible/cost of goods.

Pricing is Magic

Even after you've done the analysis, pricing is still a bit of magic. They don't teach formulas that work at any business school I know of. Although there are some basic parameters, you'll find pricing is a combination of educated guessing, art, and reality plus a little luck. With that as an introduction, here are some thoughts to consider.

Having been a consultant to and participant in small business for years, I believe most entrepreneurs are far more likely to underprice than overprice. Don't low-ball yourself. If you are a manufacturing company, you should be able to calculate your physical cost of goods and know your real costs, including marketing and administration, and make sure you make a decent profit.

For example, a retail software publisher's product may benefit by keeping the price slightly higher than its competitors. However, the retailers know their customers, and this sales channel is critical to the software publisher's success. The retailers may require the products's price to remain below $100 to keep their sales volume at an acceptable level. In this situation the software publisher must be very careful in their product pricing. One criteria encourages them to price above one point while another criteria requires that they price below it.

You can research what others are doing with prices, percentages of gross margin and related information, and from this information you can estimate their pricing structure.

The Risk Management Association (formerly Robert Morris Associates) is a membership organization sponsored by banks which publishes an annual listing of standard financial ratios, developed by polling member banks, for actual business results of thousands of different companies in small business.

The RMA has a publication called *Annual Statement Studies* which is a very valuable source of information. That study showed, for example, that shoe retailers selling less than $1 million per year make an average of 42 percent gross margins, they spend an average of 40 percent on operating expenses, and they net about one percent of sales as profits. As of this writing, this publication sells for $30 to members and $135 for nonmembers, in either hard copy or CD-ROM.

You can find out more about RMA by calling (215) 446-4000, or visit their website, as shown in Illustration 16-2.

Other pricing resources you can experiment with include direct telephone sales, interviews, and mock products, to see how people react. The Internet also provides opportunity for experimenting.

Illustration 16-2: Risk Management Association Website

Visit www.rmahq.com for more information.

CHAPTER 17:

ADVERTISING

Awareness proceeds change. You are seeking to change the current buying habits of your target market, and you must determine how are you going to reach that group in the most effective way possible.

Advertising Fundamentals

Nearly everybody in the world is subjected to advertising. We talk about the good ads and sometimes about the bad ones. For some people, the advertisements debuting during the Super Bowl broadcast are a bigger attraction than the game itself. Memorable ads are part of the culture of the last three or four generations of humanity, as our civilization is awash with advertising.

Advertising is Communication

Advertising sends a message. Your advertising campaign, regardless of its scope or size, portrays your organization, your products and services, and your values. Each attribute will be tested with each new customer you acquire. This is one area of business where you do not want to take unnecessary risks. Your advertising should enhance your credibility as an organization and present you as the best solution to meet your customers' needs.

You can see from our abbreviated list in the section entitled **Advertising Options**, that the number of advertising alternatives is enormous. To sort through it all, you need to constantly relate your advertising to your strategy. It's not a matter of clever ads or large budgets. You'll get much better results if you focus on the message you want to send and reaching the people you want to receive that message.

Take Proper Aim

As you build your plan, you will benefit from your previous focus on the development of your market segmentation (**Chapter 15: Segmentation**) and target marketing strategy (**Chapter 8: Target Marketing**). Your advertising tactics should take your message to that target market. If your target is a small group, easily identifiable by factors like geography or demographics, don't spend the money to reach a large group. The Fortune 500 companies that reach millions of people use national television advertising, while local restaurants may use the telephone directory and newspapers.

Creativity comes into play here as you look for ways to spend just enough to reach just the right people. Testing with small, more trackable groups first may serve as a way to gain information and experience. Later you can use this broader base of knowledge to effectively implement advertising tactics that are tailored to your target market segment.

The Message

Every advertising campaign has to involve a message. Make sure you understand the message you want to send to your target customers. Read your positioning statement and review your strategy. Does your message match the strategy? Does it fit your situation analysis? For example:

- The sign on the highway tells you there's a fast food restaurant off the next exit. That's a simple informational message.

- The television advertisement shows a woman and a child in a car driving at night through a rainstorm on a deserted road. Whatever product being advertised, the message involves safety and peace of mind.

- Advertising may contain simple informational messages, such as name, address, price list, or location.

- The late John Crawford, former dean of the University of Oregon School of Journalism and an executive with Leo Burnett Advertising, used to tell his students that the best ad campaign ever created was "Colgate cleans your breath while it cleans your teeth." He said that was a simple, easy-to-understand advertising message that sold products.

Food for Thought

For some thought-provoking Internet reading on the subject, *Advertising Age* magazine has a website on the best advertising of the 20th century. Illustration 17-1 shows the editor's page, at the time of this writing.

Illustration 17-1: Advertising Age Website

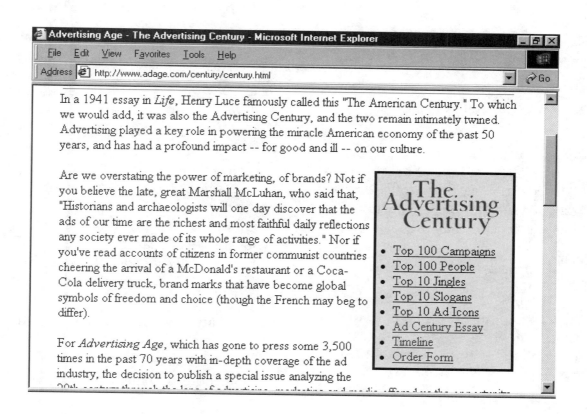

Visit http://www.adage.com/century/ for more information.

Advertising Options

It's amazing to consider how many different ways there are for you to advertise your product or service. We can only scratch the surface in this discussion. For more promotional and advertising ideas check out Jay Conrad Levinson's series of books including "The Guerilla Marketing Handbook" and "Guerilla Marketing Online."

Advertising Specialties

- Pens and pencils
- Pads of paper and sticky notes
- Mouse pads
- Magnets
- Coffee mugs.

Consider these more for branding and overall awareness than for generating sales leads. Specialty items like pens, calendars, and coffee cups are good for keeping your name in front of your customers, as a reminder.

Articles and Columns

The best columns and articles are free, and nothing has greater credibility than coverage in magazines, newspapers, radio, or television. Sometimes public relations can help.

Billboards

Not for everybody, billboard advertisements are usually extremely local (a motel, restaurant, or event at the next exit) or for cigarettes or liquor, whose advertising options are limited. The Yahoo! listing on billboards is a good place to look for more information:

http://dir.yahoo.com/
Business_and_Economy/
Business_to_Business/
Marketing_and_Advertising/Advertising/
Outdoor_Advertising/

Brochures and Circulars

Sales literature, brochures, circulars, and other so-called "collaterals" have their specific place in a marketing mix. This is a huge topic, a place where people spend their entire careers, yet others will design their own brochures on their computer. They are used mainly as informational supplements, a take-home sales accessory, rather than to generate new leads. People judge your company by the brochures, so unless you are very local and have specific information to pass on, like a price list, make sure they look very good.

For an Internet view, consider the following websites:

- Brochures Online:

http://www.look-on.com

- Desteo lets you search among thousands of already-published free travel brochures, and place online orders:

  http://www.desteo.com/

- Auto Sales Literature lets you look at automobile brochures:

  http://members.aol.com/lccjerry/asl.html

Canvassing

Door-to-door selling? Good luck! The political advertisers and nonprofit fund raisers use it effectively, but has anybody seen a Fuller Brush man recently? One of the most famous door-to-door sales organizations in the U.S. has now become the Fuller Brush online catalog, as shown in Illustration 17-2.

Illustration 17-2: Fuller Brush Online Catalog

Visit http://www.fuller.com for more information.

Note that websites change their look and content regularly to stay fresh and contemporary.

Illustration 17-3: Amway Website

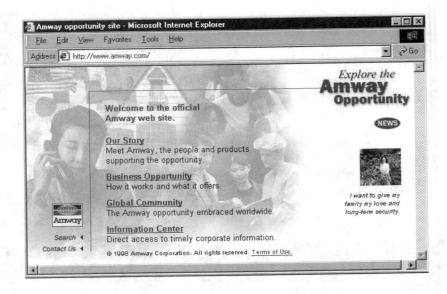

Visit http://www.amway.com/ for more information.

Illustration 17-4: Anti-Multi-Level Marketing Links

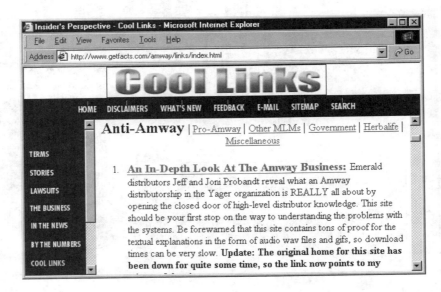

Visit http://www.getfacts.com/amway/links/index.html for more information.

Amway was once famous for door-to-door selling. Illustration 17-3 shows their website opening page. But take a look at the anti-Amway site links, shown in Illustration 17-4. It doesn't look encouraging, does it?

The cost of operations, and subsequent customer irritation combined with home security fears have made door-to-door an almost obsolete sales approach.

Catalogs

Design, print, and distribute your own catalog and, if you can get people to read it and buy from it, you have a powerful marketing tool. The mailing list is a critical component in the successful use of catalogs. Catalogs boomed in the 1980s and early 1990s, but a lot of the same effort is now going into the Internet. The following Yahoo! search lists several online catalog sites:

http://dir.yahoo.com/
business_and_economy/
shopping_and_services/retailers/
directories/catalogs/

With luck, hard work, a good product, and a marketing budget, you can also get your product into somebody else's catalog.

One of our sample marketing plans, the Willamette Furniture plan, involves a company that enjoyed huge growth prospects after winning spots in office supply catalogs.

Most of these catalogs charge the manufacturers hefty fees for placing their products on the catalog pages. With the right audience and products, it can be a hit.

Classified Advertisements

The classifieds are not just your first advertising experience, and the marketplace for used cars, houses, and apartments; some companies use classifieds as an important part of their marketing mix.

Consider the classifieds in *Inc. Magazine*, *Business Week*, *Sunset*, or *USA Today*; these are major marketing opportunities for certain kinds of specialty products and services.

The local newspaper's classifieds are one of the best places to advertise services such as hauling, painting, and gardening.

Coupons in Newspapers, Magazines, and on Receipts

Are you looking to get customers in the door? Coupons can generate local business and new customers. Offers an attractive deal to get customers in the door once, and gives them reasons to come back. An effective technique for years and years, and for the right kinds of businesses, it still works. A significant advantage of coupons is the tracking they offer, with each coupon dated and identified by the source.

Demonstrations

Demonstrations work best when crowds are already gathered, such as at a trade show. Have you ever seen the airplane toys flying around a toy store? A video of the product in use? One of the biggest uses of demos these days is in the software market. The Internet has made demo software an excellent tool for selling software.

Direct Mail

Direct mail is an industry itself, one of the bastions of old-fashioned hard selling. Direct mail is the junk mail envelope with printed brochures and order forms, asking you to call a toll-free number and order something. It is also the coupons and catalogs in your mailbox. It has fallen from favor recently, and to some extent, been replaced by the Internet, but the postal bulk rates are still there and some companies still swear by direct mail. Direct mail response rates have fallen in recent years, often producing results below one percent.

The following Yahoo! search brings up a list of sites on direct mail:

http://dir.yahoo.com/
Business_and_Economy/
Business_to_Business/
Marketing_and_Advertising/
Direct_Marketing/Direct_Mail/

Direct-response Radio

You've heard these commercials, offering a product and a toll-free number to call. Repetition is critical here.

Direct-response Television

This is the venue of the so-called infomercials, which take 30 minutes or more to sell exercise machines and cosmetics. It also includes advertisements that urge you to call a telephone number to order a product, whether they are 30-minute infomercials or 30-second commercials. Here's the Yahoo! search page:

http://dir.yahoo.com/
Business_and_Economy/
Business_to_Business/
Marketing_and_Advertising/Advertising/
Television/Infomercials/

Exhibits and Fairs

A relatively old-fashioned way to promote products and services, but still effective for some products in some targeted markets.

Fax Marketing

Faxes sent to lists of fax machines. Does anybody buy from these? A list of qualified and repeat buyers will be necessary to make this work.

Free Samples

Free toothpaste in small packages, cosmetics, cheese and crackers, demo software. Free samples work as advertising, particularly at the point of sale.

Inserts

Envelopes, boxes, and other packaging is vital for retail sales. Boxes make a difference to customer impressions, and many companies advertise on the outside of envelopes.

Magazine Advertisements

One of the stalwarts of advertising, magazine advertisements offer excellent audience targeting and a good medium for communicating a message.

Newsletters

A regular newsletter keeps your company name in front of your customers, or potential customers, and can be an excellent fit to stimulate repeat purchases and customer loyalty.

Newspaper Advertisement

Newspaper ads are the mainstay for advertising by local retailers and local services. The Wednesday paper is normally full of grocery ads, and weekend papers are full of ads for consumer electronics. There are also newspaper classified ads. Newspapers are a key medium for time-sensitive local advertising.

Personal Letters

Some companies still advertise via personal letters (a variation on direct mail), but this is rarer every day. Select and high-ticket items may justify this approach.

Postcard Decks

These are common in the electronics industry. In theory, the target person receives a deck of complementary advertising cards in the mail and looks through them. The goal is to generate leads and sales by making it easy for the potential customer to order the product, receive a discount or request additional information by simply mailing back the postage paid reply card.

Radio Advertisements

Radio advertising is a strong and effective medium, vital to many businesses. As the world spends more time in cars and offices, it spends more time with radio, too. Again, frequency of exposure is critical to the customer receiving, retaining and acting on the message.

Seminars or Educational Settings

Be careful. You can't turn seminars or educational events into sales or advertising mediums without risking serious backlash from some of the audience. Still, there are businesses that sponsor informational seminars that are based on exercise programs, investment strategies, child raising, and other topics, as part of their advertising strategy.

Signage

In many businesses, the sign outside the door is a vital part of communication with your customers. A retail store, restaurant, coffee shop, tire store or whatever, the sign says who you are, and in many cases what you sell and how you've positioned yourself. For walk-in businesses, signage can be vital.

Statement Stuffers

Statement stuffers advertise products in small pieces that come with your telephone bill, credit card bill, cable bill, and other regular mail.

Telemarketing

Telemarketing involves telephoning people to offer them products, services, or information about products or services. Telemarketers buy lists of phone numbers, and pay people to deliver their message. More and more, people view this as an invasion of their privacy, and increasing resistance to this approach is making it a less efficient promotional tool.

Television

A 30-second spot on a national television show costs tens and sometimes hundreds of thousands of dollars for placement, in addition to the production costs of the ad. This equates to big money for a big audience.

Television advertising also includes fringe ads on late-night cable and daytime cable that cost a lot less, and be more targeted, than the major national airings.

The Internet

Internet advertising is booming. Internet usage is booming. This is a vital new advertising medium (among other things) that grew up almost overnight. The targeting capabilities of the Internet combined with its affordability makes it a powerful marketing resource. Information about advertising on the Internet can be found at this link:

http://dir.yahoo.com/
Computers_and_Internet/Internet/
Business_and_Economics/
Advertising_on_Web_and_Internet/

Trade Shows

- Trade shows are vital in some industries. Buyers and sellers get together in one place, the sellers put up booths, and the buyers wander the floor. A trade show can be the best place to introduce a new product, and line up distribution, and impress potential buyers:

http://dir.yahoo.com/
Business_and_Economy/
Business_to_Business/
Conventions_and_Trade_Shows/
Directories/

- Event Marketing can be huge for certain kinds of businesses:

http://dir.yahoo.com/
Business_and_Economy/
Business_to_Business/
Marketing_and_Advertising/
Event_Marketing/

Yellow Pages and Directory Listings

The telephone directory is probably the first and most important advertising program for a majority of local businesses looking for local customers. Are you a retail business? Do you have your ad in the yellow pages?

Advertising: Make or Buy?

Do you develop your own ads? Can you? Can you afford to use an advertising agency? Can you afford not to?

Deciding on how to create your advertising is a decision each business must make. Your available resources will determine how difficult a decision this will be.

It is important that the creative aspects of your advertising communicate the look and feel of your business to build the image you desire. What is the "persona" of your business? Is it an image that is fun, formal, secure, functional, intellectual, reliable or a combination of these qualities? Your advertising must capture and communicate the optimal attributes. If you cannot accomplish this goal in-house, your decision to buy these resources is already made.

What resources does your organization possess to contribute to this process? You may want to "inventory" those resources before you look outside the organization for the creation of the advertising materials you need to promote your business. The list may begin with these skill areas:

- Graphic design

- Copy writing

- Web design

- Photo manipulation

You may have the luxury to then take on the tasks that match your in-house skills and have other work done by an agency or other resource to fill the voids.

When going through the "make or buy" decision process, ask for references from those companies with advertising that you like and that seem consistent with a look and feel that is going to be best for your business. You may be surprised where some of these referrals lead you. You may not want or need a "full service" advertising agency. An independent graphic artist may be a good solution for your needs, be more responsive, and more affordable.

If you already know where you want to advertise, explore what might be available to you through the organization selling the advertising. They may have resources to do your creative work that can be included with the purchase of your ad. The newspaper you are working with may have graphic artists that are on staff to assist you with your advertisement. Television and radio stations may offer support to assist with the production of your commercial. If there is a cost associated with the creation of the ad, ask if there are arrangements where the cost, or a portion of that cost, can be credited to the broadcast time or space you are buying. Using the advertiser's services may involve additional time, so plan ahead and ask about required lead times.

Consider investigating innovative options to compensate for creating and buying advertising. For example, based on the products or services you offer, bartering may be a solution to keep costs down and leverage the expertise of others.

The goal of the "make or buy" process is to acquire the best ad possible with your available resources. Keep in mind how important it is to have an ad that produces optimal results. It can be one of your most significant investments in your marketing efforts.

Dealing with an Advertising Agency

Most organizations need to have access to external graphic resources. A logo is critical, most need stationery, some will use collateral, and others will need to have a Web page.

Advertising agencies offer a variety of services. Most agencies offer a source for your "creative" work, including the graphics associated with your ad, letterhead, collateral or website. Agencies also offer additional services, including the option to place your ad with the media source, and some also offer public relations work.

It is important to determine what you need from the agency before they attempt to make that choice for you. In most cases, the agency will be excited to do everything they can for your business, and you may not be able to afford their level of enthusiasm.

Here are some questions that you may want to consider regarding the aspects of dealing with an advertising agency.

How much will it cost?

Get a bid regarding the work they will be performing before anything billable begins. Open-ended arrangements can lead to surprises for and from both you and the agency. Establishing a fixed cost or "not to exceed" amount can avoid difficult and expensive problems later.

Who owns the creative?

Before your project begins, determine who owns the creative, them or you. In some cases, the agency will retain ownership of their work, and you must depend on them and compensate them each time you use the graphic, the ad, or the photo. In most cases, it will be an advantage for you to have ownership of the creative so you can go to other sources with the work they have done.

Who is going to be the point of contact?

Arrange for a primary point of contact within your organization to work with the agency. This will add consistency in dealing with the agency and can save a tremendous amount of time to assess progress, build on previous work, or deal with billing questions.

Are you using the best skills for the task?

You may find creative resources that are better at some things than others. Some have incredible skills at logo design; others in ad layout. Don't assume that one agency or resource is going to do everything well. However, trade-offs do exist here. You will need to weigh the increased burden of dealing with multiple resources against the benefits accrued from optimal work on each type of project.

Who should place your ad?

If your ad agency creates the ad, you may need to decide who places the ad with the advertiser. If the agency places the ad, there may be percentage increases included, such as a commission. You may get a discount for placing the ad directly with the advertiser. Regardless, you may have to arrange to prepare disk, electronic file, or film for the ad, depending on the specification of the advertiser. Most agencies will offer you options regarding how you work with them on these types of activities.

How do you assess their performance?

Take a critical view of what the agency is doing for you on a regular basis. Don't stay with an agency out of loyalty alone. Check with other agencies if you feel you are not getting the level of performance you need. Letting your agency know that you are no longer going to use them can be difficult and it happens all the time. Tell them why, and if they are professionals, they will focus on satisfying your needs, knowing that they are at risk of losing you as a client.

The goal is to identify and leverage the creative resources you need to complement your business and produce high quality promotional experiences. Advertising agencies can account for a significant percentage of your marketing budget. Make sure you are using them wisely.

CHAPTER 18:

PUBLIC RELATIONS

Public relations involves a variety of programs designed to maintain or enhance a company's image and the products and services it offers. Successful implementation of an effective public relations strategy can be a critical component to a marketing plan.

Public Relations Marketing

A public relations (PR) strategy may play a key role in an organization's promotional strategy. A planned approach to leveraging public relations opportunities can be just as important as advertising and sales promotions. Public relations is one of the most effective methods to communicate and relate to the market. It is powerful and, once things are in motion, it can be the most cost effective of all promotional activities. In some cases, it is free.

The success of well executed PR plans can be seen through several organizations that have made it a central focus of their promotional strategy. Paul Newman's Salad Dressing, The Body Shop, and Ben & Jerry's Ice Cream have positioned their organizations through effective

PR strategies. Intel, Sprint and Microsoft have leveraged public relations to introduce and promote new products and services.

Similar to the foundational goals of marketing, effective public relations seeks to communicate information to:

- Launch new products and services.

- Reposition a product or service.

- Create or increase interest in a product, service, or brand.

- Influence specific target groups.

- Defend products or services that have suffered from negative press or perception.

- Enhance the firm's overall image.

The result of an effective public relations strategy is to generate additional revenue through greater awareness and information for the products and services an organization offers.

Goals and Objectives

An effective public relations strategy will leverage the areas of press relations, product and service promotion, firm communications, lobbying, and internal feedback to assist the organization in reaching its marketing goals. Good strategy begins with identifying your goals and stating your objectives (Chapter 14: Mission and Objectives). What are the goals and objectives behind your public relations strategy? Can they be measured and quantified?

Each of these areas may reflect the goals your public relations campaign may seek to accomplish.

Press relations

Communicating news and information of interest about organizations in the most positive light.

Product and service promotions

Sponsoring various efforts to publicize specific products or services.

Firm communications

Promoting a better and more attractive understanding of the organization with internal and external communications.

Lobbying

Communicate with key individuals to positively influence legislation and regulation.

Internal feedback

Advise decision makers within the organization regarding the public's perception and advising actions to be taken to change negative opinions.

Assessing Resources

The most commonly used public relations resources include news items, publications, events, presentations, and public service activities. Determine how your market's information resources match with these five areas.

News

One of the major tasks of public relations is to create favorable news about the company, its products, its services, or its people. Don't expect the press to be as excited about the event as you are. News generation requires skill in developing a story or concept, researching it, and writing a press release. Each effort must be executed in a way that makes it of interest to the media's audience. It must be "news" to make the cut.

Publications

Organizations can use a variety of promotional tools to reach and influence their target markets. This includes annual reports, websites, brochures, articles, company newsletters, magazines, audio tapes, videos, CDs, multimedia presentations, and other communication tools.

Events

Organizations can attract attention to new products or services and other organizational activities by arranging special events. These include news conferences, seminars, exhibits, contests, anniversaries, a variety of fund-raising activities, sporting events, and cultural sponsorships that "connect" with the target market in a positive and meaningful way.

Presentations

Sharing expert or unique information is another tool of public relations. Seminars and educational environments can enable a company spokesperson to communicate with the media in a way that adds credibility and a personal and interactive element to the organization and their products. Again, be cautious in the "selling" process. It may not fit in this venue.

Public Service Activities

"Cause marketing" is used by a growing number of companies to build public goodwill and enhance the firm's image. Cause marketing is typically associated with public service activities that have a wide-range public appeal.

The best "causes" are those that everyone in the target markets can embrace. These causes enhance the condition of life or the environment that virtually everyone can support. Causes that battle cancer, pollution, child abuse, and support Special Olympics events are examples of winning causes worth considering. Associating an organization, brand, or product with these efforts can be powerful and enduring.

In most cases you will attempt to generate coverage from all available resources and then assess your response. Tailor your message to get the most attention possible from each resource.

Example of PR Strategy

Determine what areas may best serve your organization and incorporate them into your public relations strategy. For example, the public relations goals for "Upper Crust," a single location, retail gourmet food store, may take this approach to their publicity campaign:

1. Develop two stories about key products they carry that have established cause-related images.

2. Create one story about their community involvement that leverages the efforts of their key suppliers.

3. Tailor these stories to connect with their key target markets, including "The Country Clubbers," the "Under 30 Women" and "Health Conscious Retired" that account for the majority of the store's revenues.

4. If follow up coverage does occur, such as a television interview after a newspaper or radio coverage, use this exposure to announce a

promotion where 10% of all sales for the next 10 days will be contributed to the cause cited in the press release.

Review Marketing Objectives with Your PR Strategy

Next, review your overall marketing strategy and objectives to make certain they complement one or more of the areas you want to impact. This process is a challenging one when you are working to change something that is intangible. Attempting to quantify your objectives whenever you can will add focus and will reinforce your investment in this area.

Let's return to our example. The measurable objectives for "Upper Crust" might include the following:

1. Have at least one of the stories about their products or the store itself picked up by the local newspaper or radio.

2. You may be able to leverage this exposure by co-sponsoring an event to a community group comprised of one or more of the target markets. Presenting the contribution to representatives of the cause may offer additional exposure.

3. Expect to receive comments from at least 10 customers regarding the exposure.

4. "Test" for a 10% increase in revenues within 14 days of the initial exposure.

The more specific you can be with your goals and objectives, the more targeted you will be in designing your public relations campaign and the more objective you will be in assessing your impact.

Future action: Repeat successes and modify or discontinue the failures based on your results.

The Role of the Champion

Another part of an effective public relations strategy is identifying a "champion" that will design and manage the public relations promotional activities.

Who is going to be responsible for implementation? Is it incorporated into the marketing milestones and on the marketing calendar? These are important questions that must be addressed and the answers will play a key role in the success of the public relations activities.

For most businesses, public relations marketing has to be planned, otherwise it may not take place at the right time, or at all. The "champion" will develop relationships with members of the press, editors, and others who determine what is, and what is not, going to make the news. The "who you know" also enters into the complex equation of public relations.

The responsible person will need to be diligent. This is a process that resembles more of a "journey" than a "cause and effect" experience. Creativity, tenacity, and patience are cornerstones of fruitful public relations work.

The Control Factor

When it comes to public relations and control, you don't have it. "When you don't pay, you don't have a say."

You can write the most impressive press release, offer great photos, provide visuals that would excite any publication, and even give a great interview, and it may not be used. Ever. You have virtually no control over what you are "given" by the press. You need to do what you can to give them "news," and then sit back and see what happens.

Create different angles and perspectives on events or issues that didn't get press the first time. Taking on this perspective can save you a tremendous amount of frustration. Do all the right things to gain attention and then be prepared for anything, or possibly nothing.

Once your public relations programs are implemented, the fate of their exposure lies in the hands of the reviewers, journalists, and Web masters. The trade-off for "free" public relations is the lack of control regarding when, where, and how this information will be shared with your targeted audience.

CHAPTER 19:

PRODUCT MARKETING

Going back to the basics, keep in mind your target user needs and how your product or service meets those needs. This is fundamental.

The Offering Concept

An offering consists of the benefits or satisfaction provided to target markets by an organization. An offering consists of a tangible product or service, plus related services. This may include installation, warranties, guarantees, and packaging.

Focusing on the offering, rather than on the actual product or service itself, can be valuable to analyze the consumers' alternatives, to better identify the unmet needs and wants of the target markets, and to enhance the development of new products or services. This approach allows you to think beyond the tangible "product" entity and consider what the consumer is actually buying and their reasoning behind that purchase.

In a larger sense, an organization's offerings are a part of who they are as a business. Their offerings illustrate the buyer needs served, the types of customer groups sought, and the means for satisfying their needs. Your marketing plan should address how that offering is communicated and what value it holds for the consumer.

Offering Mix

Most organizations sell more than one product. A multi-product approach often adds value, leverages economies of scale and expertise, and increases revenue generation potential. Banks offer dozens of services. Most retail stores offer hundreds of products to meet the breadth of needs of their customers. General Electric has over 200,000 products. The combined offerings of an organization is known as their offering mix.

This offering mix can be classified according to the width, length, depth, and consistency of the products. These four dimensions are the tools for developing the company's marketing strategy and deciding which product line to grow, maintain, harvest, or divest. Strong products should be grown or maintained. Weak or unprofitable lines should be sold or discontinued.

Four basic factors are critical in the decision to manage individual product lines.

1. Consumer demand.

2. Cost to produce.

3. Gross margin.

4. Total sales volume.

Analyzing a product line and deciding how many resources should be invested should be conducted when change occurs in any of these areas.

What is a Product Brand?

Branding has become a popular term. For generations, however, the process of branding has been a basic element of product marketing.

A brand identifies the seller or the producer of a product. A brand can be a name, a term, a trademark, a logo, a symbol, a design, or a combination of all. The objective of a brand is to identify the products of one provider in a way that differentiates them from their competitors. Branding is especially important with products that are considered a "commodity" like toothpaste, gasoline or computer disks.

Successful brands are easily identifiable. This is measured by their level of brand awareness, and is most notable when a single symbol or logo is highly recognizable on its own. Think about the information the following logos communicate:

- Do you know each organization's name?

- Do you know what products they produce?

- Do you know some attributes of their target customers?

Consistent advertising with a targeted and clear theme can be one of the most dramatic testimonies to successful advertising.

Once brands are established and recognized, they communicate various levels of meaning. Brands seek to describe a product's attributes, benefits, values, and personality in a way that connects with the targeted user.

Multiple aspects of a product, the organization, and its customers can be "understood" by a brand.

It is this strong association that gives branding such power. Most of us have a radically different perception of a brand like "Budweiser" compared to how we feel about the products and customers of "Neiman Marcus." A brand is commonly referred to as "deep" when it successfully communicates a broad range of these meanings.

Brand identity can be developed through sheer exposure rather than via an intuitive connection. For example, the association of a double-tailed mermaid with specialty coffee drinks is a highly recognizable symbol for a market leader like Starbucks, largely resulting through repeated and successful exposure.

Part of the branding strategy involves how to assign brands. A producer must decide whether to assign brand names to: all of the offerings; each line of offerings; or individual names to each offering.

This decision should be based on the degree of commonality between the needs each offering satisfies. Closely related offerings indicate that a common, or a family, brand strategy is often selected. Meeting a diverse range of needs indicates individual brands will fit best.

Above all, branding is about communicating benefits, regardless of how intangible or seemingly disconnected they may be with the product and its function.

Again, brands differentiate. Brands set the product and the producer of that product apart from the competition. This differentiation may have very little to do with the product itself. It has a great deal to do with the perception around that product. Your marketing plan should capture your branding strategy and support the overall marketing strategy.

Product Manager

The product manager often stands between the product development team and the marketing team, bringing the concepts together throughout the implementation process. Some organizations have the resources and the need to have a position dedicated to manage the one or more product lines. The role of the product manager is to develop product plans, implement them, monitor the results, and take corrective action when necessary.

What is the Goal?

The product manager's goal is to intimately know the target markets the product or products serve and understand how these markets perceive the product. There are critical customer questions the product manger must answer:

- What needs are our customers satisfying when they buy our product?

- Why do they buy it?

- What do they consider to be viable product alternatives or substitutes?

- How do our products compare to those other potential choices?

What are the Tasks to Achieve the Goal?

The product manager's tasks most often can be described by these activities:

1. Develop an enduring competitive strategy.

2. Prepare and maintain a product marketing plan with a sales forecast.

3. Work with advertising and merchandising agencies to develop copy, programs and campaigns.

4. Stimulate an understanding of the product and support among the sales force and distributors.

5. Gather product performance data from customers, resellers, dealers and others in the sales channel regarding attitudes, new problems, and opportunities.

6. Initiate product improvement to meet changing market needs.

The focus and specialization a product manager offers an organization can prove to be a valuable resource in making certain that the return on investment for each product is optimized.

Packaging and Labeling

Product packaging must be appealing in order to attract and hold the consumers' eye and attention, and serve as an efficient and functional shipping container.

Most physical products require packaging. This involves the design of a box or wrapper that contains the product. In addition to the function it performs—to hold and protect the product—it is also a powerful selling tool.

Products can have multiple packages. This includes the container itself, such as a bottle, can, or case. This is often enclosed in a box for protection purposes. The product may also have a case or larger container to ship multiple products within one box. Each of these packages, particularly those that the consumers see before their purchase, offers the opportunity to communicate information to consumers at a critical point in their decision making process.

Packaging offers the opportunity to:

Protect the Product

- Reduce costs due to breakage.

- Protect the product in transit: for example breakable or perishable items such as perfume, light bulbs or food.

- Protect the product on the shelf: from theft, damage or tampering (i.e., pharmaceuticals or CDs).

Promote the Product

- Complement other promotional activities.

- Communicate information: core benefits, "why to buy" testimonials, Internet addresses and toll-free telephone numbers, for products like tools or software.

- Display the product: attach to display hardware or stand upright as with gloves or cell phones.

Provide Additional Value and Differentiation

- To provide increased purchase justification.

- Dispense the product: ease of use or the size of recommended portions, as with spray paint, hair care products, etc.

- Preserve the product: seal and reseal perishables. Examples are food products and cleaning supplies.

- Offer consumer safety: warn of hazards due to improper use of dangerous substances (such as the information on cigarette packaging) or design considerations (such as not standing on the top step of a ladder).

- Serve other uses: containers that can be used for other after-purchase purposes. Film canisters might carry a couple days' vitamins or aspirin in a backpack. A current foldable bicycle ships and travels in a suitcase, which then converts into a trailer to be pulled behind the bike.

Retail products purchased on an impulsive basis depend heavily on packaging to communicate information and encourage a buy decision. Music CDs, perfume, and software are examples of this. An increasing number of products are purchased without the assistance from a store employee, magnifying the opportunity and impact of the package.

Well-designed packages offer a promotional tool and convenience value to the user. This can result in another form of product differentiation. Packaging can offer after-purchase value to store the product, or be used for other uses. Razors that are packaged in travel cases are an example of this.

Product Bundling

Product bundling is combining two or more products or services together, creating differentiation, greater value and therefore enhancing the offering to the customer. Bundling is based on the idea that consumers value the grouped package more than the individual items.

Bundling can enhance an organization's offering mix while minimizing costs. This is attractive to consumers who will benefit from a single, value-oriented purchase of complementary offerings. Bundling is attractive to producers by increasing efficiencies, such as reducing marketing and distribution costs. It can also encourage customers to look to one single source to offer several solutions.

Product bundling may also incorporate products from multiple producers. For example, Palo Alto Software may include one of their business planning products with an accounting software package, or participate in a "small business bundle" through a major computer manufacturer whose customers would have the opportunity to purchase with their new PC. In these situations, bundles may cost effectively open doors to new marketing channels.

If the product combination is right, the decision to bundle often involves taking these four variables into consideration:

1. **Volume**: Bundling typically increases unit sales volume.

2. **Margins**: Bundling can reduce margins.

3. **Exposure**: Bundling may offer new channel opportunities or exposure to new potential customers.

4. **Risk**: If executed incorrectly, bundling may cannibalize more profitable sales, resulting in lower contribution margins and potential channel conflict.

These factors must be considered in terms of the revenue opportunity and exposure potential bundles offer. Determine if bundling has a place in your marketing plan and how it will provide value for your customer and your organization.

It is important to be selective, but with the right bundle, everyone can win.

Adaptations for Global Marketing

The topic of "global marketing" is as large as its name suggests. The following offers some key points of consideration that may assist in addressing a global marketing strategy within your marketing plan.

The concept of global marketing is grounded in the notion that enhanced communication and other technologies have resulted in parallel needs and tastes of consumers around the world. Some feel that this level of commonality is overstated and that consumers' tastes and needs should be examined on a market-by-market basis. Global marketing is different from international marketing. Global marketing seeks to develop a uniform marketing strategy, rather than a separate marketing strategy tailored for each country or region.

Internet marketing strategies represent some of the most successful and low-risk global marketing strategies today. Marketing campaigns are measured by their success in various regions and countries and are modified to attract the greatest number of customers, regardless of their location. More individualized strategies may spin-off to improve results in areas that do not have common needs.

Global positioning and branding decisions follow the problems and opportunities of international and global marketing. Depending on the product or service, it may or may not be possible to develop truly global brand positions and equity.

Products that can be globally marketed most easily are those that are subject to economies of scale in manufacturing and those that are used and accepted across a wide array of cultures.

CHAPTER 20:

DIRECT MARKETING

An organization that markets directly to their end users to sell their products or services is benefiting from direct marketing. Based on the characteristics and resources of the organization and their target markets, direct marketing may be an attractive approach to generate revenue.

What is Direct Marketing?

Direct marketing occurs when the "producer" connects with the end user. The end user may be a consumer or a business.

Direct marketing applies to product and service-oriented businesses, and to nonprofit organizations. In all situations, there is no intermediary involved. Direct marketing describes this interactive communication with the end user.

Direct marketing is not synonymous with mass marketing. The most effective direct marketing takes place when there is a clear connection to reach the target market.

Organizations may use several ways to leverage direct marketing as they communicate with and deliver products to their customers. This may include using a direct sales force, catalogs, websites, email, direct mail, telemarketing, seminars, trade shows, and other "one-to-one" techniques to communicate and sell to their customers and clients.

Some of these direct marketing methods have grown dramatically, especially with the growth of marketing over the Internet. There is evidence that other direct marketing approaches have diminished, such as reports that the response to direct mail is often below one percent compared to the five percent+ response rate numbers more commonly experienced in the past.

Companies may choose to leverage direct marketing exclusively.

Examples are:

- Lands' End
  http://www.landsend.com
- Mary Kay Cosmetics
  http://www.marykay.com/
- Prepaid Legal Services
  http://prepaidlegal.com/

Many local nonprofit organizations also use direct marketing exclusively.

http://www.nonprofit.net/

Other businesses use direct marketing in concert with other marketing channels.

Examples are:

- Dell Computers
  http://www.dell.com/
- NordicTrack
  http://www.nordictrack.com
- Neiman Marcus
  http://www.neimanmarcus.com/
- General Electric
  http://www.ge.com/

Types of Direct Marketing

The most common forms of direct marketing are:

- Internet marketing
- Face-to-face selling
- Direct mail
- Catalogs
- Telemarketing
- Direct-response advertising
- Kiosk marketing

Let's look at these in more detail.

Internet Marketing

The Internet has revolutionized direct marketing for promoting the sale of products and services to targeted audiences. Access to the Internet provides users with services in four basic areas:

1. Information

2. Entertainment

3. Shopping

4. Individual and group communication

Online channels can eliminate geographic considerations. With this capability people around the world have the same access as the person across the street. Many businesses that can sell their products and services through downloading, or who can economically ship those products, have discovered an entirely new way to market.

The Internet makes direct marketing easier, more targeted, more flexible, more responsive, more affordable, and potentially more profitable than ever. Virtually every business should seriously consider the Internet as a part of their marketing mix and determine if it is a viable fit for their direct marketing efforts.

Face-to-Face Selling

The most traditional direct marketing involves the in-house sales force personally contacting potential and established consumers. Examples of organizations that use face-to-face selling include:

- Mary Kay

    http://www.marykay.com

- Avon

    http://www.avon.com

- Amway

    http://www.amway.com

Direct Mail

Direct mail is described as sending information about a special offer, product or sale announcement, service reminder, or some other type of communication to a person at a particular street or electronic address. Historically direct mail has existed in the form of printed materials, but CDs, audio tapes, video tapes, fax mail, email, and voice mail are also used in direct mail campaigns. For example, America Online experienced a highly successful campaign through mailing out CD-ROMs to prospective customers. Direct mail permits high target-market selectivity; it can be personalized, it is flexible, and it allows early testing and response measurement to take place. A highly selective and accurate mailing list often determines the success of direct mail efforts to enhance response rates and control costs.

Catalogs

Product catalogs are another version of direct mail where the catalogs are the communication tool. The most common use of this approach involves featuring a variety of products that target the needs of a specific audience who have shown a propensity to order from catalogs. An increasing number of business-to-business marketers are sending catalogs on CD-ROM to prospects and customers. The average U.S. household receives more than 50 catalogs each year, ranging from general merchandise to specialty goods.

Examples of general merchandise catalogs are:

- Spiegel

    http://www.spiegel.com

- J.C. Penny

    http://www.jcpenny.com

Examples of specialty goods catalogs are:

- Pottery Barn

    http://www.potterybarn.com

- PC Connection

    http://www.pcconnection.com

Telemarketing

The process of contacting people on a qualified list to sell services over the phone has grown in popularity to the point that the average household receives 19 telemarketing calls each year. Successful telemarketing campaigns depend on a good calling list, an effective script and contact structure, and well-trained people that are compensated and rewarded for making calls that result in sales.

The telecommunications industry, for example, has used telemarketing extensively to attempt to increase their market share.

This includes:

- AT&T

    http://www.att.com

- MCI WorldCom

    http://www.worldcom.com

- Sprint

    http://www.sprint.com

Direct-Response Advertising

Direct-response advertising is communicating with potential buyers through television, radio, magazines, and newspapers. The prospective consumer watches, hears, or reads about the product or service and initiates a call to a toll-free number to place their order. Television, for example, offers a wide range of exposure, from a 30-second commercial to a 60-minute infomercial.

Kiosk Marketing

Customer order machines, versus vending machines that actually provide products, are another form of direct marketing. Examples are:

- Eddie Bauer

  Stores place computer terminals to order from the entire line of products not available in the retail store.

  http://www.eddiebauer.com

- Florsheim Shoe Company

  http://www.florsheim.com

Your bank's automatic teller machines (ATMs) placed in convenient and high traffic areas are another example of kiosk marketing. A combination of these direct marketing techniques may offer the optimal revenue generating solution.

Assessing the Criteria

The criteria for direct marketing begins with a reliable customer database. Other factors include offering greater customer value through a more customized and personalized approach for product and service offerings, distribution processes tailored to meet the needs of customers, and the opportunity to build customer loyalty.

One of the first criteria for direct marketing is to have a consistent customer profile available which describes the dominant target markets. This information must have sufficient detail to support a customer database.

A customer database quantitatively captures the key characteristics of prospects and customers who are most ready, willing, and able to purchase your product or service. It may offer demographic information about their age, income, education, gender, and previous mail order purchases. In concert with this information, this customer database identifies customers who possess these characteristics:

- Have purchased most frequently.

- Purchased recently.

- Spend the most at each transaction.

This database is used to accomplish the following.

- Identify prospects.

- Decide when a customer needs a specific offer.

- Enhance customer loyalty.

- Stimulate repeat purchases.

Access to a customer database is the first step. The next set of criteria includes enhancing customer value through one or more of the following factors:

- Customized product and service solutions.

- Personalized interaction before or during the actual transaction.

- The development of expertise within an industry or based on specific issues.

- Individualized distribution processes accompanied by customized marketing offerings.

When these criteria are met, the organization may be able to leverage areas of expertise, economies of scale, and have the potential to build customer loyalty. An organization may be able to achieve greater target market precision through direct marketing than it can experience through a mass marketing or channel marketing approach.

Before You Begin, Decide How to Measure

Successful direct marketing campaigns plan their efforts, determine their objectives, target their markets, determine the offers' key elements, test those elements, and establish measurements to assess the campaign's success. Measuring your success is key.

Begin by gathering information about your fixed costs relating to overhead expenses and the variable costs relating to how many pieces are going to be sent. Then prepare to track revenues generated. Each of these areas offers valuable information to assess the results of the direct marketing campaign.

Conducting a simple break-even analysis can be a valuable tool in this process. For example;

Dental Data Co. is an organization that offers specialized patient management software to dentists. They would like to determine what their break-even point would be if they mailed CD-ROM demos with printed materials to 2,000 selected dentists. Their estimated expenses for the direct mail campaign follow.

This information will help determine what Dental Data's response rate needs to be to break even on the campaign. The 43 units to break-even equates to a 2.15% response rate. This response rate is determined by dividing the 43 units at break-even by 2,000, the total number mailed.

Illustration 20-1:
Dental Data Co. Examples

Fixed Costs	
Creation of printed material graphics and text	$3,450
Creation of CD-ROM graphics	$750
Intitial set up fee for CD	$1,600
Initial set up fee for printed materials	$1,500
Production of 2,000 demo units	$30,750
Distribution of demo units	$2,500
Estimated Fixed Costs	$40,550
Per-unit variable costs (to fulfill orders sold)	$45
Per-unit revenue	$995
Break-even (in units)	43

Break Even Analysis: Assumptions	
Average Per-unit Revenue	$995.00
Average Per-unit Variable Cost	$45.00
Estimated Fixed Costs	$40,550.00
Units Break-even	43
Sales Break-even	$42,471.00

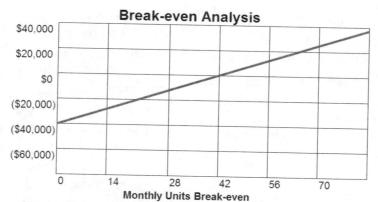

Break-even Analysis

Units break-even point = where line intersects with $0

Therefore, if Dental Data does not have a response rate higher than 2.15% over the time period they have determined, they will not realize profit from this direct marketing effort.

You can test the anticipated response rate, based on establishing a break-even sales point, to better understand the possible combinations of potential results. Information regarding general direct mail response rates, industry standards, or your past direct marketing experiences may be used to predict reasonable response rates.

Analyzing your direct marketing campaign can allow you to steadily improve direct marketing performance. If multiple direct mail pieces are used, analyze the response rates from each.

This measurement may consider the results that occur after the conclusion of the campaign. Some direct marketing campaigns produce results months or years after the campaign has been assessed. Initial "failure" may change into a successful campaign if results are tracked and measured over time.

Ethical Considerations and Responsibilities

Not all marketing is good marketing. It is important to recognize that some direct marketing techniques contain negative attributes that impact the targeted group. This may include invasion of privacy, deception, or fraud.

Invasion of privacy issues are often associated with telemarketing. How many long distance provider calls have you received in the middle of dinner? "Spam" email messages sent to numerous computer mail addresses clutter inboxes. How many are you receiving each day? These activities can create negative impact on a potential customer. And it costs money that could be more effectively spent elsewhere.

Direct marketing can also involve using communication vehicles that exaggerate information and mislead buyers through deceptive claims about a product size, performance, or price. Products that fail to meet the claim, and nonprofit organizations that use funds for other purposes, are guilty of inaccurate or misleading direct mail promotion tactics.

Consider the potential ramifications a direct marketing campaign may have on your product, service, and organization when selecting, designing, and implementing the campaign.

CHAPTER 21:

CHANNEL MARKETING

How do you most efficiently get your product or service to the people that need it and are willing to pay for it? Using a marketing channel may be a solution. Channel marketing describes the organizations that work together to get your product or service to the end user.

Extending Your Reach

Many producers of products and services do not sell directly to their end users. They use a marketing channel. In its most simplistic form, a marketing channel performs the work of moving goods from producers to consumers.

A marketing channel includes one or more marketing intermediaries who perform a variety of functions. Each channel member:

1. Provides value.

2. Performs a function.

3. Expects an economic return.

Channel marketing most often relates to the sale of products. However, it is not limited to the distribution of physical goods. Providers of services and ideas also benefit from channel marketing. For example, banks and credit unions depend on a network of ATMs to offer their services. Health and medical organizations depend on a network of providers to offer their services. Financial management and insurance organizations disseminate information through systems provided by other vendors. In the cases above, channel marketing offers better services at costs lower than offerings without the assistance of channel members.

Organizations can achieve differentiation through their distribution channels. Each of these channels may offer different coverage, expertise, and performance. They may also realize economies of scale that channels of distribution often offer.

Marketing channel decisions are among the most critical decisions facing an organization. The chosen channels intimately affect all other marketing decisions. The organization's pricing depends on whether it uses mass merchandisers or high-quality boutiques. The firm's sales force and advertising decisions depend on how much training and motivation the dealers need.

NOTE: A glossary of common channel marketing roles and functions can be found on the last page of this chapter.

Channel Members Provide Value

Channel marketing intermediaries exist because they offer value in making goods and services more available and accessible to the targeted markets.

Channel intermediaries offer contacts, experience, specialization, and economies of scale to organizations that cannot offer these attributes on their own. Marketing channels allow producers to realize the benefits that only larger organizations may be able to support.

Each channel intermediary provides value in the form of:

• **Information**

Collect and disseminate marketing information about potential and current customers, competitors, and other aspects of the marketing process.

• **Promotion**

Develop and share marketing communications designed to inform and attract customers.

• **Negotiation**

Reach final agreement on the price and other terms of the transaction.

- **Funding**

  Acquire access to funds to finance inventories at different levels of the marketing channel.

- **Risk taking**

  Take on risks associated with performing the functions of the channel. Obsolete or damaged inventory, bad debt, and slow payment are a few examples of this risk.

- **Physical possession**

  Store and move products from raw materials to the final customers.

- **Payment options**

  The buyers' payment of their bills to the sellers through banks and other financial institutions.

- **Title**

  Transfer title of ownership from one organization or person to another.

Channel Resources

In a functional sense, these are some examples of the types of resources that marketing channels offer. Each adds value to the promotion, the transaction, or the services associated with the purchase:

- Accounting services
- Advertising planning assistance
- Catalog services
- Co-op advertising programs
- Consumer advertising
- Data processing programs and systems
- Dealer shows and events
- Drop-ship programs
- Employee training
- Financing
- Forms and printing assistance
- Insurance programs
- Inventory control systems
- Management consultation services
- Merchandising assistance
- Ordering and processing systems
- Point-of-sale identification
- Private-label merchandise
- Store planning and layout

Through their acquired expertise and economies of scale, channel members offer these activities more efficiently than organizations, particularly smaller ones, could provide on their own. The marketing channel allows the producer and the channel members to do what they each do best in higher volumes.

Channel Criteria

An important step in determining if channel marketing is beneficial is to assess if it better meets the desires of the target market.

Channel marketing proves to be a "fit" if the process better responds to the desires of the target market than the organization could do alone. An organization must answer the question, "Will our customers or clients be better served by channel members rather than having us perform these functions?"

- **Lot size**

    How many "units" does the end user want per transaction? A household may purchase one personal computer per transaction. The customer service department of Eddie Bauer may purchase 20 personal computers at a time. Channel members may have systems designed to address the needs of both.

- **Waiting time**

The speed of providing faster service may be magnified through the systems that channel members offer.

- **Location**

    Getting the product in the right place and time is important. Arranging for "authorized dealerships" throughout a wide geographic area allows products to be conveniently and affordably accessible to customers.

- **Product variety**

    The ability to purchase other products from a retail store may enhance the sales and/or margins of all products offered by attracting customers who appreciate the variety of products.

- **Service support**

    Channel members may be better equipped to offer add-on services. This may include advertising, credit, delivery, installation, and repair to enhance the overall value provided to the customer.

The first step is to select intermediaries that complement the product or service. These channel members should have the goal of offering attractive attributes to the end user. Channel members also need to be motivated to continue to provide value. Motivation typically exists in the form of profitability through stimulating sales.

The overall goal is to build long-term and supportive relationships among channel members that are successful for all involved.

Channel Conflict

Marketing channels inherently have the potential for conflict. However, with proper planning it can be minimized or avoided.

Of all the factors, the most common source of channel conflict relates to pricing. It is important that the producer creates the foundation for a pricing structure where each member is able to make a profit from the value they bring to the marketing channel process. Each member's price must reflect his or her role within the channel. For example, if a retailer is able to purchase directly from the producer at a cost equal to or less than what they buy from their distributor, channel conflict will occur.

Other sources of channel conflict may result from goal incompatibility, poorly defined roles and rights, perceptual differences, and interdependent relationships. All of these factors must be taken into consideration, addressed when necessary, and "managed" whenever possible.

The member that has the greatest control--and that may not be the producer--is in the best position to influence the channel.

Channel Marketing - Roles and Functions

Channel marketing has its own set of terminology regarding each of the players. It often varies by industry. Here is a list of some of the most common terms:

TITLE	ROLE	CARRY INVENTORY	OFFER FINANCING
Broker	Brings buyers and sellers together.	No	No
Distributor	Allocates goods to wholesalers or to retailers, depending on the industry.	Yes	Potentially
Facilitator	Assists in the distribution process.	No	No
Manufacturer's representative	Represents and sells for several manufacturers to perform the same functions of an internal salesforce.	No	No
Merchant	Purchases inventory to resell.	Yes	Potentially
OEM	Original Equipment Manufacturer - Initial producer of a product who agrees to allow another entity to include, remanufacture, or label products or services under their own name and sell through their distribution channels.	No	Potentially
Retailer	Sells directly to the end user.	Yes	Potentially
Sales agent	Searches for customers and negotiates on the producers behalf.	No	No
Wholesaler	Sells to merchants who then resell to end users.	Yes	Potentially

Part 6:

FORECASTING

Forecasting

The process of developing a sales forecast begins with gathering data, continues with making informed guesses, and then follows up by testing thoses guesses against reality.

CHAPTER 22:

SALES FORECAST

The mechanics of sales forecasting are relatively simple. Break your sales down into manageable parts, and then forecast the parts. Guess your sales by line of sales, month by month, then add up the sales lines and add up the months.

A Standard Sales Forecast

The content takes work, but not the design of the table. It's built on common sense and reasonable guesses, without statistical analysis, mathematical techniques, or any past data.

This example shows a simple forecast of consulting sales by month, with cost of sales by month as well. Add up 12 months to get the totals for the year. The educated guessing might be hard, but the math, and the spreadsheet work, is simple.

Illustration 22-1 is a sample spreadsheet that shows vertical columns and horizontal rows. Each line of sales occupies a row, and the months and years occupy columns. The Total Sales row sums the individual sales rows for each month. The annual sales column sums the months for each row, including the total rows.

Illustration 22-1: Standard Sales Forecast by Month

| Sales Forecast | Plan | | | | | |
Sales	Jan	Feb	Mar	Nov	Dec	2000
Retainer Consulting	10000	$10,000	$10,000	$20,000	$20,000	$200,000
Project Consulting	$0	$0	$10,000	$50,000	$15,000	$270,000
Market Research	$0	$0	$0	$20,000	$20,000	$122,000
Strategic Reports	$0	$0	$0	$0	$0	$0
Other	$0	$0	$0	$0	$0	$0
Total Sales	$10,000	$10,000	$20,000	$90,000	$55,000	$592,000
Direct Cost of Sales	Jan	Feb	Mar	Nov	Dec	2000
Retainer Consulting	$2,500	$2,500	$2,500	$2,500	$2,500	$30,000
Project Consulting	$0	$0	$1,500	$8,500	$2,500	$45,000
Market Research	$0	$0	$0	$14,000	$14,000	$84,000
Strategic Reports	$0	$0	$0	$0	$0	$0
Other	$0	$0	$0	$0	$0	$0
Subtotal Cost of Sales	$2,500	$2,500	$4,000	$25,000	$19,000	$159,000

For the purpose of illustration, the spreadsheet hides the monthly columns for April through October so you can see the annual total. Those other months are there, even if they don't show.

Forecasting depends on how well you know your business and your market. Sales forecasting starts when the research is done. Ultimately a forecast is a guess, but we want it to be an educated guess.

Build on Past Data When you can

We talked about and illustrated the value and use of past data in **Chapter 6: Business Forecasting**, and we'll remind you of the salient points now.

- When you have past data to call on, use it.

- Always compare your forecast to past results.

- Look to the past as a reality check.

- Understand what's changing and why, and what may remain the same.

While mathematical and statistical analyses are great, a simple forecast-to-past data comparison is quick, practical, and very powerful. Every professional analyst knows to look first to real past results before projecting into the future.

Units-Based Sales Forecast

This more detailed sales forecast is still relatively simple. Guess your sales by units, and your price per unit, and cost per unit. The math to produce sales and cost of sales is not complex. Illustration 22-2 shows the row and column format, broken down as follows:.

- Unit sales rows are estimates; total unit sales adds estimated unit sales for each column.

- The unit price rows estimate prices for each kind of sales unit.

- The total sales rows contain the product of multiplying the units times the price for each kind of unit sales. The total sales sums the individual sales rows.

- The annual sales column sums the months for each row, including the total rows.

Units-based sales forecasting has the advantage of breaking your assumptions down into meaningful parts. Depending

Illustration 22-2: Units-Based Sales Forecast by Month

Sales Forecast Unit Sales	Jan	Feb	Mar	Nov	Dec	2000	2001
Exective Desk Oak	14	16	16	27	25	209	350
Exective Desk Cherry	2	3	3	3	2	31	35
Other Furniture Oak	3	4	4	5	4	45	50
Other Furniture Cherry	0	1	0	1	1	7	10
Custom Designed Furniture	1	0	0	1	0	6	10
Total Unit Sales	20	24	23	37	32	298	455
Unit Prices	Jan	Feb	Mar	Nov	Dec	2000	2001
Exective Desk Oak	$1,600	$1,600	$1,600	$1,600	$1,600	$1,600	$1,600
Exective Desk Cherry	$1,750	$1,750	$1,750	$1,750	$1,750	$1,750	$1,750
Other Furniture Oak	$900	$900	$900	$900	$900	$900	$900
Other Furniture Cherry	$1,000	$1,000	$1,000	$1,000	$1,000	$1,000	$1,000
Custom Designed Furniture	$2,500	$2,500	$2,500	$2,500	$2,500	$2,500	$2,500
Sales	Jan	Feb	Mar	Nov	Dec	2000	2001
Exective Desk Oak	$22,400	$25,600	$25,600	$43,200	$40,000	$334,400	$560,000
Exective Desk Cherry	$3,500	$5,250	$5,250	$5,250	$3,500	$54,250	$61,250
Other Furniture Oak	$2,700	$3,600	$3,600	$4,500	$3,600	$40,500	$45,000
Other Furniture Cherry	$0	$1,000	$0	$1,000	$1,000	$7,000	$10,000
Custom Designed Furniture	$2,500	$0	$0	$2,500	$0	$15,000	$25,000
Total Sales	$31,100	$35,450	$34,450	$56,450	$48,100	$451,150	$701,250

For the purpose of illustration, the spreadsheet hides the monthly columns for April through October so you can see the annual total. Those other months are there, even if they don't show.

on your type of business, most people find it easier to guess units and price per unit than to guess total sales values. Also, you can adjust either unit sales or price per unit, and then consider the impact of changes either way.

The quality of the forecast depends on how well you know your business and your market.

Projecting Cost of Sales

Normally a sales forecast includes not just sales, but cost of sales as well. Although not all marketing plans include cost of sales, it's actually a good idea to include these estimates now while you're doing your forecast rather than later on. The previous illustrations of sales forecasting also included cost of sales. As with the sales in the top block, the costs are projected as educated guesses, row by row, and summed in the last row.

Illustration 22-3 shows the unit cost projection portion of the same forecast table shown in Illustration 22-2. Just as the unit sales forecast projects price per unit and multiplies price times units for sales, the cost projection estimates cost per unit and multiplies units times unit cost to calculate total cost of sales for each item. The bottom row adds up the item rows to calculate total direct cost of sales.

You don't need to calculate all of your costs in a marketing plan. Your direct cost of sales might not be your total cost of sales. For example, at Palo Alto Software the direct cost of sales includes the packaging, disks, manuals, and assembly of software products. The total cost of sales also includes additional costs of shipping, fulfillment, and royalties.

This units-based cost forecast has the advantage of breaking your assumptions down into meaningful parts. Depending on your type of business, most people find it easier to guess units and cost per unit than to just guess cost values. Also, as you review and adjust your forecast, you can adjust either unit sales or price per unit as you make changes. And you can consider the impact of changes in either way.

A sales forecast is difficult for many people because they are unsure of how to project future revenue. Don't worry, if you know your business, you can still give an educated guess of future sales. You can then modify the forecast as you learn more through research or experience. Remember, one thing harder than creating a sales forecast is running a business without one.

Illustration 22-3: Unit Costs of Sales Forecast

Sales Forecast Unit Sales	Jan	Feb	Mar	Nov	Dec	2000	2001
Executive Desk Oak	14	16	16	27	25	209	350
Executive Desk Cherry	2	3	3	3	2	31	35
Other Furniture Oak	3	4	4	5	4	45	50
Other Furniture Cherry	0	1	0	1	1	7	10
Custom Designed Furniture	1	0	0	1	0	6	10
Total Unit Sales	20	24	23	37	32	298	455
Direct Unit Costs	Jan	Feb	Mar	Nov	Dec	2000	2001
Executive Desk Oak	$400	$400	$400	$400	$400	$400	$400
Executive Desk Cherry	$525	$525	$525	$525	$525	$525	$525
Other Furniture Oak	$180	$180	$180	$180	$180	$180	$180
Other Furniture Cherry	$300	$300	$300	$300	$300	$300	$300
Custom Designed Furniture	$625	$625	$625	$625	$625	$625	$625
Direct Cost of Sales	Jan	Feb	Mar	Nov	Dec	2000	2001
Executive Desk Oak	$5,600	$6,400	$6,400	$10,800	$10,000	$83,600	$140,000
Executive Desk Cherry	$1,050	$1,575	$1,575	$1,575	$1,050	$16,275	$18,375
Other Furniture Oak	$540	$720	$720	$900	$720	$8,100	$9,000
Other Furniture Cherry	$0	$300	$0	$300	$300	$2,100	$3,000
Custom Designed Furniture	$625	$0	$0	$625	$0	$3,750	$6,250
Subtotal Cost of Sales	$7,815	$8,995	$8,695	$14,200	$12,070	$113,825	$176,625

For the purpose of illustration, the spreadsheet hides the monthly columns for April through October so you can see the annual total. Those other months are there, even if they don't show.

This page is intentionally blank.

CHAPTER 23:

MARKET FORECAST

A market forecast is a core component of a market analysis. It projects the future numbers, characteristics, and trends in your target market. A standard analysis shows the projected number of potential customers divided into segments.

Market Forecast - Example

The AMT computer store sample marketing plan has a simple market forecast. The plan defines two target market segments, and the forecast projects how many potential customers in each of those segments by years, for five years. (**Note:** the complete plan is printed in the appendix of this book.)

In the market forecast the AMT sample plan numbers indicate that there are 25,000 home offices included in the market, and that number is growing at an estimated five percent per year. There are also 10,000 small businesses in the area, and that number is also growing at five percent per year.

These numbers are estimates. Nobody really knows, but we all make educated guesses. The developers of the AMT plan researched the market as well as they could, then estimated populations of target users in their area and the annual growth rates for each. Illustration 23-1 shows the market forecast described for AMT.

You can use your market forecast numbers to create a chart of projected market growth, like the one shown in Illustration 23-2. It offers a visual view of the AMT market forecast table.

Illustration 23-1: Market Forecast Table

Target Market Forecast Potential Customers	Growth	2000	2001	2002	2003	2004	CAGR
High-end Home Office	10%	25,000	27,500	30,250	33,275	36,603	**10.00%**
Small Business	5%	10,000	10,500	11,025	11,576	12,155	**5.00%**
Other	6%	1,000	1,060	1,124	1,191	1,262	**5.99%**
Total	**8.57%**	**36,000**	**39,060**	**42,399**	**46,042**	**50,020**	**8.57%**

Illustration 23-2: Market Forecast by Year

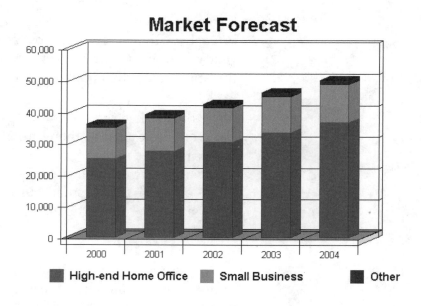

Market Value

Normally you would also look at market value, not just market size. For example, even though AMT's high-end home segment is 2.5 times larger than its small business segment as measured by number of customers, the small business customer spends almost four times as much as the home office customer. Therefore the small business market is a more important market in terms of dollar value. Illustration 23-3 shows AMT's table for tracking market value.

The important numbers in this table are the average purchase per customer and the market value.

- Average purchase per customer is an educated guess based on AMT's experience. Sales managers got together to make the estimate. Although AMT would have liked some external source of information to use for this, there was none available. Notice that the home office customer tends to purchase much less overall than the small business customer.

- The market value is simple mathematics. Multiply the number of potential customers in the market by the average purchase per customer. In this case they took the average number of customers in each segment over the five-year forecast period and multiplied that by the average purchase per customer, to calculate the market value.

Illustration 23-3: AMT Market Value Table

Market Segments	Avge. $ per cust.	Market Value	Product Attitude	Loyalty Status	Buyer readiness
High-end Home Office	$3,200	$98Million	Positive	Medium	Medium
Small Business	$12,500	$138Million	Indifferent	None	Defensive
Other	$4,800	$5Million	Depends	Strong	Informed

The other items in this market analysis table are subjective qualities that help with marketing. AMT assigns these points to people charged with preparing marketing materials.

Reality Checks

A market forecast should always be subject to a reality check. When you think you have a forecast, you need to find a way to check it for reality. In AMT's case, if the total market is worth some estimate they could estimate sales of all the competitors and see if the two numbers relate to each other. In an international market, you might check production and import and export figures to see whether your estimates for annual shipments appear to be in the same general range as published figures. You might check with vendors who sold products to this market in some given year to see whether their results check with your forecast. You might look for macroeconomic data to confirm the relative size of this market compared to other markets with similar characteristics.

Review Target Focus

The market analysis should lead to developing strategic market focus. That means selecting the key target markets.

This is the critical foundation of strategy. We talk about it as segmentation and positioning.

Under normal circumstances, no company will attempt to address all the segments in a market. As you select target segments, think about the inherent market differences, keys to success, competitive advantage, and strengths and weaknesses of your company. You want to focus on the best market, but the best one is not necessarily the largest one or the one with the highest growth. It might be the one that matches your own company profile.

How Do I Make a Market Forecast Estimate?

Relatively few marketing plans are blessed with budgets for professional market research. When you can't pass the problem to professionals, then you have to make some intelligent estimates.

Get comfortable with the idea of making good educated guesses. Many people think there is something magic about this, some technique they don't know that the experts learned in graduate school. Don't worry about it. Having gone through graduate business school and worked as a vice president in a marketing research firm, I can reassure you: sophisticated data analysis rarely works very well for business forecasts. No matter how elaborate the forecasting model, mathematical forecasts are based on past results. Nobody knows the future.

In most situations, the best way to create a market forecast estimate is to find an expert forecast, estimate from past data, find parallel data or apply a model.

Finding an Expert Forecast

If you can find an expert forecast already published, or if you have a budget to pay for an expert forecast, that's a luxury. This probably means you don't have to do your own.

Many expert forecasts are published where you can obtain their results for free. Some of these are government forecasts intended to be free, some are expert forecasts made during interviews or news media coverage, and some are professional forecasts whose highlights are released to the media as teasers to sell the more expensive research.

You can look for these forecasts in published news reports, on the Internet, in library reference materials, and in trade association publications. Where

yours might be found depends on your industry and the exact nature of your business. Unfortunately, nobody but you can pinpoint exactly where to look for your industry and your plan, but at least you can consider some examples:

Forecast Examples

• U.S. Bureau of Labor Statistics

http://www.bls.gov

The BLS regularly publishes job outlooks that include forecasts of the numbers of certain kinds of jobs into the future. If your marketing plan needed to project growth in the number of accountants, chief executives, or heavy machinery operators, you could find that at the BLS site.

http://www.bls.gov/emptab21.htm

The link shown above shows the projected growth of computer industry jobs to be 108% from 1996 to 2006.

• Datamonitor

http://www.datamonitor.com
http://www.nua.ie/surveys

As another example, in late Spring of 1999 a market research firm named Datamonitor published a study saying Western European consumer online shopping markets will be worth $775 million by the end of 1999, increasing to a total value of $8.6 billion by 2003. If your marketing plan involved this market, you could use this as an expert forecast.

- Beverage World Publications

http://www.beverageworld.com/bevinfo.html

If you are working on a marketing plan involving soft drinks, you could go to the national soft drink association for a five-year forecast of soft drink consumption.

- Business Week

http://www.businessweek.com/

Several major business magazines publish economic forecasts regularly. You could go into a reference library and use the *Reader's Guide* to find published data related to your data needs. The *Business Week* magazine link listed here has a column on business outlooks and quarterly surveys of industry outlooks.

For more ideas on where to find these forecasts, try the following chapters in this book:

- Chapter 9: Market Analysis

- Chapter 11: Competitive Analysis

Both of those chapters include website links to the same kinds of information sources that will provide expert forecasts.

Estimating from Past Data

Although the past doesn't really predict the future, it can indicate trends. Sometimes you can find past data on a market and use that to project into the future.

The principle of using past data as a guideline for the future is one of the fundamentals of forecasting that we presented in **Chapter 6: Business Forecasting**.

It is particularly important for market forecasting because you'll frequently find ample data about the recent past of your market even when you can't find a market forecast. Using the past data will give you a good starting point and a sense of reasonableness for your forecast.

Past Data Estimate - Example

For example, say I want to project the market for restaurant equipment in Lane County, Oregon. I can go to the U.S. Census Bureau, County Business

Patterns to find out that Lane County had 611 "eating and drinking places" in 1993 and 639 in 1996:

http://tier2.census.gov/cbp/cbp_sts.htm

I used this example earlier in **Chapter 6: Business Forecasting**, to show calculations of compound growth rates. I don't particularly like the fact that these numbers are several years old, but they are the latest available and they are also better than any other numbers I can find. I could count eating and drinking establishments by using the Yellow Pages in the telephone directories, but any alternative would be impractical and expensive.

So I accepted the latest available census data. I calculated the growth rate for 1993 to 1996 and applied that same rate into the future to create a market forecast, as shown in Illustration 23-4.

Illustration 23-4: Calculating Compound Annual Growth Rate (CAGR)

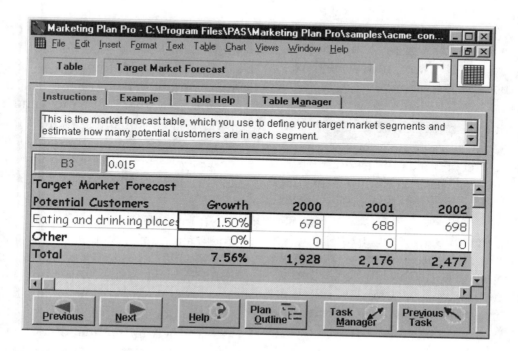

Adding Common Sense and Educated Guessing

Is this the best I can do? Maybe not. I can probably take the past data as a base number, and then add my own research and common sense to improve on it. For example:

- I could contact the local Chamber of Commerce or restaurant association and ask for an expert opinion about the fate of eating and drinking establishments in the recent past and foreseeable future. If the local expert says there has been a boom in restaurants, or a problem with restaurants, then I can use that information to adjust my growth rate up or down. In my marketing plan text I would explain what the past growth rate was and why I was expecting it to change.

- I could also check with the Chamber of Commerce or local governments to find economic growth numbers. I could compare general economic health in the 1993-1996 period to the 1996-2000 period as well as projections for the foreseeable future. I would then revise my projected growth rate accordingly and explain in my text about the source of the growth rate figure.

The important point is that I wouldn't have to just take a wild guess about the restaurant population. By starting with past numbers, I improve the overall quality of the forecast. This is mainly just common sense and educated guessing.

Parallel Data

You may also be able to use data from another industry or another business. This is a twist on "benchmarking" that attempts to establish performance standards based on common issues with other businesses.

For example, the entrepreneurs of a new retail store selling clothing to females between the ages of 18 to 24 may want to look at other businesses in their market that sell to this same target group. These businesses may include stores selling beauty products, CDs, or shoes, where a portion of their sales is to the same target market.

Information about the quantity sold, the average transaction value, and the seasonality of sales may be helpful to create your sales forecast. Theses businesses may be more willing to share information if they feel that you will not be competing in their market. In the best-case scenario, they may anticipate that your complementary products may provide the opportunity to refer customers or combine the marketing efforts of both stores.

The Idea Adoption Model

The use of a model may be a good resource for creating a market forecast. Social scientists have studied adoption of new ideas by many different groups. They have studied how a group of doctors adopt a new treatment technique, how farmers accept a new farming idea, and many other examples of the process of groups of people absorbing innovation.

Most of these studies show a common pattern in adoption of new ideas. They are accepted first by the innovators, who seldom make up more than 2-3 percent of the larger group. The innovators prove the idea works, but they have relatively little influence on the group as a whole. The idea takes off when it is taken up by the early adopters (who tend to be the opinion leaders) who are a second group of roughly 13 percent of the larger group. These are people smart enough to see what those innovators are doing, and influential enough to spread that idea into the next group, the early majority, which comprises approximately 24 percent of the larger group. This pattern continues through the remaining groups, as the bell chart shows in Illustration 23-5, with the percentages in reverse as the number of people reached increases.

Illustration 23-5: Idea Adoption Model

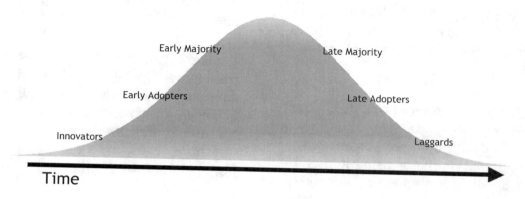

The Idea Adoption Model shows how an idea can spread between different groups of people, from Innovators to Laggards.

When you're forecasting your market, particularly if you are looking at a new product and a new idea, the idea adoption model can help you improve your educated guessing. It's not magic, not even strictly mathematical, but it can help.

Adoption Model-Examples

Calculate what percent penetration your market has at present, how long the market has taken to get there, and extrapolate based on the adoption model to calculate the rest of the curve.

Example: If the Internet took six months to spread to three percent of the market (Innovators), you might expect it to reach 16 percent of the market in another six months (Innovators and Early Adopters), and 50 percent of the market in another six months (Innovators, Early Adopters, and Early Majority). That would be an extremely fast ramp-up, but it still might be valuable to help you estimate.

Another example: Look at another technology that took a long time to spread. If only three percent of the potential market is using it after 10 years, then it might take another 10 years to reach 16 percent of the market.

You have to be careful how you apply the basic idea to your market. If you define your potential market as 12 million people and after five years only 200,000 own this new type of product, then the product doesn't appeal to nearly as many people as you imagined, and you may have overestimated the potential market.

The Diffusion Model

You can model the spread of a product or idea on the spread of a disease, passed from one person to another. This is called diffusion. It can help you forecast a market.

Diffusion models were first used by health organizations to understand and predict the spread of contagious diseases. Market forecasters use them to simulate the spread of ideas, products, and techniques through groups of people.

The formula that follows is taken from James G. March's published work, **An Introduction to Models in the Social Sciences**, which includes research into the use of diffusion models to market questions. It assumes that for a given population of size N, there is a diffusion factor a, which, when n is the number of people who already have the disease, the change in *n* during a time period is equal to the following formula:

$$an(N-n/N)$$

Example: If the total population **N** is 50,000, and there are 5,000 people **n** who already have the disease, the formula would look like this:

a5,000(50,000-5,000/50,000)
5,000 * (.9) = 4,500

Diffusion Model-Examples

In the early 1980s I headed a consulting group asked by Apple Computer to analyze the spread of personal computers into the Latin American market. We used a diffusion model to do it. This is a good example of practical use of diffusion calculations.

Our analysis started with estimates of the U.S. population of knowledge workers. Apple had contracted an earlier study on this and had given us the estimate of 50 million. Using standard idea adoption research, as outlined earlier, we redefined our total population into the classifications of 1) Innovators, 2) Early Adopters, 3) Early Majority, and 4) Late Majority.

Illustration 23-6 shows the breakdown for these diffusion group categories. Our forecast ignored the eight million so-called laggards and late adopters, which gave us a target market population of 42 million. In this case the diffusion factors were estimates. The standard idea adoption research gave us a breakdown of the population into various adoption groups, and from there we developed diffusion factors for each

Illustration 23-6: Diffusion Group Categories

	A	B	D	E	F	G
1	Population Numbers in Millions		Assumed Diffusion Factors			
2				Factor 1	Factor 2	
3	Innovators	1.5		1.50		n.a.
4	Early Adopters	6.5		1.00		0.50
5	Early Majority	17.0		0.60		0.30
6	Late Majority	17.0		0.20		0.10
7	Total Population	42.0				

Assigning diffusion factor values to targeted market segments.

group. We didn't have primary research on diffusion, but we did have data on the early spread, and we manipulated the assumed factors to match the first six years' market data we already had. Illustration 23-7 shows the early years of the forecast.

For spreadsheet experts only--you don't have to follow this--the selected cell on the spreadsheet, E12, has the formula:

=MIN(D12+(((D12*$E4)+(D11*$G4))*((Early_Adopters-D12)/Early_Adopters)),Early_Adopters)

The related ranges are shown in Illustration 23-7 for the cell references, and *Early_Adopters* is a spreadsheet range name for the 6.5 million early adopters included in the model.

Illustration 23-8 follows this model up through 1999. We see an interesting picture of the spread of personal computers through the population of U.S. knowledge workers, as it might have been. This isn't history, it is a market estimate using the diffusion model.

Illustration 23-7: Diffusion Category Forecast

A	B	C	D	E	F	G	H
9	76	77	78	79	80	81	82
10 Users (thousands)							
11 Innovators	5	12	31	77	186	430	890
12 Early Adopters		3	11	38	114	317	822
13 Early Majority			1	5	19	64	197
14 Late Majority				0	1	3	9
15 Total	5	15	43	119	319	813	1,918
16 New Users							
17 Innovators	5	7	19	46	109	244	460
18 Early Adopters		3	9	27	76	203	506
19 Early Majority			1	4	14	45	133
20 Late Majority			-	0	0	2	7
21 Total	5	10	28	76	199	494	1,105

Applying past data in developing a forecast.

What's interesting, however, is how closely this matches the real market data as we know it. The curve shows an increase in computer usage among knowledge workers, reaching 40 million in the middle 1990s. It also shows that the knowledge workers who were new to computing in any given year reached its maximum in about 1988. By that time most of the market penetration was over.

This isn't a complete analysis of market units because it doesn't include replacement units and the second and third computers of the knowledge workers. Some of them have desktop computers at their offices and in their homes, and some have laptops. The replacement and add-on unit market drives the forecast after the middle 1980s.

Illustration 23-8: Diffusion Model Graph

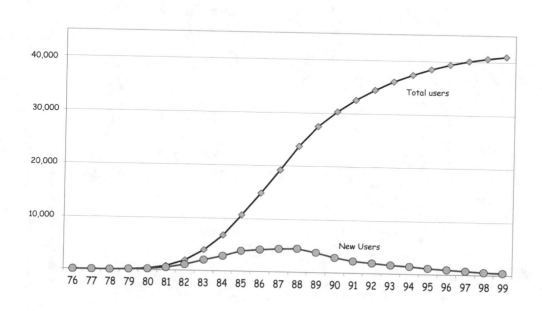

A market estimate comparing yearly growth in new users and cumulative total users.

As a second example, consider the spread of Internet use during the 1990s, beginning in 1994. In this case, the spread was much quicker and the population was greater, so we revised our assumptions as shown in Illustration 23-9. We still ignored the laggards, but we made the total population 60 million. The diffusion factors are greater because the spread was faster.

Illustration 23-9: Diffusion Assumptions

Population Numbers in Millions			Assumed Diffusion Factors	
			Factor 1	Factor 2
Innovators	1.8		8.00	n.a.
Early Adopters	7.8		4.00	8.00
Early Majority	20.4		2.50	4.00
Late Majority	20.4		2.00	2.50
Total Population	60.0			

Illustration 23-10: Diffusion Results Data

	94	95	96	97	98	99
Users (thousands)						
Innovators	5	45	395	1,800	1,800	1,800
Early Adopters		40	556	5,558	7,800	7,800
Early Majority			160	2,765	20,400	20,400
Late Majority				400	7,962	20,400
Total	5	85	1,111	10,524	37,962	50,400
New Users						
Innovators	5	40	350	1,405	-	-
Early Adopters		40	516	5,002	2,242	-
Early Majority			160	2,605	17,635	-
Late Majority			-	400	7,562	12,438
Total	5	80	1,027	9,412	27,438	12,438

This table displays the yearly number of adopters per category based on the diffusion model.

Illustration 23-10 shows the resulting data as if it were a forecast. Illustration 23-11 follows this model through the periods 1994 through 1999. We can see how the idea spread more quickly through the population.

In this case we have over 40 million of the total 60 million knowledge workers already operating on the Internet by 1999. The same diffusion that took more than 20 years for personal computing took only five years for the Internet. The mathematics are the same, but the assumptions changed.

You will probably also notice in the chart that the basic phenomenon is the same. The overall market of users shoots up in an S-curve, but the new users reaches a peak and then trails off as the idea spreads through the population.

Illustration 23-11: Diffusion Results Graph

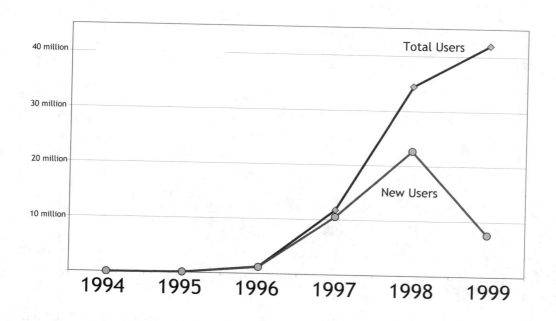

A graph of the diffusion model illustrates results as the number of adopters changes.

Product Life Cycle

Most products go through different stages of development, and those stages are reflected in the different growth rates expected at different stages. The important points are the takeoff point and the market saturation point.

The normal model of the product life cycle looks a lot like the same curve we use for tracking idea adoption, or the S-curve produced by the diffusion model. See Illustration 23-12.

In the early development stage, growth rates may be high, but very few units are involved. This is a new market just beginning to reach its potential consumers' minds and is even further from their pocketbooks. At this point, a few magazine articles begin to address this new technology. As Innovators begin to look for the product, the channels of distribution are set up.

Takeoff is when the market turns upward. Pioneer buyers have spread the word and the general public begins to buy. This is what happened when, for

Illustration 23-12: Product Life Cycle

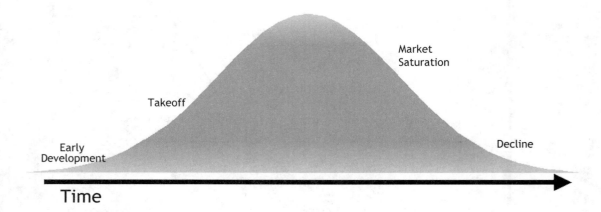

This graph shows how product recognition and acceptance and consumer demand waxes and wanes over time, from introduction to market saturation.

example, mall merchandisers began to sell a lot of home computers in 1982, or when color television sets took off in the 1960s. This is the stage all those people who invested in the early market are waiting for. Growth rates are still attractive, and volume has skyrocketed.

Growth rates decline when the market approaches saturation. At this point, most of the buyers who want the product have it. The market turns into a low-growth and replacement market, just as the markets for stoves and refrigerators did.

Using the Life Cycle in Forecasts

There are three keys to remember in using the product life cycle in your market forecasts:

- First, takeoff resembles a snowball, as it rolls down the hill gaining momentum, and the situation changes enormously.

- Second, once markets get going, saturation will occur.

- Third, each product has a different life cycle, some fast, some slow, and some unlike the normal pattern.

Takeoff is the trickiest stage. There are markets that never take off at all. Some companies spend years waiting for the snowballing affect to get started, and it never does. There are also markets that take off at odd moments, at times you would not normally expect, or after long periods of apparent smoldering.

For example, the home computer boom was predicted as early as 1978, but didn't happen until 1982. Some companies went broke waiting for it. Others left this market and were not participating when the boom finally happened.

After takeoff, it's too easy to forget that market growth rates will eventually approach saturation and decline. Some of the color television people projected increasing growth through the 1970s and were caught off guard when the market moved up to about 10-15 million units per year and then stopped. The video market drew a crowd of new entrants in 1982 and then virtually stopped growing.

The speed of a life cycle is also hard to predict. The video game industry boomed and faded like a typical fad. The home computer industry will probably last longer before saturating its market; then it will become a replacement market. Much depends on what the product does for its buyers and on who those buyers are. Sometimes the standard idea adaptation research will help.

Mature markets are by far the easiest to forecast. These have slow growth rates and little change from year to year. In these markets, the old-fashioned forecasting methods – such as taking the average growth rate of the last five years and projecting it into the next five years – work reasonably well.

Web Links for Market Data

You can find an amazing wealth of market data on the Internet. The hard part, of course, is sorting through it all and knowing what to stress. As the Internet explosion increases, the hardest part about gathering market data is digesting all that's available.

In **Chapter 7: Market Research** we introduced you to many Internet information sites where you can research data for United States and international markets. Take a moment now and review some of these sites. Perhaps you saw some and wondered at their usefulness. You may find that with the knowledge and insight you've gained in these additional chapters, the value of these sites is more readily apparent.

CHAPTER 24:

EXPENSE BUDGET

Spending levels are strategic and tactical. Some companies spend 50% of sales on marketing, some spend 10%, and some spend nothing at all.

Your Budget is a Marketing Tactic

There are several benefits of creating and using a marketing budget:

- The goal of your marketing budget is to control your expenses and project your revenues.

- It also assists in the coordination of your marketing activities within your organization.

- A realistic budget establishes a standard of performance for your actions, and communicates those standards to others responsible for implementing your marketing strategy.

- A well-designed budget is also a tool to keep you on target and indicate when there is needed modification of your marketing plan, especially if something goes really right or very wrong.

A Simple Expense Budget

Budgets are plans. They are spending plans, activity plans, sales plans, marketing plans, all linked to the disciplines of careful projection and resource allocation.

The math of the expense budget is very simple. The content takes work, but not the design of the table. It's built on common sense and reasonable guesses, without statistical analysis, mathematical techniques, or any past data. The mathematics are also simple, sums of the rows and columns.

In the example below, rows are horizontal, columns are vertical. Each line of expense occupies a row, and months and years occupy columns. The source spreadsheet hides the monthly columns for March through October for the purpose of illustration, so you can see the annual total without scrolling. Those other months are there, even if they don't show.

The total expense row sums the individual expense rows. The annual expense column sums the months for each row, including the total rows.

As you develop a budget, think of it as educated guessing. Consider your plan objectives, your sales and marketing activities, and how you'll relate your spending to your strategy. Remember, as you budget you want to prioritize your spending to match your priorities in sales and target marketing.

Illustration 24-1: A Simple Expense Budget

Marketing Expense Budget	Jan	Feb	Nov	Dec	2000	2001
Advertising	$15,000	$15,000	$20,000	$10,000	$150,000	$250,000
Catalogs	$2,000	$3,000	$2,000	$2,000	$25,000	$28,000
Websites	$3,000	$11,800	$8,000	$5,000	$113,300	$125,000
Promotions	$0	$0	$15,000	$0	$16,000	$18,000
Shows	$0	$0	$0	$0	$20,200	$22,000
Literature	$0	$7,000	$0	$0	$7,000	$8,000
PR	$0	$0	$0	$0	$1,000	$1,000
Seminars	$1,000	$0	$0	$0	$31,000	$34,000
Service	$2,000	$1,000	$500	$250	$10,250	$11,000
Training	$5,000	$5,000	$5,000	$5,000	$60,000	$66,000
Other	$1,000	$1,000	$1,000	$1,000	$12,000	$15,000
Total Sales and Marketing Expenses	$29,000	$43,800	$51,500	$23,250	$445,750	$578,000
Percent of Sales	6.24%	9.36%	6.77%	3.75%	7.48%	8.82%
Contribution Margin	$144,310	$123,238	$80,161	$72,035	$913,563	$1,108,926
Contribution Margin / Sales	31.07%	26.33%	10.54%	11.63%	15.33%	16.92%

The emphasis in your strategy should show up in your actual detailed programs.

Budgeting is hard for many people because they are unsure of how to project the future. Don't worry, if you know your business, you can give an educated guess of future expenses. One thing harder than budgeting is running a business without a budget.

Budgeting Approaches

Where do you get budget numbers? How do you set a budget and organize it? What are some standard ways to measure your budget?

There are several approaches you can take to create your budget. Examples of these approaches may include basing your budget on:

- Percent of projected gross sales.
- Percent of past gross sales.
- Per unit sales.
- Seasonal allocation.
- Projected cash flow.

Select a budget methodology that will work best for your business. You may want to make this choice based on how you track your sales and revenues, or based on industry standards.

Keep the Process in Perspective

Don't forget your fundamentals, **Chapters 4 through 8**. A budget is an educated guess and a management tool.

Keep the budget process in perspective. You are making a series of educated guesses. If it makes you feel better, remind your audience how you came up with your projections in your marketing plan. For this same reason, it is important to review your budget throughout the year and make adjustments when necessary. Reviewing your marketing plan throughout the plan period will be addressed in **Chapter 25: Print and Publish** and **Chapter 26: Keep it Alive**.

One of the best ways to create your budget may be to build your projections on the previous year's performance. If you have this information, the foundation is in place. Look at trends and expectations in each area and modify these numbers based on your expectations for the upcoming year. Look at industry performance and trends and take those factors into consideration. Once you get to the bottom line, ask yourself if it is realistic, or if you need to go back and modify revenues or expenses to more closely capture what you expect to happen in the year ahead.

When You Don't Have Past Data to Compare

Yes, it is harder to set budgets when you don't have past budgets to go on. Still, even a new company needs a budget.

If you do not have historical data available, the process is more challenging, but still doable. Your reliance on industry information is going to be greater and it will require more research to formulate your projections. Take advantage of the tremendous amount of marketing information through resources that may be available at no cost. In most cases, each industry will have a trade association, a website, and at least one publication in existence.

You may also be able to leverage information from other industries that might provide you additional insight. For example, a restaurant may want to know more about new home construction projections in their immediate area as they attempt to predict next year's growth.

Creativity is a Budget's Best Friend

There are ways to reap enormous marketing benefits from free activities, barter, alliances, and public relations.

You may also want to consider some non-traditional ways of maximizing your budget dollars and including those into your budget projections. A large percentage of advertising on the radio is on a barter basis. Manufacturers may offer co-op dollars for advertising efforts. Magazines may extend your payment schedule to allow you to generate sales from the ad before you pay the balance.

Part 7:

MAKE IT HAPPEN

Make It Happen

The value of your marketing plan will be realized through its successful implementation, which produces your stated results.

CHAPTER 25:

PRINT AND PUBLISH

The worst danger in developing a plan is not having it implemented. That's a waste. You must make sure a plan is properly distributed and accepted within its target management group. That's what we mean by publishing a plan.

Publishing is Management

So you're about ready to print your plan. Please make sure to run it through a final critical edit. Then, make sure to publish it so that commitments made by managers are clearly known and acknowledged. In this case, publishing means distributing the plan where all the managers can see it. People who make commitments as part of the plan need to see those commitments on record. They need to know that the plan will be tracked and that the difference between planned and actual results will be calculated and discussed.

Final Edit

Always, **always** edit your plan. Misspelled words and number errors will *certainly* not impress your readers. Or perhaps create a decidedly negative impression on them. Read it over again. Have some other people read and review it for you. Sometimes you don't see the errors that others will because you are too close.

Check the numbers in your charts and tables. Make sure they match each other, and go back and check the references to numbers in the text. People often change numbers after writing objectives, which results in conflicting information. For example, your text might set sales objectives of $500,000, but your plan tables show sales projections of $400,000.

If you can, tighten your text. Shorten it, get to the point, make it sharper.

Presentation

A good presentation of your marketing plan enhances and highlights information. It adds clarity and aids understanding. Presentation is important but only to communicate content. Expensive paper, expensive bindings, and excessive presentation are not really needed. Make the paper whatever quality necessary to make the plan easy to read, and avoid some of the more fibrous papers that can interfere with the printed content. Make the binding a good coil, or some other binding that will hold up to use, but keep it practical. Impress with content, not expense.

Good text formatting should make the text easy to read. Use a legible font with a mix of headings and subheadings to make the organization visible. Bullet points are generally easier to read than long paragraphs and the variation adds interest. Color is impressive for charts, when it makes numbers easier to understand, but gets in the way when used for text. Good charts are dynamite when they make numbers easier to read quickly, and they can be essential when numbers are complex.

Bring Together in Print

With the computer tools available, you should be able to produce a good looking plan, with text, tables, and charts merged together into a design that's easy to read and to follow.

- A cover page and table of contents is recommended.

- Keep the tables and charts together with the related text so that your readers can refer to them while they read.

- Keep your plan in a vertical (portrait) layout that is easier to read, with summary tables. Then put your monthly forecasts into horizontal (landscape) format to display all the months on a single page.

- Appendices are a good way to include backup details, such as monthly forecasts. They are also a good way to handle problems of page layout.

Illustration 25-1: Printed Page of a Sample Plan

Acme Consulting

4.2.1 Sales Breakdown by Partner

As the projection shows, we expect our billing to come from all three of our main partners first. The partners have relationships that should create these billings at that level.

Later on, we expect the billing to come from additional resources and additional partners, so the billings attributed to the main three go down as a percentage of the total.

The detail for this table is included in the appendices.

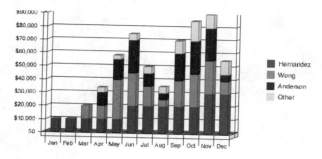

Table 4.2.1: Sales by Partner

Sales by: Sales	Partner	2000	2001	2002	2003	2004
Hernandez		$210,000	$250,000	$350,000	$450,000	$600,000
Wong		$175,000	$200,000	$250,000	$350,000	$450,000
Anderson		$140,000	$175,000	$200,000	$250,000	$350,000
Other		$67,000	$275,000	$350,000	$450,000	$425,000
Total		$592,000	$900,000	$1,150,000	$1,500,000	$1,825,000
Average		$148,000	$225,000	$287,500	$375,000	$456,250

Page 18

Illustration 25-1 shows a sample page from a printed marketing plan.

This page is intentionally blank.

CHAPTER 26:

KEEP IT ALIVE

The decisions you make and the steps you take to put your plan into action benefit from focused planning as well.

Start with the Right Plan

Some plans are more likely to be implemented than others. Successful implementation starts with a good plan, one that is full of specific information on milestones, managers, responsibilities, dates and budgets. Beyond the plan itself, however, there are other factors also critical to implementation. Are you going to track results, comparing the planned results to the actual results? Are you going to follow up with your management team, making revisions and checking on performance?

Illustration 26-1 shows a view of what it takes to develop and implement a marketing plan. We call this "planning for implementation." There are some important factors beyond the plan that are also critical:

1. Is the plan simple? Is it easy to understand and to act on? Does it communicate its contents easily and practically?

Illustration 26-1: Implementation Isn't Automatic

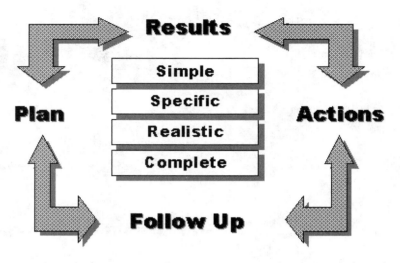

A marketing plan should be simple, specific, realistic and complete.

Even if it is all these things, a good plan will need someone to follow up and check on it.

2. Is the plan specific? Are its objectives concrete and measurable? Does it include specific activities, with dates of completion, people responsible, and specific budgets?

3. Is the plan realistic? Are the sales goals, expense budgets, and milestone dates realistic? Nothing stifles implementation like unrealistic goals.

4. Is the plan complete? Does it include all the necessary elements? Requirements of a marketing plan vary, depending on the context. There is no guarantee that the plan will work if it doesn't cover the main bases.

Track and Follow-Up

A good plan alone isn't enough. As the illustration indicates, other elements are also critical. Even a good plan means virtually nothing if somebody doesn't follow-up on its concrete and specific milestones or results. A plan won't be implemented unless responsibilities are assigned to specific people, milestones are established and agreed upon, and the people responsible know that somebody will follow up to check on results. If you don't follow up, your plan will not be implemented.

Implementation Milestones

At this point, you've been through the main thinking and analysis. It is time to put some bite into your plan, and management, by listing specific actions to be taken.

Each action is called a milestone. This is where a business plan becomes a real plan, with specific and measurable activities, instead of just a document. Give as many milestones as you can to make it more concrete. Give each milestone a name, a person responsible, a milestone date, and a budget. Then make sure that all your people know that you will be following the plan and tracking plan-vs.-actual results.

Milestones Table

The Milestones table should be the most important section of the entire marketing plan. Each marketing and sales-related program you plan should be listed in the table and explained in the related text. You want to cement your sales strategy with programs that make it real. How is this strategy to be implemented? Do you have concrete and specific plans? How will implementation be measured?

If created using computer software, a milestones table can be set up to track the difference between plan versus actual results for each program. You can also track actual spending and dates of

Illustration 26-2: Milestones Table

Milestones Milestone	Plan Start Date	End Date	Budget	Manager	Department
Seminar implementation plan	1/3/00	2/15/00	$1,000	Jan	Sales
Tech99Expo	4/12/00	4/21/00	$15,000	Jan	GM
Service Revamp	2/25/00	3/16/00	$2,500	Kelly	Product
6 Presentations	2/25/00	3/7/00	$0	Leslie	Sales
3 Accounts	3/17/00	4/8/00	$0	Leslie	Sales
Direct Mail	2/16/00	3/2/00	$3,500	Leslie	Marketing
Upgrade Mailer	1/16/00	2/6/00	$5,000	Leslie	Sales
Business Plan Review	1/10/00	2/16/00	$0	Ralph	GM
VP S&M Hired	6/11/00	6/25/00	$1,000	Ralph	Sales
New corporate brochure	1/16/00	3/16/00	$5,000	Ralph	Marketing
Corporate identity	1/3/00	3/15/00	$10,000	Ralph	Marketing
Advertising	1/15/00	11/30/00	$150,000	Ralph	GM
X4 Testing	3/6/00	3/19/00	$1,000	Sonny	Product
X4 Prototype	2/25/00	3/15/00	$2,500	Sonny	Product
L30 Prototype	3/26/00	4/4/00	$2,500	Sonny	Product
Delivery vans	3/25/00	4/15/00	$22,500	Sonny	Service
Mailing Systems	7/25/00	11/15/00	$10,000	Leslie	Service
Totals			$231,500		

These are the milestones, the heart and core of the marketing plan.

completion, and sort the table by person responsible, milestone date and budget, and by department.

Regular Modifications and Corrections

The decisions you make and the steps you take to put your plan into action benefit from focused planning as well.

A marketing plan should be a live document. As you review your implementation results with the people responsible, you will often find the need to set new goals and make course corrections. Keep track of the original plan and manage changes carefully. Although changes should be made only with good reason, don't be afraid to update your plan and keep it alive.

We recommend using a computer for your budgets and forecasts so you can easily make changes, as described below.

Prescription for Live Planning

1. After your plan starts, type actual results into the sales forecast, expense budget, and milestones. Compare what the plan vs. actual worksheets tell you.

2. Note when actual results indicate you need to make changes to your plan.

3. Make adjustments to future months of your cash plan, based on the actual results for the months already completed.

4. As each month closes, type actual results over your revised plan numbers.

Sales Forecast - Example

The following example shows how a hypothetical company keeps its marketing plan alive.

The Starting Sales Plan

The example begins in Illustration 26-3 with the sales forecast portion of a finished marketing plan.

Illustration 26-3: Beginning Sales Plan

Unit Sales	Jan	Feb	Mar
Systems	85	115	145
Service	200	200	200
Software	150	200	250
Training	145	155	165
Other	160	176	192
Total Unit Sales	740	846	952

Unit Prices	Jan	Feb	Mar
Systems	$2,000.00	$2,000.00	$2,000.00
Service	$75	$69	$58
Software	$200	$200	$200
Training	$37	$35	$39
Other	$300	$300	$300

Sales			
Systems	$170,000	$230,000	$290,000
Service	$15,000	$13,846	$11,667
Software	$30,000	$40,000	$50,000
Training	$5,365	$5,500	$6,500
Other	$48,000	$52,800	$57,600
Total Sales	$268,365	$342,146	$415,767

To set the scene, this illustration shows the sales forecast as the marketing plan is finished.

Actual Results for Sales

In Illustration 26-4, we see the actual results for the same company for the first three months of the plan.

Illustration 26-4: Actual Sales Results

Unit Sales	Jan	Feb	Mar
Systems	63	74	108
Service	168	171	174
Software	174	235	289
Training	156	171	183
Other	162	151	220
Total Unit Sales	723	802	974

Unit Prices			
Systems	$1,782.57	$1,801.20	$1,791.14
Service	$102.52	$106.13	$88.83
Software	$223.57	$185.39	$276.77
Training	$48.35	$38.77	$46.17
Other	$291.23	$370.82	$221.96

Sales			
Systems	$112,302	$133,289	$193,443
Service	$17,223	$18,148	$15,456
Software	$38,901	$43,567	$79,987
Training	$7,543	$6,629	$8,449
Other	$47,179	$55,994	$48,832
Total Sales	$223,148	$257,627	$346,167

The actual sales flow at the end of March shows actual sales numbers plus adjustments and course corrections.

Plan vs. Actual Sales

Illustration 26-5 shows you the plan-vs.-actual results (or variance) for our hypothetical company.

Illustration 26-5 : Sales Variance

Unit Sales	Jan	Feb	Mar
Systems	(22)	(41)	(37)
Service	(32)	(29)	(26)
Software	24	35	39
Training	11	16	18
Other	2	(25)	28
Total Unit Sales	(17)	(44)	22
Unit Prices			
Systems	($217.43)	($198.80)	($208.86)
Service	$27.52	$36.90	$30.49
Software	$23.57	($14.61)	$76.77
Training	$11.35	$3.28	$6.78
Other	($8.77)	$70.82	($78.04)
Sales			
Systems	($57,698.00)	($96,711.00)	($96,557.00)
Service	$2,223.00	$4,302.00	$3,789.00
Software	$8,901.00	$3,567.00	$29,987.00
Training	$2,178.00	$1,129.00	$1,949.00
Other	($820.74)	$3,194.00	($8,768.00)
Total Sales	($45,216.74)	($84,519.00)	($69,600.00)

The variance view shows plan vs. actual results. This discussion focuses on the sales forecast variance.

As you look at the variance for the sales forecast for the first three months, you should see several important trends:

1. Unit sales of systems are disappointing, well below expectations.

2. The average revenue for systems sales is also disappointing.

3. Unit sales for service are disappointing, but dollar sales are way up.

4. Sales are well above expectations for software and training.

Variance Analysis

Variance is the frequently forgotten other half of budgeting.

Many businesses, especially the small, entrepreneurial kind, ignore or forget the other half of the budgeting. Budgets are too often proposed, discussed, accepted, and forgotten. Variance analysis looks after the fact at what caused a difference between plan and actual numbers. Good management looks at what that difference means to the business.

Variance analysis ranges from simple and straightforward to sophisticated and complex. Some cost-accounting systems separate variances into many types and categories. Sometimes a single result can be broken down into many different variances, both positive and negative.

The most sophisticated systems separate unit and price factors on materials, hours worked, cost-per-hour on direct labor, and fixed and variable overhead variances. Though difficult, this kind of analysis can be invaluable in a complex business.

Look for Specifics

This presentation of variances shows how important good analysis is. In theory, the positive variances are good news because they mean spending less than budgeted. The negative variance means spending more than the budget.

Variance Analysis for Sample Company

Illustration 26-6 shows a variance analysis for the company's Expense Budget table.

Illustration 26-6: Expense Budget Planned vs. Actual

	Jan	Feb	Mar
Sales	($45,217)	($84,519)	($69,600)
Direct Cost of Sales	$43,116	$72,786	$67,561
Production payroll	$192	$276	($259)
Other	$467	($282)	$64
	------------	------------	------------
Total Cost of Sales	$43,775	$72,780	$67,366
Gross Margin	($88,991)	($157,299)	($136,966)
Gross Margin %	196.81%	186.11%	196.79%
Sales and Marketing Exp.			
Payroll	$544	($529)	$129
Ads	$5,000	($17,674)	($896)
Catalog	($200)	($100)	($95)
Mailing	$1,127	($275)	($1,121)
Promo	$0	$0	$0
Shows	$0	$0	$0
Literature	$0	$7,000	($6,401)
PR	$0	$0	$0
Seminar	$0	$0	$0
Service	$2,000	($2,023)	($23)
Training	$450	($550)	($50)
Total Expenses	$8,921	($14,151)	($8,457)

This illustration shows a portion of the Expense Budget Variance for our example. March results showed sales below plan and costs above plan, for a large negative variance. Marketing expenses were also above plan in March, causing another negative variance.

In our example, the $5,000 advertising variance in January means $5,000 less than planned was spent, and the $7,000 positive variance for literature in February means $7,000 less than planned was spent. The negative variance for advertising in February and March, and the negative variance for literature in March, show that more was spent than was planned for those items.

Evaluating these variances takes thought. Positive variances aren't always good news. For example, the positive variance of $5,000 in advertising means that money wasn't spent, but it also means that advertising wasn't placed. System sales are way below expectations for this same period--could the advertising missed in January be a possible cause? For literature, the positive $7,000 in February may be evidence of a missed deadline for literature that wasn't actually completed until March. If so, at least it appears that the costs of completion were a bit less than the $7,000 planned.

Every variance should stimulate questions. Why did one project cost more or less? Were objectives met? Is a positive variance a cost saving or a failure to implement? Is a negative variance a change in plans, a management failure, or an unrealistic budget?

A variance table can provide management with significant information. Without this data, some of these important questions might go unasked.

More on Variance

Variance analysis on sales can be very complex. There can be very significant differences between higher or lower sales because of different unit volumes, or because of different average prices. For purposes of example, Illustration 26-7 shows the sales table (including costs) in variance mode, for the sales forecast of our sample company.

The units variance shows that the sales of systems were disappointing. In the expenses outlined in Illustration 26-6, we saw that advertising and mailing costs were below plan. Could there be a correlation between the saved expenses in mailing, and the lower-than-planned sales? Yes, of course there could.

The mailing cost was much less than planned, but as a result the planned sales never came.

In this example, the positive expense variance is not good for the company.

Illustration 26-7: Sales Forecast Variance

Unit Sales	Jan	Feb	Mar
Systems	(22)	(41)	(37)
Service	(32)	(29)	(26)
Software	24	35	39
Training	11	16	18
Other	2	(25)	28
Total Unit Sales	**(17)**	**(44)**	**22**
Unit Prices			
Systems	($217.43)	($198.80)	$208.86
Service	$27.52	$36.90	$30.49
Software	$23.57	($14.61)	$76.77
Training	$11.35	$3.28	$6.78
Other	($8.77)	$70.82	($78.04)
Sales			
Systems	$57,698.00	($96,711.00)	($96,557.00)
Service	$2,223.00	$4,302.00	$3,789.00
Software	$8,901.00	$3,567.00	$29,987.00
Training	$2,178.00	$1,129.00	$1,949.00
Other	($820.74)	$3,194.00	($8,768.00)
Total Sales	**($45,216.74)**	**$84,519.00**	**$69,600.00**
Direct Unit Costs			
Systems	$65.95	$10.99	$42.67
Service	($2.75)	($4.71)	$7.77
Software	$16.87	$25.97	$4.44
Training	$4.59	($0.15)	$1.95
Other	$3.66	$17.29	$13.19
Direct Cost of Sales			
Systems	$41,555.00	$70,513.00	$67,508.00
Service	$498.00	$935.00	$2,912.00
Software	$55.00	$1,902.00	($3,398.00)
Training	$594.50	($203.50)	$157.50
Other	$413.00	($361.00)	$381.00
Subtotal (DCoS)	**$431.16**	**$72,786.00**	**$67,561.00**

The illustration shows the sales variance for the same example set used in other illustrations in this section.

This page is intentionally blank.

Part 8:

APPENDICES

Appendices

The Appendices support the main text.

SAMPLE PLAN: All4Sports, Inc.

This sample marketing plan has been made available to users of *Marketing Plan Pro*™, marketing planning software published by Palo Alto Software. It is based on a real marketing plan of an existing company. Names, numbers, and substantial portions of text may have been omitted to preserve confidential information.

You are welcome to use this plan as a starting point to create your own, but you do not have permission to reproduce, publish, distribute, or even copy this plan as it exists here.

Requests for reprints, academic use, and other dissemination of this sample plan should be addressed to the marketing department of Palo Alto Software.

Table of Contents

1.0 Executive Summary

All4Sports is a tax-exempt not-for-profit organization that provides the community with a complete youth sports program. All4Sports offers participants from kindergarten to high school positive learning and team experiences along with the opportunity to create life-long memories.

All4Sports continues to be the premier provider of youth sports experiences, and seeks to make this experience affordable and available for all interested participants. This is done through a series of successful fund-raising activities, the role of the Fund-Raising Foundation, and a solid financial approach to managing these resources. All4Sports now serves more than 24,000 participants in seven sports throughout the Jackson County area with additional youth participating on an out-of-district basis. Ongoing efforts are in place to continue to improve the quality and integrity of the program. The success of these efforts has been documented through studies that confirm the positive perception of the program within the Jackson County area.

Major challenges face All4Sports for the future. These include the uncertainties brought on by property tax changes, facility and capital requirements, the impact of alternative programs, and volunteer training and educational needs, to name a few. The Board of Directors, staff, and volunteers continue to work toward providing a quality experience in the most effective and efficient manner possible with optimism for the future of this exceptional organization.

2.0 Situation Analysis

The need for youth sports programs is validated and magnified by information that attributes long-term value to participants in these programs. Numerous studies document the direct value of youth participation in sports. These studies indicate a direct correlation demonstrating that involvement in sports reduces the potential to become involved in drugs, sex, crime, and gang-related behaviors. Research indicates the economic, social and personal value of "investing" in the lives of children in a positive and constructive manner avoids the social and penal system costs that may later result. To meet this need, All4Sports offers an experience that serves as a personal "sports reference" for participants throughout their lives. These important benefits continue to validate the All4Sports concept.

1

2.1 Market Summary

All4Sports provides valuable team and social experiences for the increasing population of public, private, and home-schooled youth. All4Sports offers young people the opportunity to participate in a variety of team sports throughout the calendar year. Beginning in kindergarten, these experiences provide a source of recreation and simultaneously improve athletic skills, health and fitness as they offer experiences in teamwork, sportsmanship, fair play, cooperation and leadership. Increased self confidence is just one of the many intangible benefits this program offers.

Target Market Forecast

Potential Customers	Growth	2000	2001	2002	2003	2004	CAGR
Public School Students	6%	1,947	2,064	2,188	2,319	2,458	6.00%
Private School Students	9%	388	423	461	502	547	8.97%
Home School Students	17%	107	125	146	171	200	16.93%
Total	**7.03%**	**2,442**	**2,612**	**2,795**	**2,992**	**3,205**	**7.03%**

Target Markets

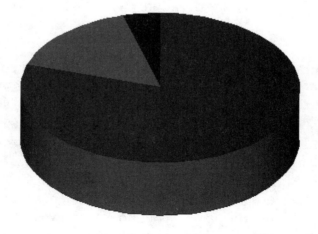

■ Public School Students   ■ Private School Students   ■ Home School Students

2

2.1.1 Market Demographics

Market Geographics—All4Sports serves the Jackson County area with a total population in excess of 170,000 people. With a majority of participants from Medford, the program also has participation from surrounding communities, including Central Point, Jacksonville, White City, and Ashland.

Market Demographics—An estimated 45% of households in this area contain children under the age of 18. Each of these households averages 2.1 children. Therefore, an estimated 39,000 children under the age of 18 are potential All4Sports participants. This number is determined annually from grade school enrollment within the areas served. Past data indicates that the highest level of participation occurs after Grade 2. Participation begins to drop in the middle school years, with a significant reduction in participation at Grade 9. A total of 59% of the participants are male and 41% female. Boys dominate football and girls dominate volleyball. These percentages constantly change due to trends in choice of sports, other alternatives offered in the market place, and other factors impacting participation and availability of these experiences.

Market Psychographics—One of the most typical profiles of families interested in this type of program can be described by the following:

- The parent/guardian works full-time in a traditional "8 to 5" schedule.
- They have more than one child living at home.
- They are relatively active in their child's life, but feel they have limited time.
- They value the physical and social experience their child receives more than actual sports and skill-development aspects of the experience.

Market Behaviors—All4Sports continues to enjoy a positive perception within the community. Studies report solid support of the concept and purpose of the organization and an awareness of the problems inherent in a program that involves thousands of volunteers. Based on research conducted in April of 1997, more than 86% of the population in Jackson County area has some awareness of All4Sports. Most people report they are familiar with All4Sports through knowing a young person who has participated in an All4Sports program. Individual awareness levels are highest among adults in the 25-54 age range, and business owners and managers have a 93% awareness level. More than 82% of this group feels our program has a positive influence on youth and a potential deterrent to violence and other anti-social behavior. This is a primary reason people continue to support this program.

3

Target Market Analysis

Market Segments	Age Focus	Dominate Gender	Lead Sport	Multi-Programs	Out-of-Area
Public School Students	K-12	Male 51%	Soccer	12%	5%
Private School Students	Grade 1-12	Male 54%	Basketball	28%	8%
Home School Students	Grade 2-12	Female 52%	Soccer	54%	14%

2.1.2 Market Needs

The initial reasons for All4Sports remain constant. School-sponsored sports programs are severely limited in terms of age and range of events. Based on the April 1997 study, 59% of the people in the Jackson County area surveyed believe the public school system fails to meet their sports experience expectations. Driven by economics, most notably with the passage of state legislation limiting school funding, many sports programs have not survived increasing economic pressures on the public school system. Property tax modifications may further impede the public school system's ability to offer any more than the most basic classroom experiences. All4Sports seeks to serve all interested children from kindergarten through high school regardless of what their school offers. There are no expectations regarding skill or experience, only the desire to participate. The All4Sports program is orchestrated to be as accessible and affordable as possible to this audience.

4

2.1.3 Market Trends

· Diminishing financial support at all grade levels from public schools to facilitate sports activities for students.
· Increasing demands from children and their families to offer sports experiences at early ages, beginning at kindergarten.
· Heightened awareness of the positive correlation with involvement in sports and reduced potential for involvement in violent activities.
· Increasing interest from corporations to sponsor and support these types of community activities when they receive attribution for this involvement.

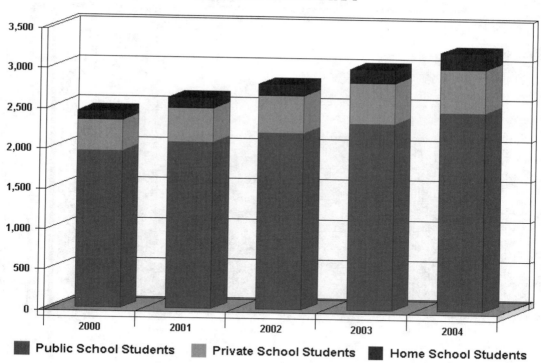

Market Forecast

Public School Students   Private School Students   Home School Students

5

2.1.4 Market Growth

The program has experienced an average annual participation growth rate of 6% for the past five years. This is indicative of the growing needs of the market we serve. Based on school attendance projections, we expect to experience increased participation growth between 9% and 11% annually over the next three years. The most dramatic growth is expected in the soccer programs, with relatively static participation expected in most other sports. These trends are monitored, and to the degree possible, used to help predict future program demands.

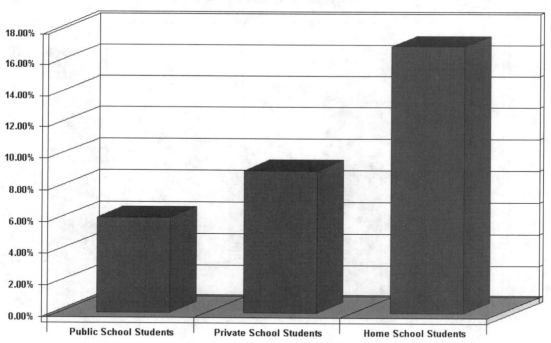

Target Market Growth

6

2.2 SWOT Analysis

The following outlines the most significant strengths and weaknesses internal to All4Sports, and the opportunities and threats that exist in our environment. Our objective is to leverage our strengths to take advantage of the opportunities our market presents, develop those areas that are weaknesses, and devise contingency plans to address threats if those should become a reality.

2.2.1 Strengths

The following outlines key strengths of the organization:

Program Reputation—All4Sports is considered to be the premier choice for youth sports related experiences. There is now a generation of participants that send their children to participate in the program.

Donor Base—We have developed a stable and loyal donor base from both private and corporate sources.

Facilities Relationships—We depend on access to athletic facilities including gyms, soccer fields, football fields, softball and baseball fields. Close relationships and reciprocal maintenance agreements with public and private schools and church facilities are an invaluable asset to the organization.

The Internet—Our website, www.all4sports.com, promises to be a significant technological solution for All4Sports in the area of registration, communication, and information delivery. The website has demonstrated the ability to provide more extensive and current information at reduced costs. We can reduce the need for printed materials, voice mail communication equipment, and staff payroll time. It has also allowed us to reallocate volunteer hours to better serve our program.

2.2.2 Weaknesses

Capital Requirements—All4Sports continues to make impressive improvements in the management of financial resources. Additional funds are needed to maintain the quality of the experiences offered and meet future program demands. The Fund-raising Foundation's strategy is to provide significant financial resources for All4Sports. The future depends on these resources in addition to revenues from participants and traditional fund-raising events.

7

Facilities—Our need for facilities is growing beyond what is now available. This is one of the most urgent challenges facing All4Sports. This essential component is threatened from several aspects. Increasing program needs, combined with recent restrictions and fees for the use of public school facilities, is an issue. Indoor facilities are virtually at capacity for basketball and volleyball games and tournaments. They are insufficient to support flexible and convenient practice schedules. Outdoor facilities are adequate, but the increasing demands of soccer presents concerns in this area as well. New and innovative alternatives must be explored and implemented to provide additional facilities to support the demands of the program. One alternative is to form "alliances" with public facilities to take on the management and maintenance of these facilities in exchange for scheduled use. Other potential options may include establishing relationships with private schools, churches and other institutions with available gym space. For example, successful experiences have occurred where All4Sports has taken the lead in the development and maintenance of outdoor fields on property owned by other not-for-profit organizations.

Training and Education for Coaches and Officials—Individuals often have their first coaching experience with All4Sports. This presents the need to adequately train these individuals to enable them to better understand All4Sports' philosophy, their responsibilities, potential liability issues, and appropriate behavior with participants. A more positive experience for participants, coaches and officials with an increased awareness of responsibilities are some of the goals. The resource demands of this training effort are tremendous.

Staff Challenges and Attrition—The All4Sports' staff experiences tremendous pressure due to workloads, dealing with parents, and addressing the issues of the program. These factors, combined with concerns regarding compensation, have resulted in undesirable turnover in important positions.

2.2.3 Opportunities

All4Sports competes for resources in a community with a high number of not-for-profit organizations per capita. Numerous organizations target personal and corporate dollars to augment other revenue sources. Based on this challenge, All4Sports must continue to demonstrate that it successfully offers a meaningful experience to participants, with short and long-term benefits, in a manner that effectively meets community needs. The following summarizes potential opportunities:

8

Geographic Serving Area Issues—All4Sports continues to be a precedent-setting organization that attracts attention from surrounding communities. Decisions regarding the serving area will impact financial requirements and potentially open new revenue opportunities. This growth strategy must be managed and orchestrated in a manner that will add strength to the program.

Soccer Interest—Soccer is the single fastest growing sport in terms of participation. With some participation trade-offs with boy's football, this increasing interest in soccer is the most predominant reason for program growth and has added a more even balance to gender participation. There is an increasing demand for indoor soccer programs.

Program Expansion—Program expansion also requires consideration and evaluation. This may include adding sports to the current venue or looking at offering these sports to older age groups, potentially including adult sports programs.

Community Education—All4Sports must continue to tell its story to the community it serves. This message is one that reinforces the philosophy and the purpose for its existence. A well-informed community may effectively ensure public facilities are available for use based on reasonable expectations placed on All4Sports.

2.2.4 Threats

The major challenges All4Sports currently face include the following:

Property Tax Changes—The impact of property tax modifications on the public school systems, their support of sports programs, and their willingness to provide their facilities for use by All4Sports has not been determined. The precise ramifications of this measure may not be known for months, but all potential outcomes must be considered as plans are made for the coming year.

Alternative Programs—The increasing impact from other programs, ranging from organization-sponsored to club sports, poses a threat to a segment of All4Sports' market. These organizations target the highly skilled and committed players and coaches and are eroding the depth and breadth of All4Sports' participant and coach resources.

9

Legal and Liability Issues—All4Sports continues to be exposed to liability issues in many aspects of the experience it provides. The potential concerns range from health and safety issues to various forms of verbal or physical abuse. In an increasingly litigious society, there is always potential for legal action.

The "Elite/Advanced" Sports Dilemma—Providing competitive environments for athletes with higher skill levels who seek to be in an intentionally competitive arena is in question. The threat of not offering this option is that these athletes may be drawn away from All4Sports by alternative programs. Some of the most highly trained and experienced coaches can also be attracted to these other programs. This issue challenges some of All4Sports' most basic philosophies.

2.3 Alternative Providers

A number of other programs offer youth sports experiences. None of these programs offers the extensive range of experiences or infrastructure of All4Sports. Some programs do, however, offer specific attributes some participants and parents find attractive. This is particularly true for those who seek a higher level of competition and competitive screening of participants.

These alternatives programs include the following:

- Babe Ruth Baseball/American Legion Baseball
- Southern Oregon Volleyball
- Rogue Valley Athletic Club Volleyball
- AAU Basketball
- YMCA Basketball
- ASA Softball
- Oregon Youth Soccer
- AYSO Soccer
- National Gymnastics Academy

Other programs are also available through schools and other organizations. Although some variables are now in place, there are questions regarding the future of indoor soccer organizations.

All4Sports possesses a commanding percentage of the total market share. This is based on the estimated number of participants compared to participation levels in other programs, both public and private. This share percentage drops in high school due to increased competition from other organizations as well as in-school programs offered through the public school system.

10

Growth and Share

Competitor	Price	Growth Rate	Market Share
Babe Ruth Baseball	$120	3%	2%
So. Oregon Volleyball	$150	5%	3%
AAU Basketball	$90	4%	5%
ASA Softball	$95	2%	5%
Oregon Youth Soccer	$110	22%	4%
AYSO Soccer	$105	22%	5%
All4Sports	$85	7%	75%
Total	**$755.00**	**65.00%**	**99.00%**
Average	$107.86	9.29%	14.14%

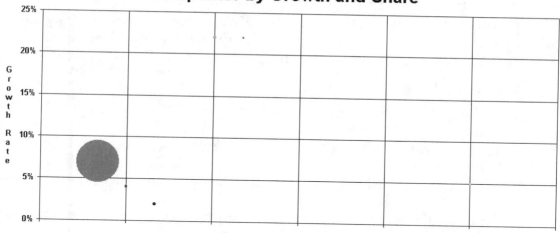

Competitor by Growth and Share

Relative Price (lower to higher)
Diameter = market share

- Babe Ruth Baseball
- So. Oregon Volleyball
- AAU Basketball
- ASA Softball
- Oregon Youth Soccer
- AYSO Soccer
- All4Sports

11

2.4 Services Offered

All4Sports is a tax-exempt, not-for-profit organization dedicated to presenting sports opportunities that are an integral part of each participant's learning experience. This is done with the belief that every child should be able to participate in the program of his or her choice regardless of race, religion, creed, sex, ability, or financial status. This spirit is fostered in an environment where everyone has a chance to play and learn, regardless of skill. All4Sports' long-term goal is to give its participants positive life-long memories of their youth sports experience.

The "All4Sports experience" is designed to offer the following to each participant:

·   Recreation through participation in organized team sports.
·   The opportunity to learn and experience a variety of sports.
·   A means to improve athletic skills.
·   A means to learn teamwork, sportsmanship, and fair play.
·   A source of fun and enjoyment to enrich their lives.
·   An opportunity to enhance their health and fitness.

The parents and guardians of the participants also realize benefits. They are able to offer their children a positive, well-supervised experience as they learn the skills described above that does not necessarily require their time.

2.5 Keys to Success

·   Expand into new areas within Jackson County that desire access to All4Sports activities.
·   Leverage the growth offered by the increasing interest in soccer in the Fall and Spring programs.
·   Identify additional facilities to support future growth and offer greater flexibility in scheduling.
·   Continue to develop the donor base and corporate contributions that add to the financial resources of the participant fees.

2.6 Critical Issues

Our strengths are impressive. Our weaknesses are identified and have potential solutions. All4Sports could be described as in a "speculative" situation. We are presented with numerous opportunities and also have threats that present a level of risk. However, we have a chance to experience large returns on our efforts if we can continue to capture the largest market share and are not negatively impacted by the

12

alternative programs in our market. We are well positioned in the market. We have the ability to offer the greatest value and we take advantage of our economies of scale.

The critical issues include the following:

- Continuing to offer programs that are perceived to be positive, enriching, and affordable compared to the alternatives in our area.
- Attract participants on a return basis from kindergarten through their high-school years.
- Be perceived by public, private, and home schooling providers as a valuable resource that complements the academic experiences they offer.

3.0 Marketing Strategy

All4Sports strives to be the premier provider of sports experiences for children in the areas served. Programs are in place to simultaneously serve the needs of out-of-district participants in a manner that is positive for these participants and enhances revenue streams for All4Sports with minimal additional costs.

The marketing strategy attempts to successfully communicate the unique value the program offers participants. This strategy redirects the focus from the "cost" issue to the benefits that participants and their guardians experience from involvement in the program. The marketing strategy will continue to identify the needs of the market and communicate with this audience in the most effective and positive manner possible.

Ongoing efforts continually attempt to understand how All4Sports can maintain the quality and integrity of the program within the finite financial resources of participants and the community of donors and supporters. This challenge is increasing. As costs continue to increase in a number of areas, the demands and expectations of the participants and their parents do as well. All4Sports is constantly working to improve the program through improvements and changes in its structure and implementation. Quality and efficiency are just two goals of these changes.

The growth strategy is based on continued attention to the quality of the experience in conjunction with identifying opportunities to expand the participation of the programs where possible. Recent changes in key areas, such as the facilities used for events, present ominous challenges for all aspects of the program.

13

3.1 Mission

All4Sports is dedicated to providing all youth with the highest quality education and team experience through sports participation. Participants are treated with respect through the opportunity to experience growth in the areas of interacting with others, teamwork, sportsmanship, fair play, and skill development. The goal is to create a positive environment that fosters improved self-confidence and self-esteem through experiences in sports activities.

3.2 Marketing Objectives

The objective is to provide this valuable experience to as many children as possible in a positive and supportive manner. A positive, constructive and meaningful experience is the sought-after result of the All4Sports experience. This experience may assist individuals to better understand the necessary skills that life demands and empower them to realize the choices and options available to them.

1. Provide a positive experience to 27,500 youth through the academic year 1999-2000 and enable their parent/guardian to appreciate the value of this experience for their child.
2. Accomplish our program goals within the allocated budget of $1,510,000.
3. Expand the program to two new schools within our serving area by August, prior to the 2000-2001 academic year.

3.3 Financial Objectives

1. Raise a minimum of $575,000 through non-participation fees from sources including donations, contributions, special events, gifts-in-kind, and grants.
2. Increase corporate donations and contributions to exceed 12% of the total revenues.
3. Accomplish our program goals within the allocated 1999-2000 budget of $1,510,000.

3.4 Target Markets

The target market for All4Sports continues to be youth between the ages of 5 and 18 who have some interest in participating in competitive sports. This may be their first organized sports experience, and All4Sports strives to make it the most positive and successful experience possible. Another area of the target market focuses on addressing the growing interest and demands for outdoor and indoor soccer.

14

3.5 Positioning

All4Sports offers a unique experience for children that want to have an enjoyable sports experience. All youth between the ages of 5 and 18 can participate in one or more sports throughout the year. Their participation is not dependent upon their previous experience, skill level, or athletic ability. Everyone can play. The breadth, depth and overall quality of the sports experience we offer cannot be matched within our market. We work with parents and guardians to add to their child's sports experiences. All4Sports exists to create a cherished childhood memory for each participant.

3.6 Strategy Pyramid

All4Sports focuses on achieving success in these four basic areas with the resources available to our program:

- Equal opportunity to participate, regardless of skill level.
- A wholesome, positive, safe, and value-oriented atmosphere in which participants learn teamwork, sportsmanship and interactive skills.
- An acceptable outlet for youthful energy.
- A broad variety of sports experiences to further develop self-esteem and personal confidence.

```
STRATEGY #1    Program expansion
    Tactic #1-A School expansion
        Program 1-A    New school campaign
        Program 1-B    Jacksonville campaign
    Tactic #1-B "All4Soccer"
        Program 2-A    School presentations
        Program 2-B    Free soccer clinics
        Program 2-C    Participation in high school regional soccer playoffs
        Program 2-D    Special needs scholarship program
STRATEGY #2    Fund-raising
    Tactic #2-A Corporate donor base
        Program 1-A    "Taking Care of Donors" committee
        Program 1-B    Corporate contact program
    Tactic #2-B Special events
        Program 2-A    Taste of Medford to add Spring event
        Program 2-B    Grant application program focus
```

15

4.0 Financials

All4Sports is committed to balancing its operating budget and operating on a solid financial foundation. These efforts are based on a mixture of fund-raising, charitable gifting, tournaments, and fees. Just as revenues are tracked, internal expenses are closely monitored. The goal of All4Sports is to continue to provide a quality youth sports experience at an affordable cost. This is a tremendous challenge, due to the size of the program, unpredictable costs in areas such as facilities, and uncertainties in participant revenues.

All4Sports is intentionally emphasizing the need to reduce reliance on fee-based revenues and look toward contributions from other sources, particularly businesses, to support the program. This approach will enable the program to realize the objective of keeping fees affordable while continuing to offer a quality program for all participants.

All4Sports has an independent auditor's report conducted annually that includes financial statements and additional information. The following information is based on the 1997 and 1998 Independent Auditor's Report. The following summarizes key facts regarding the financial status of All4Sports and its 1998 results:

- Revenues in 1998 totaled $1,732,658.
    - A total of 65% of those revenues are from participation fees, donations and contributions, special events, and gifts-in-kind.
    - Supervision Grants account for a combined 34%.
- Expenses for 1998 were $366 over revenues.
    - "People-related" expenditures represent 47% of expenditures.
    - Non-program operations account for 9% of the total expenditures.

16

4.1 Break-even Analysis

Our break-even analysis is based on the ongoing overhead costs we incur to keep the doors of All4Sports open. Fixed costs including the building lease, payroll, utilities, and marketing costs are an estimated $10,250. This number level is due to our dependence on volunteers to run our program. Our assumptions on the average unit revenue are based on the average participant fee. The result of this analysis offers general insight regarding the number of average participants we must have involved in the program each month.

Break-even Analysis

Assumptions

Average Per-Unit Revenue	$85.50
Average Per-Unit Variable Cost	$35.00
Estimated Fixed costs	$10,250.00
Monthly Units Break-even	**203**
Monthly Revenue Break-even	**$17,354**

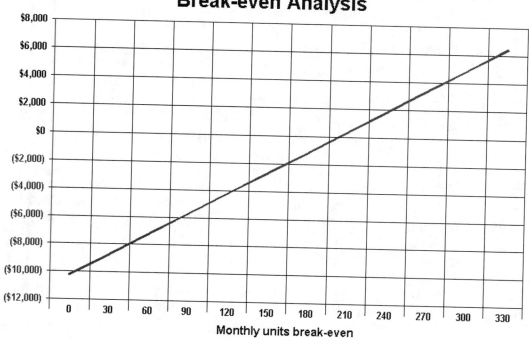

Break-even Analysis

Units break-even point = where line intersects with $0

17

4.2 Funding Forecast

Monthly revenues for the 2000 calendar year will fluctuate based on the seasonality of the sports offered and the projected level of participation in each sport. The forecasted revenues range from a dramatic low of $16,535 in September as schools are getting started, to a high of $115,360 in November with the Fall Soccer, Tackle Football, and Volleyball seasons overlapping.

Donor Drive—The Donor Drive effort depends on the commitment of key volunteers to raise funds through corporate and individual contributors throughout the area. This includes leveraging the resources of corporate sponsors and initiating an adopt-a-school scholarship fund sponsors program where businesses are partnered with specific schools. Sponsors and donors are recognized in numerous ways for the valuable role they play in the organization.

A Taste of Medford—All4Sports has created a culinary tradition with the fundraising event "A Taste of Medford." Restaurants from throughout the area come together to offer a taste of their menu, and businesses and individuals pay admission to sample their cuisine throughout the evening. Since its inception, this highly publicized event has become an annual highlight and a financial success for more than a decade. This is due to continued public appeal, corporate sponsorships, and experienced volunteer leadership.

Value Checks—Since 1993, All4Sports t-ball, baseball, and softball participants have sold these sought-after coupon books. The relationship with and support of numerous businesses throughout the area also provide an effective promotional medium for marketing efforts.

Grants—All4Sports continues to identify grants on a national and local basis that complement the goals and efforts of the program. Grant sources have included the U.S. Department of Housing & Urban Development, Recreational Activities Valuing Education and Sports (RAVES), and the Willard Family Foundation.

Work continues to expand the impact of the All4Sports Foundation. The recent adoption of bylaws further recognizes and empowers this entity. The Foundation will establish relationships with key individuals and organizations that desire to provide financial support to All4Sports on an ongoing basis. The long-term objective is to provide financial stability to support program quality and expansion and reduce dependence on program fees.

18

Funding Forecast

Funding	2000	2001	2002	2003	2004
Participation Fees	$935,000	$938,500	$948,000	$983,000	$995,000
Private Donations & Contributions	$131,500	$138,000	$144,000	$148,000	$157,000
Corporate Contributions	$180,000	$200,000	$225,000	$250,000	$275,000
Special Events	$162,000	$215,000	$225,000	$236,000	$240,000
Gifts-in-Kind	$51,500	$100,000	$110,000	$120,000	$130,000
Grants	$50,000	$60,000	$60,000	$75,000	$80,000
Total Funding	**$1,510,000**	**$1,651,500**	**$1,712,000**	**$1,812,000**	**$1,877,000**

Direct Cost of Funding

	2000	2001	2002	2003	2004
Participation Fees	$7,800	$8,200	$8,450	$8,650	$9,000
Private Donations & Contributions	$15,000	$17,500	$20,000	$22,500	$25,000
Corporate Contributions	$11,100	$12,500	$14,000	$16,000	$18,000
Special Events	$31,600	$34,000	$38,000	$43,000	$48,000
Gifts-in-Kind	$7,200	$8,000	$8,750	$9,500	$10,000
Grants	$1,250	$1,400	$1,500	$1,600	$1,700
Subtotal Cost of Funding	**$73,950**	**$81,600**	**$90,700**	**$101,250**	**$111,700**

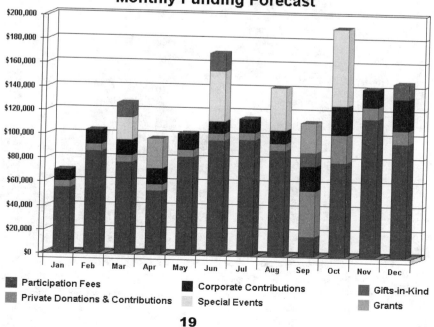

Monthly Funding Forecast

Legend:
- Participation Fees
- Private Donations & Contributions
- Corporate Contributions
- Special Events
- Gifts-in-Kind
- Grants

19

4.2.1 Funding by Participant Fees

The following summarizes the projected revenue from participant fees on a monthly basis for the upcoming year. Note the variance based on sports season and overlapping sports.

Funding by: Participant Fees

Funding	2000	2001	2002	2003	2004
Fall Soccer	$215,920	$360,000	$380,000	$400,000	$425,000
Flag Football	$14,253	$24,000	$24,500	$25,000	$26,000
Tackle Football	$34,476	$53,000	$53,500	$54,500	$55,000
Volleyball	$47,829	$102,000	$105,000	$106,000	$108,000
Basketball	$215,809	$365,000	$367,000	$368,000	$370,000
Spring Soccer	$179,000	$355,000	$358,500	$370,000	$390,000
Baseball/Softball	$229,960	$412,000	$413,000	$414,000	$416,000
Other	$572,753	($19,500)	$10,500	$74,500	$87,000
Total	**$1,510,000**	**$1,651,500**	**$1,712,000**	**$1,812,000**	**$1,877,000**
Average	$188,750	$206,438	$214,000	$226,500	$234,625

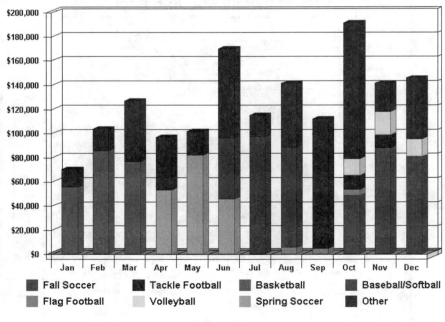

Funding by Participant Fees Monthly

20

4.2.2 Funding by Fund-Raising Events

Our fund-raising events are a critical component to our revenue base, particularly in relation to the "Taste of Medford" and "Value Checks" efforts.

Funding by: Fund-Raising Events

Funding	2000	2001	2002	2003	2004
A Taste of Medford	$85,000	$96,000	$102,000	$115,000	$124,000
Value Checks	$136,500	$142,000	$150,000	$160,000	$170,000
Other	$1,288,500	$1,413,500	$1,460,000	$1,537,000	$1,583,000
Total	**$1,510,000**	**$1,651,500**	**$1,712,000**	**$1,812,000**	**$1,877,000**
Average	$503,333	$550,500	$570,667	$604,000	$625,667

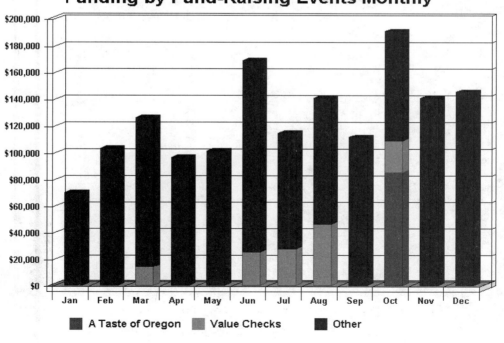

Funding by Fund-Raising Events Monthly

Legend: A Taste of Oregon • Value Checks • Other

21

4.2.3 Funding by Donations

Donations from private and corporate sources are one of the most stable and predictable sources of income. Our objective is to increase corporate contributions. Gifts-in-kind offset program costs, such as when sports equipment is donated, and goods are also supplied for the various auction events held.

Funding by: Donations

Funding	2000	2001	2002	2003	2004
Private	$131,200	$134,000	$136,000	$138,000	$140,000
Corporate	$177,000	$280,000	$310,000	$330,000	$350,000
Gifts-in-Kind	$98,700	$100,000	$108,000	$118,000	$123,000
Other	$1,103,100	$1,137,500	$1,158,000	$1,226,000	$1,264,000
Total	**$1,510,000**	**$1,651,500**	**$1,712,000**	**$1,812,000**	**$1,877,000**
Average	$377,500	$412,875	$428,000	$453,000	$469,250

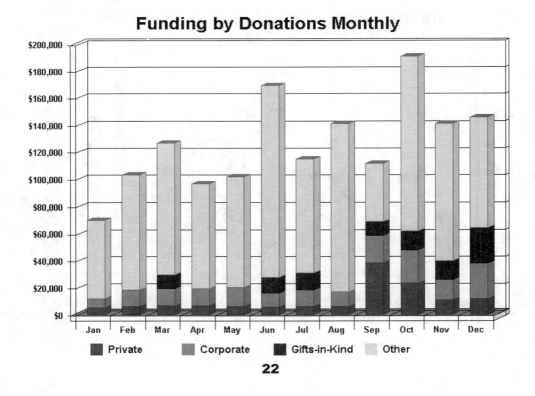

Funding by Donations Monthly

22

4.3 Expense Forecast

Our expense budget is based on maximizing the return from our marketing and promotion efforts. We must closely monitor this return to determine what events are generating the most revenue based on the actual dollar investment. Another resource we consider is the number of volunteer hours required, based on a "ceiling" of hours, that we have access to each year from our volunteer base.

Marketing Expense Budget

Marketing Expense Budget	2000	2001	2002	2003	2004
Special Events	$9,300	$14,800	$15,500	$17,500	$18,800
Private Donations & Contributions	$5,900	$6,200	$7,400	$8,000	$8,500
Corporate Campaign	$8,810	$12,000	$12,500	$13,000	$14,000
Other	$3,600	$4,000	$4,300	$4,500	$4,800
Total Funding and Marketing Expenses	$27,610	$37,000	$39,700	$43,000	$46,100
Percent of Funding	1.83%	2.24%	2.32%	2.37%	2.46%
Contribution Margin	$7,940	$2,900	$3,600	$12,750	$1,200
Contribution Margin/Funding	0.53%	0.18%	0.21%	0.70%	0.06%

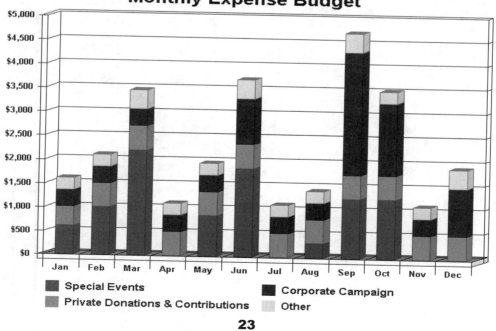

Monthly Expense Budget

23

4.3.1 Expenses by Program

Program expenses are contained due to volunteer hours. It is clear that All4Sports is a volunteer-driven organization. The work of volunteers is an integral part of All4Sports. For example, 1998's programs consisted of 2,045 teams with an estimated 4,230 head and assistant coaches volunteering an estimated 300,000 hours. Based on the April 1997 study by Anderson Research, All4Sports enjoys a positive perception among the coaches involved in the program. The number of teams and coaches is greater for 1999 and the perceptions are anticipated to be as positive. All4Sports could not survive without this invaluable and committed resource. Annual recognition programs, awards, and events are designed to acknowledge the irreplaceable roles these volunteers play.

Expenses by Program

Expenses	2000	2001	2002	2003	2004
Fall Soccer	$900	$1,000	$1,200	$1,350	$1,500
Flag Football	$500	$600	$800	$900	$1,250
Tackle Football	$350	$450	$650	$750	$900
Volleyball	$500	$650	$750	$1,000	$1,250
Basketball	$900	$1,000	$1,200	$1,350	$1,500
Spring Soccer	$900	$1,000	$1,200	$1,350	$1,500
Baseball/Softball	$900	$1,000	$1,200	$1,350	$1,500
Other	$22,660	$31,300	$32,700	$34,950	$36,700
Total	**$27,610**	**$37,000**	**$39,700**	**$43,000**	**$46,100**
Average	$3,451	$4,625	$4,963	$5,375	$5,763

24

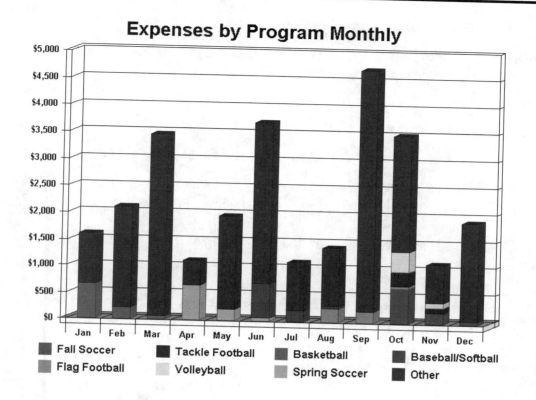

4.3.2 Expenses by Administrative

Administrative expenses are based on supporting our staff, along with temporary employees that are brought on to meet seasonal demands.

Expenses by Administrative

Expenses	2000	2001	2002	2003	2004
Staff	$3,450	$4,000	$4,400	$4,800	$5,100
Temporary	$1,100	$1,200	$1,300	$1,400	$1,500
Other	$23,060	$31,800	$34,000	$36,800	$39,500
Total	**$27,610**	**$37,000**	**$39,700**	**$43,000**	**$46,100**
Average	$9,203	$12,333	$13,233	$14,333	$15,367

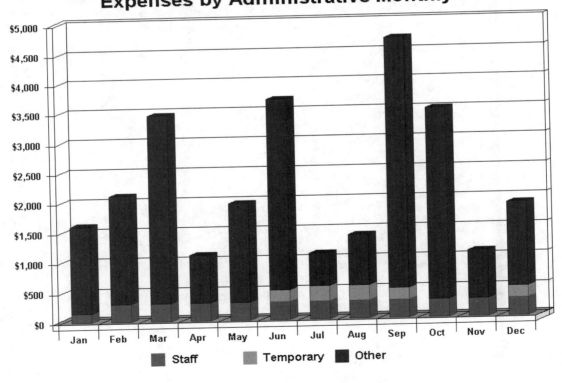

Expenses by Administrative Monthly

26

4.3.3 Expenses by Fund-Raising

Fund-raising expenses relate to costs incurred to identify, communicate, and receive donations from private and corporate donors.

Expenses by Fund-Raising

Expenses	2000	2001	2002	2003	2004
Private	$1,790	$1,900	$2,150	$2,300	$2,450
Corporate	$3,800	$4,000	$4,250	$4,500	$4,700
Other	$22,020	$31,100	$33,300	$36,200	$38,950
Total	**$27,610**	**$37,000**	**$39,700**	**$43,000**	**$46,100**
Average	$9,203	$12,333	$13,233	$14,333	$15,367

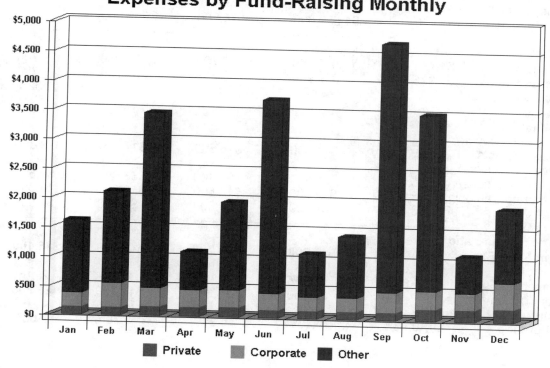

Expenses by Fund-Raising Monthly

27

4.4 Contribution Margin

Based on past performance, our fund-raising efforts are realistic. We enjoyed a $20,000 surplus last year and hope to have a similar experience in the year ahead. The challenges will be to develop greater revenue streams from corporate sponsors and to become proportionately less dependent on participation fees. This is expected to offer a more stable source of revenue for the future and reduce the efforts to secure these funds. We expect our special-event fund-raising activities and individual contributions to remain relatively constant as a percent of total revenues. The involvement of the Board of Directors and the formation of the foundation committee will be critical to our success in this area.

Contribution Margin

	2000	2001	2002	2003	2004
Funding	$1,510,000	$1,651,500	$1,712,000	$1,812,000	$1,877,000
Direct Cost of Funding	$73,950	$81,600	$90,700	$101,250	$111,700
Other Variable Costs of Funding	$1,400,500	$1,530,000	$1,578,000	$1,655,000	$1,718,000
Total Cost of Funding	$1,474,450	$1,611,600	$1,668,700	$1,756,250	$1,829,700
Gross Margin	$35,550	$39,900	$43,300	$55,750	$47,300
Gross Margin %	2.35%	2.42%	2.53%	3.08%	2.52%
Marketing Expense Budget					
Special Events	$9,300	$14,800	$15,500	$17,500	$18,800
Private Donations & Contributions	$5,900	$6,200	$7,400	$8,000	$8,500
Corporate Campaign	$8,810	$12,000	$12,500	$13,000	$14,000
Other	$3,600	$4,000	$4,300	$4,500	$4,800
Total Funding and Marketing Exp.	**$27,610**	**$37,000**	**$39,700**	**$43,000**	**$46,100**
Percent of Funding	1.83%	2.24%	2.32%	2.37%	2.46%
Contribution Margin	$7,940	$2,900	$3,600	$12,750	$1,200
Contribution Margin/ Funding	**0.53%**	**0.18%**	**0.21%**	**0.70%**	**0.06%**

28

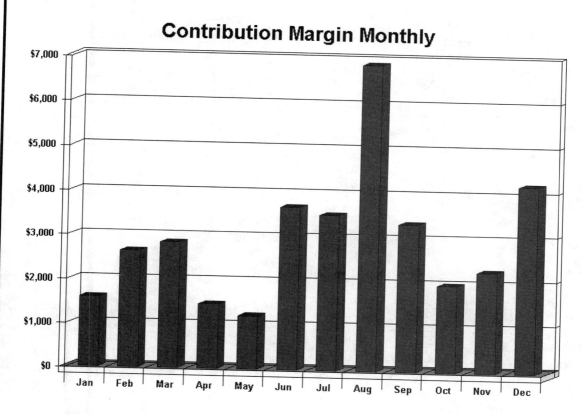

Contribution Margin Monthly

5.0 Controls

The purpose of the All4Sports marketing plan is to serve as a guide to the staff, the Board of Directors, and the volunteers to continue to improve the organization and its ability to serve the youth of Jackson County. We must take action to accomplish our goals. Failing to implement even one of the programs could be devastating to our success.

5.1 Implementation

The following chart and table identify the key marketing programs. Dates and budgets are specified, and the "Chairpeople" are informed of the programs. We will track plan-vs.-actual results for each of these programs and evaluate them at our quarterly Board of Directors meetings. If necessary, the programs will be revised if we discover they are not accomplishing the intended goal.

29

Milestones Plan

Milestone	Start Date	End Date	Budget	Manager	Department
Individual Donor Drive	1/4/00	4/1/00	$3,750	Tamarra	Marketing
A Taste of Medford	4/4/00	6/23/00	$18,500	Tamarra	Marketing
Value Checks	9/5/00	12/1/00	$9,500	Chris	Programs
Grant Proposal-USDHUD	1/5/00	2/15/00	$625	Cindy	Staff
Corporate Drive	5/1/00	11/1/00	$2,100	Jan	Executive
Grant-Willard Fd.	7/5/00	8/4/00	$625	Cindy	Staff
Program Develop.	6/19/00	7/31/00	$550	Rob	Programs
Promotional Scholar.	8/1/00	8/31/00	$300	Rob	Programs
End-of-Year Campaign	12/1/00	12/31/00	$450	Tamarra	Marketing
Other	12/1/00	12/1/00	$0	N/A	N/A
Totals			**$36,400**		

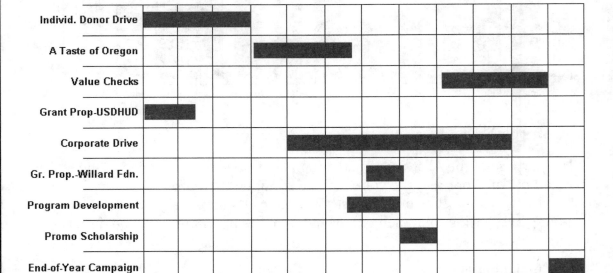

Milestones

30

5.2 Marketing Organization

Our marketing organization consists of one paid staff person, Tamarra McNeil. Tamarra interfaces with the Board of Directors and the Marketing Committee to coordinate our marketing efforts. Tamarra has key responsibilities in marketing implementation. It is also Tamarra's goal to provide direction and encouragement to those that take on specific marketing responsibilities. She attends all Board of Directors' meetings to report status and progress and she chairs the monthly meetings of the Marketing Committee.

5.3 Contingency Planning

The following lists, in order of probability beginning with the highest potential for change that will impact this marketing plan, the future of All4Sports:

- Major philosophy shift regarding the use of public and/or private school facilities.
- The rapid growth of one of the alternative programs that significantly reduces our market share and our ability to operate one or more of our programs.
- Legal action due to injury or negligence that causes severe financial damage to the organization.

31

This page intentionally blank.

All4Sports - Appendix Tables

Table 4.2: Funding Forecast

Funding	Jan	Feb	Mar	Apr	May	Jun	Jul	Aug	Sep	Oct	Nov	Dec
Participation Fees	$54,700	$85,125	$75,984	$52,400	$81,400	$95,750	$96,520	$87,890	$16,535	$78,466	$115,360	$94,870
Private Donations & Contributions	$5,500	$6,000	$6,250	$6,050	$6,000	$5,750	$6,000	$6,000	$38,500	$23,500	$10,500	$11,450
Corporate Contributions	$9,500	$12,000	$13,000	$13,000	$14,000	$10,000	$12,000	$11,000	$20,000	$24,000	$15,000	$26,500
Special Events	$0	$0	$18,500	$0	$0	$42,500	$0	$36,000	$0	$65,000	$0	$0
Gifts-in-Kind	$0	$0	$12,500	$0	$0	$15,000	$0	$0	$11,500	$0	$0	$12,500
Grants	$0	$0	$0	$25,000	$0	$0	$0	$0	$25,000	$0	$0	$0
Total Funding	**$69,700**	**$103,125**	**$126,234**	**$96,450**	**$101,400**	**$169,000**	**$114,520**	**$140,890**	**$111,535**	**$190,966**	**$140,860**	**$145,320**

Direct Cost of Funding	Jan	Feb	Mar	Apr	May	Jun	Jul	Aug	Sep	Oct	Nov	Dec
Participation Fees	$650	$650	$650	$650	$650	$650	$650	$650	$650	$650	$650	$650
Private Donations & Contributions	$1,250	$1,250	$1,250	$1,250	$1,250	$1,250	$1,250	$1,250	$1,250	$1,250	$1,250	$1,250
Corporate Contributions	$600	$600	$600	$600	$1,800	$600	$600	$600	$1,800	$600	$1,200	$1,500
Special Events	$0	$0	$3,600	$0	$0	$18,500	$0	$9,500	$0	$0	$0	$0
Gifts-in-Kind	$0	$0	$1,300	$0	$0	$1,200	$0	$0	$1,500	$0	$0	$3,200
Grants	$625	$0	$0	$0	$0	$625	$0	$0	$0	$0	$0	$0
Subtotal Cost of Funding	**$3,125**	**$2,500**	**$7,400**	**$2,500**	**$3,700**	**$22,825**	**$2,500**	**$12,000**	**$5,200**	**$2,500**	**$3,100**	**$6,600**

Table 4.2.1: Funding by Participant Fees

Funding	Jan	Feb	Mar	Apr	May	Jun	Jul	Aug	Sep	Oct	Nov	Dec
Fall Soccer	$0	$0	$0	$0	$0	$0	$0	$0	$0	$48,070	$87,500	$80,350
Flag Football	$0	$0	$0	$0	$0	$0	$0	$5,000	$4,220	$5,033	$0	$0
Tackle Football	$0	$0	$0	$0	$0	$0	$0	$0	$12,315	$11,562	$10,599	$0
Volleyball	$0	$0	$0	$0	$0	$0	$0	$0	$0	$13,800	$19,509	$14,520
Basketball	$54,700	$85,125	$75,984	$52,400	$0	$0	$0	$0	$0	$0	$0	$0
Spring Soccer	$0	$0	$0	$0	$81,400	$45,200	$96,520	$82,890	$0	$0	$0	$0
Baseball/Softball	$0	$0	$0	$0	$0	$50,550	$0	$0	$0	$0	$0	$0
Other	$15,000	$18,000	$50,250	$44,050	$20,000	$73,250	$18,000	$53,000	$95,000	$112,501	$23,252	$50,450
Total	**$69,700**	**$103,125**	**$126,234**	**$96,450**	**$101,400**	**$169,000**	**$114,520**	**$140,890**	**$111,535**	**$190,966**	**$140,860**	**$145,320**
Average	**$8,713**	**$12,891**	**$15,779**	**$12,056**	**$12,675**	**$21,125**	**$14,315**	**$17,611**	**$13,942**	**$23,871**	**$17,608**	**$18,165**

Table 4.2.2: Funding by Fund-Raising Event

Funding	Jan	Feb	Mar	Apr	May	Jun	Jul	Aug	Sep	Oct	Nov	Dec
A Taste of Oregon	$0	$0	$0	$0	$0	$25,000	$27,500	$46,000	$0	$85,000	$0	$0
Value Checks	$0	$0	$14,000	$0	$0	$0	$0	$0	$0	$24,000	$0	$0
Other	$69,700	$103,125	$112,234	$96,450	$101,400	$144,000	$87,020	$94,890	$111,535	$81,966	$140,860	$145,320
Total	**$69,700**	**$103,125**	**$126,234**	**$96,450**	**$101,400**	**$169,000**	**$114,520**	**$140,890**	**$111,535**	**$190,966**	**$140,860**	**$145,320**
Average	**$23,233**	**$34,375**	**$42,078**	**$32,150**	**$33,800**	**$56,333**	**$38,173**	**$46,963**	**$37,178**	**$63,655**	**$46,953**	**$48,440**

Table 4.2.3: Funding by Donations

Funding	Jan	Feb	Mar	Apr	May	Jun	Jul	Aug	Sep	Oct	Nov	Dec
Private	$5,000	$6,000	$6,250	$6,250	$6,000	$5,750	$6,000	$6,000	$38,500	$23,500	$10,500	$11,450
Corporate	$6,500	$12,000	$13,000	$13,000	$14,000	$10,000	$12,000	$11,000	$20,000	$24,000	$15,000	$26,500
Gifts-in-Kind	$0	$0	$10,000	$0	$0	$12,000	$12,700	$0	$10,000	$14,000	$14,000	$26,000
Other	$58,200	$85,125	$96,984	$77,200	$81,400	$141,250	$83,820	$123,890	$43,035	$129,466	$101,360	$81,370
Total	**$69,700**	**$103,125**	**$126,234**	**$96,450**	**$101,400**	**$169,000**	**$114,520**	**$140,890**	**$111,535**	**$190,966**	**$140,860**	**$145,320**
Average	**$17,425**	**$25,781**	**$31,559**	**$24,113**	**$25,350**	**$42,250**	**$28,630**	**$35,223**	**$27,884**	**$47,742**	**$35,215**	**$36,330**

Table 4.3: Marketing Expense Budget

Marketing Expense Budget	Jan	Feb	Mar	Apr	May	Jun	Jul	Aug	Sep	Oct	Nov	Dec
Special Events	$600	$1,000	$2,200	$0	$850	$1,850	$0	$300	$1,250	$1,250	$0	$0
Private Donations & Contributions	$400	$500	$500	$500	$500	$500	$500	$500	$500	$500	$500	$500
Corporate Campaign	$350	$350	$350	$350	$350	$950	$350	$350	$2,560	$1,500	$350	$1,000
Other	$250	$250	$400	$250	$250	$400	$250	$250	$400	$250	$250	$400
Total Funding and Marketing Expenses	$1,600	$2,100	$3,450	$1,100	$1,950	$3,700	$1,100	$1,400	$4,710	$3,500	$1,100	$1,900
Percent of Funding	2.30%	2.04%	2.73%	1.14%	1.92%	2.19%	0.96%	0.99%	4.22%	1.83%	0.78%	1.31%
Contribution Margin	($25)	$525	($616)	$350	($750)	($25)	$2,420	$5,490	($1,375)	($1,534)	$1,160	$2,320
Contribution Margin /Funding	-0.04%	0.51%	-0.49%	0.36%	-0.74%	-0.01%	2.11%	3.90%	-1.23%	-0.80%	0.82%	1.60%

Table 4.3.1: Expenses by Program

Expenses	Jan	Feb	Mar	Apr	May	Jun	Jul	Aug	Sep	Oct	Nov	Dec
Fall Soccer	$0	$0	$0	$0	$0	$0	$0	$0	$0	$650	$200	$50
Flag Football	$0	$0	$0	$0	$0	$0	$0	$250	$200	$50	$0	$0
Tackle Football	$0	$0	$0	$0	$0	$0	$0	$0	$0	$250	$100	$0
Volleyball	$0	$0	$0	$0	$0	$0	$0	$0	$0	$400	$100	$0
Basketball	$650	$200	$50	$0	$0	$0	$0	$0	$0	$0	$0	$0
Spring Soccer	$0	$0	$0	$650	$200	$50	$0	$0	$0	$0	$0	$0
Baseball/Softball	$0	$0	$0	$0	$0	$650	$200	$50	$0	$0	$0	$0
Other	$950	$1,900	$3,400	$450	$1,750	$3,000	$900	$1,100	$4,510	$2,150	$700	$1,850
Total	**$1,600**	**$2,100**	**$3,450**	**$1,100**	**$1,950**	**$3,700**	**$1,100**	**$1,400**	**$4,710**	**$3,500**	**$1,100**	**$1,900**
Average	$200	$263	$431	$138	$244	$463	$138	$175	$589	$438	$138	$238

Table 4.3.2: Expenses by Administrative

Expenses	Jan	Feb	Mar	Apr	May	Jun	Jul	Aug	Sep	Oct	Nov	Dec
Staff	$150	$300	$300	$300	$300	$300	$300	$300	$300	$300	$300	$300
Temporary	$0	$0	$0	$0	$0	$200	$250	$250	$200	$0	$0	$200
Other	$1,450	$1,800	$3,150	$800	$1,650	$3,200	$550	$850	$4,210	$3,200	$800	$1,400
Total	**$1,600**	**$2,100**	**$3,450**	**$1,100**	**$1,950**	**$3,700**	**$1,100**	**$1,400**	**$4,710**	**$3,500**	**$1,100**	**$1,900**
Average	$533	$700	$1,150	$367	$650	$1,233	$367	$467	$1,570	$1,167	$367	$633

Table 4.3.3: Expenses by Fund-Raising

Expenses	Jan	Feb	Mar	Apr	May	Jun	Jul	Aug	Sep	Oct	Nov	Dec
Private	$120	$120	$150	$150	$160	$120	$120	$120	$120	$190	$200	$220
Corporate	$250	$420	$320	$300	$300	$300	$250	$250	$350	$320	$290	$450
Other	$1,230	$1,560	$2,980	$650	$1,490	$3,280	$730	$1,030	$4,240	$2,990	$610	$1,230
Total	**$1,600**	**$2,100**	**$3,450**	**$1,100**	**$1,950**	**$3,700**	**$1,100**	**$1,400**	**$4,710**	**$3,500**	**$1,100**	**$1,900**
Average	$533	$700	$1,150	$367	$650	$1,233	$367	$467	$1,570	$1,167	$367	$633

Table 4.5: Contribution Margin

	Jan	Feb	Mar	Apr	May	Jun	Jul	Aug	Sep	Oct	Nov	Dec
Funding	$69,700	$103,125	$126,234	$96,450	$101,400	$169,000	$114,520	$140,890	$111,535	$190,966	$140,860	$145,320
Direct Cost of Funding	$3,125	$2,500	$7,400	$2,500	$3,700	$22,825	$2,500	$12,000	$5,200	$2,500	$3,100	$6,600
Other Variable Costs of Funding	$65,000	$98,000	$116,000	$92,500	$96,500	$142,500	$108,500	$122,000	$103,000	$186,500	$135,500	$134,500
Total Cost of Funding	**$68,125**	**$100,500**	**$123,400**	**$95,000**	**$100,200**	**$165,325**	**$111,000**	**$134,000**	**$108,200**	**$189,000**	**$138,600**	**$141,100**
Gross Margin	**$1,575**	**$2,625**	**$2,834**	**$1,450**	**$1,200**	**$3,675**	**$3,520**	**$6,890**	**$3,335**	**$1,966**	**$2,260**	**$4,220**
Gross Margin %	2.26%	2.55%	2.25%	1.50%	1.18%	2.17%	3.07%	4.89%	2.99%	1.03%	1.60%	2.90%
Marketing Expense Budget												
Special Events	$600	$1,000	$2,200	$0	$850	$1,850	$0	$300	$1,250	$1,250	$0	$0
Private Donations & Contributions	$400	$500	$500	$500	$500	$500	$500	$500	$500	$500	$500	$500
Corporate Campaign	$350	$350	$350	$350	$350	$950	$350	$350	$2,560	$1,500	$350	$1,000
Other	$250	$250	$400	$250	$250	$400	$250	$250	$400	$250	$250	$400
Total Funding and Marketing Expenses	**$1,600**	**$2,100**	**$3,450**	**$1,100**	**$1,950**	**$3,700**	**$1,100**	**$1,400**	**$4,710**	**$3,500**	**$1,100**	**$1,900**
Percent of Funding	2.30%	2.04%	2.73%	1.14%	1.92%	2.19%	0.96%	0.99%	4.22%	1.83%	0.78%	1.31%
Contribution Margin	**($25)**	**$525**	**($616)**	**$350**	**($750)**	**($25)**	**$2,420**	**$5,490**	**($1,375)**	**($1,534)**	**$1,160**	**$2,320**
Contribution Margin / Funding	-0.04%	0.51%	-0.49%	0.36%	-0.74%	-0.01%	2.11%	3.90%	-1.23%	-0.80%	0.82%	1.60%

This page intentionally blank.

SAMPLE PLAN: AMT

This sample marketing plan has been made available to users of *Marketing Plan Pro*™, marketing plan software published by Palo Alto Software. It is based on a real marketing plan of an existing company. Names and numbers have been changed, and substantial portions of text may have been omitted to preserve confidential information.

You are welcome to use this plan as a starting point to create your own, but you do not have permission to reproduce, publish, distribute, or even copy this plan as it exists here.

Requests for reprints, academic use, and other dissemination of this sample plan should be addressed to the marketing department of Palo Alto Software.

Table of Contents

1.0 Executive Summary

Our new marketing focus, made explicit in this plan, renews our vision and strategic focus on adding value to our target market segments, the small business and high-end home office users, in our local market.

American Management Technologies, Inc. (AMT) will change its focus to differentiate itself from box pushers and improve the business by filling the real need of small businesses and high-end home offices for reliable information technology including hardware, software, and all related services. Our marketing challenge is to position our product and service offerings as the high-quality, high-value add alternative to box pushing in a vacuum.

2.0 Situation Analysis

Before we talk about strategy for future development, we have to understand where we are, and where we've been. Strategy is about playing towards strengths and away from weaknesses. Marketing is about understanding our target markets and target market needs.

Therefore, we begin this section with our market analysis, looking in detail at our target market and market needs. Then we develop our SWOT analysis, looking at strengths, weaknesses, opportunities, and threats. Afterwards we finish up with a look at some other key factors of the present situation.

2.1 Market Summary

AMT focuses on small business in the local market, with special focus on the high-end home office and the 5-20 unit small business office.

We have broken our markets into groups according to standard classifications used by market research companies: home offices and small businesses.

Exact definitions of these market segments are not necessary for our marketing planning purposes here; general definitions will suffice. We know our home office customers tend to be heavy users, wanting high-end systems; people who like computing and computers. The low-end home office people buy elsewhere. We also know that our small business customers tend to be much less proficient on computers, are more likely to need and want hand-holding, and more likely to pay for it.

1

Target Markets

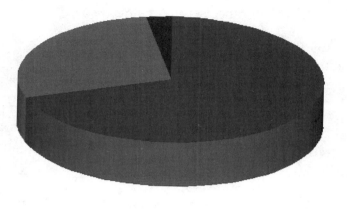

High-end Home Office **Small Business** **Other**

Target Market Forecast

Potential Customers Growth		2000	2001	2002	2003	2004	CAGR
High-end Home Office	10%	25,000	27,500	30,250	33,275	36,603	10.00%
Small Business	5%	10,000	10,500	11,025	11,576	12,155	5.00%
Other	6%	1,000	1,060	1,124	1,191	1,262	5.99%
Total	**8.57%**	**36,000**	**39,060**	**42,399**	**46,042**	**50,020**	**8.57%**

2.1.1 Market Demographics

The home offices in Tintown are an important, growing market segment. Nationally, there are approximately 30 million home offices, and the number is growing at 10% per year. Our estimate in this plan for the home offices in our market service area is based on an analysis published four months ago in the local newspaper.

Home offices include several types. For our plan, the most important are the home offices that serve as the only offices of professional firms. These are likely to be professional services such as graphic artists, writers, and consultants, also some accountants and the occasional lawyer, doctor, or dentist. There are also individuals

2

who maintain home offices for part-time use, including "moonlighters" and hobbyists. This segment is not who AMT wishes to sell to; our marketing focus consists of professionals and entrepreneurs who maintain a full-time office. In this plan, we will refer to customers in the home office segment as HOs.

Small business in our market includes virtually any business with a retail, office, professional, or industrial location outside of someone's home, and with fewer than 30 employees. We estimate 45,000 such businesses in our market area.

The 30-employee cutoff is arbitrary. We find that the larger companies turn to other vendors, but we can sell to departments in larger companies, and we shouldn't be giving up leads when we get them. We will refer to customers in the small business segment as SBs.

Target Market Analysis

Market Segments	Product Attitude	Loyalty Status	Buyer Readiness	Benefits	Value
High-end Home Office	Positive	Medium	Informed	Quality	$25m
Small Business	Indifferent	None	Defensive	Speed	$50m
Other	Depends	Strong	Informed	Depends	$1.2m

2.1.2 Market Needs

Our target HOs are on average as dependent on reliable information technology as any other business. They care more about reliable service and confidence than about the rock-bottom lowest price. They don't want to rely solely on their own expertise, so they choose to deal with us instead, with our promise of service and support when needed.

Our standard HOs will be one-system installations, without networks, and will generally be more powerful systems than the average small business. Fax modems, voicemail, and good printers are likely system component additions. They tend to be interested in desktop publishing, accounting, the Internet, and administration software as well as their job-specific software needs.

It's important that we realize we won't be selling to the price-oriented HO buyers. We'll be able to offer an attractive proposition to the service-oriented and security-oriented buyers only.

3

Our target SBs are very dependent on reliable information technology. They use their computers for a complete range of functions beginning with the core administration information such as accounting, shipping, and inventory. They also use them for communications within the business and outside of the business, and for personal productivity. They are not, however, large enough to have dedicated computer personnel such as the MIS departments in large businesses. Ideally, they come to us for a long-term alliance, looking to us for reliable service and support to substitute for their in-house people. These are not businesses that want to shop for rock-bottom prices through chain stores or mail order. They want to be sure they have reliable providers of expertise.

Our standard SBs will be 5-20 unit installations, critically dependent on local-area networks (LANs). Back-up, training, installation, and ongoing support are very important. They require database and administrative software as the core of their systems.

4

2.1.3 Market Trends

The SB buyers are accustomed to buying from vendors who visit their offices. They expect the copy machine vendor, office products vendors, and office furniture vendors, as well as the local graphic artist, freelance writer, or whoever, to come visit the SB office to make their sales.

There is usually a lot of leakage in ad-hoc purchasing through local chain stores and mail order. Often the administrators try to discourage this, but are only partially successful.

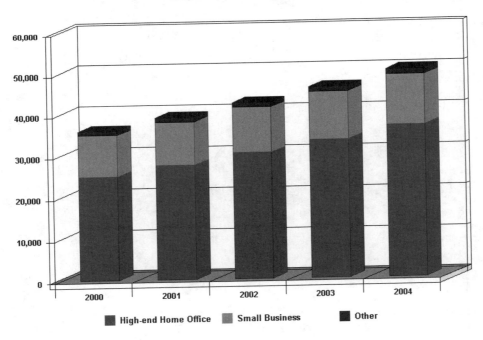

Market Forecast

5

2.1.4 Market Growth

Overall we see the number of potential customers in our small business and home office markets growing at about 8-9% per year, over the next few years. This is just a simple calculation based on locations and users. We see a more interesting market opportunity in the skyrocketing expansion in the uses of computers in business.

The next big wave is connectivity, LANs, and the Internet. The growth figures in these areas are spectacular. According to Harper's Internet Index, there are now 57 million Internet users in the United States, and that number has doubled in two years. There are currently over 6 million websites, up from 100,000 in 1996.

Meanwhile, demand for personal computers continues to grow. The IDC forecast for this quarter suggests 14.1% growth in sales of personal computers in the United States, compared to the same quarter a year ago.

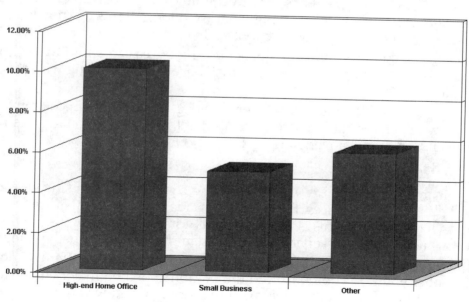

Target Market Growth

6

2.2 SWOT Analysis

As we look at our SWOT analysis to follow, we are in a sustainable overall position. We have strengths to balance our weaknesses, particularly our knowledge of what our customers need in terms of connectivity, the Internet, LANs, software, training, and service. We also have some attractive opportunities in these same areas of expertise. However, we have an inherent weakness in competing against price-oriented competition from the major brand stores.

2.2.1 Strengths

1. <u>Knowledge</u>: Our competitors are retailers, pushing boxes. We know systems, networks, connectivity, programming, all the Value-Added Resellers (VARs), and data management.
2. <u>Relationship selling</u>: We get to know our customers, one by one. Our direct sales force maintains this relationship.
3. <u>History</u>: We've been in our town forever. We have loyal customers and vendors. We are local.

2.2.2 Weaknesses

1. <u>Costs</u>: The chain stores have better economics. Their per-unit costs of selling are quite low. They aren't offering what we offer in terms of knowledgeable selling, but their cost per square foot and per dollar of sales are much lower.
2. <u>Price and volume</u>: The major stores pushing boxes can afford to sell for less. Their component costs are less and they have volume buying with the main vendors.
3. <u>Brand power</u>: Take one look at their full-page advertising, in color, in the Sunday paper. We can't match that. We don't have the national name that flows into national advertising.

2.2.3 Opportunities

1. <u>Local area networks</u>: LANs are becoming commonplace in small businesses, and even in home offices. Businesses nowadays assume LANs are part of normal office work. This is an opportunity for us because LANs are much more knowledge and service intensive than the standard off-the-shelf PC.
2. <u>The Internet</u>: The increasing opportunities of the Internet offer us another area of strength in comparison to the box-on-the-shelf major chain stores. Our customers want more help with the Internet, and we are in a better position to give it to them.

7

3. <u>Training</u>: The major stores don't provide training, but as systems become more complicated, with LAN and Internet usage, training is more in demand. This is particularly true of our main target markets.

4. <u>Service</u>: As our target market needs more service, our competitors are less likely than ever to provide it. Their business model doesn't include service, just selling the boxes.

2.2.4 Threats

1. <u>The computer as an appliance</u>: Volume buying and selling of computers as products in boxes, supposedly not needing support, training, connectivity services, etc. As people think of the computer in those terms, they think they need our service orientation less.

2. <u>The larger price-oriented store</u>: When we have huge advertisements of low prices in the newspaper, our customers think we are not giving them good value.

2.3 Competition

Our focus group sessions indicated that our target HOs consider price but they would buy based on quality customer support and service if the offerings were positioned correctly. Price is the message they're exposed to again and again; they have been trained to shop on price. We have very good indications that many would much willingly pay 10-20% more for a relationship with a long-term vendor who provides backup and quality service and support. They end up in the box-pusher channels because they aren't aware of the alternatives.

Availability is also very important. The HO buyers tend to want immediate solutions to problems. Consequently, they can be subjected to high-pressure, undertrained salespeople who may not be able to factor in all of a customer's needs.

The SB buyers understand the concept of service and support, and are more likely to pay for it when the offering is clearly stated.

There is no doubt that we compete more against all the box pushers than against other service providers. We need to effectively campaign against the idea that businesses should buy computers, the heart of their business, as plug-in appliances, that don't need ongoing service, support, and training.

Growth and Share

Competitor	Price	Growth Rate	Market Share
ABC Chain	$90	18%	35%
DEF Chain	$85	20%	30%
GHI Chain	$85	20%	20%
Local Rival	$95	0%	5%
AMT	$100	5%	10%
Other	$90	0%	0%
Average	$90.83	10.50%	16.67%
Total	$545.00	63.00%	100.00%

Competitor by Growth and Share

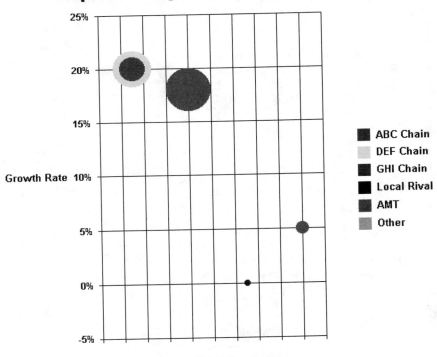

Relative Price (lower to higher)
Diameter = market share

Legend: ABC Chain, DEF Chain, GHI Chain, Local Rival, AMT, Other

9

2.4 Products Offered

In personal computers, we support three main lines:

The Super Home is our smallest and least expensive line, initially positioned by its manufacturer as a home computer. We use it mainly as a cheap workstation for small business installations. Its specifications include ...[additional specifics omitted].

The Power User is our main up-scale line. It is our most important system for high-end home and small business main workstations, because of .... Its key strengths are .... Its specifications include ....[additional specifics omitted].

The Business Special is an intermediate system, used to fill the gap in the positioning. Its specifications include ... [additional specifics omitted].

In peripherals, accessories and other hardware, we carry a complete line of necessary items from cables to forms to mousepads ... [additional specifics omitted].

In service and support, we offer a range of walk-in or depot service, maintenance contracts and on-site guarantees. We have not had much success selling service contracts. Our networking capabilities ...[additional specifics omitted].

In software, we sell a complete line of ... [additional specifics omitted].

In training, we offer ... [additional specifics omitted].

2.5 Keys to Success

The main key to success with HO buyers is making the product and marketing positioning clear. Many potential buyers would prefer our offering(s) to the box-only offerings of the chain stores and mail order sources, if only they possessed adequate information to conduct a value-added cost/benefit analysis.

Word of mouth is critical in this segment. We will have to make sure that once we gain a customer, we never lose them. To help accomplish this, we must work to reinvigorate relationships through successful database marketing, among other means. We must always remember to sell the company, not the product. They have to understand they are taking on a relationship with AMT, not just buying boxes.

2.6 Critical Issues

1. The most obvious critical issue is whether we can get over the price-oriented competition and sell our customers the idea of comparing us for the security and reliability we offer. Will our customers be willing to pay for what they need, or will they be led astray by the price-oriented advertising?

2. The second critical issue is whether or not we can redefine our business to emphasize the service and support our customers ultimately need. Can we stop focusing on price and selling computers as appliances? We need to make that happen.

3. Issue number three is fulfilling the promise. None of what we're saying is any good unless we can deliver on it. Do we provide excellence in training, fulfillment, installation, and customization? We're promising to be a strategic ally. Are we?

2.7 Historical Results

The accompanying historical results table is not strictly accurate. It is based on our best guess of what the share would have been for CPU units in our town, over the past few years.

It is valuable, however, for understanding our present position. We do believe the general trends are reflected in the table.

It is important for us to understand that we can't try to gain market share in CPU sales. We are getting into a different business. We need to emphasize training and support.

Historical Data

Variable	1997	1998	1999
Industry Revenue	$15,000,000	$21,000,000	$32,000,000
Company Market Share	25%	20%	15%
Company Revenue	$3,750,000	$4,200,000	$4,800,000
Industry Variable Costs	$13,125,000	$18,637,500	$28,800,000
Company Variable Costs	$3,187,500	$3,570,000	$4,080,000
Industry Gross Contribution Margin	$1,875,000	$2,362,500	$3,200,000
Company Gross Contribution Margin	$562,500	$630,000	$720,000
Market Expenses	$318,750	$420,000	$528,000
Company Net Contribution Margin	**$243,750**	**$210,000**	**$192,000**

2.8 Macroenvironment

Our macroenvironment is exciting. We are in the middle of an unprecedented boom in connectivity and communications, as the Internet offers spectacular new information technology. We are talking about real value here, real changes in the way we deal with information.

Meanwhile, all other signs are encouraging. The economy is in a strong growth spurt, unemployment is at an all-time low, stocks are up, and macroeconomic indicators are all positive.

2.9 Channels

We do need to keep in mind that we have two channels of distribution that are relevant to our business:

1. <u>Our sales agents</u>: Sales agents are independent consultants, mostly technical consultants helping people with computers, who channel their clients' product and service needs through our business. Each agent is registered with us first, and commissions are recorded at the time of sale and paid when accounts make payments. Agents account for roughly 10% of our sales.
2. <u>VARs</u>: The initials stand for "value-added-resellers." We have two VARs, one in Newport and one in Oakridge, who maintain small retail consulting businesses and cooperate with us for ordering and maintenance.

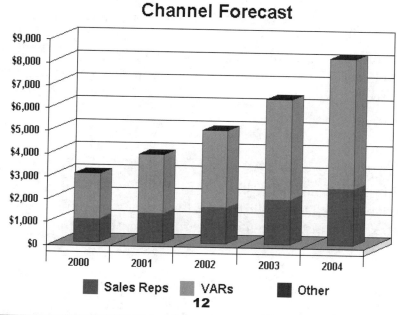

Channel Forecast

12

Channel Forecast

Channel	Growth	2000	2001	2002	2003	2004	CAGR
Sales Reps	25%	1,000	1,250	1,563	1,954	2,443	25.02%
VARs	30%	2,000	2,600	3,380	4,394	5,712	30.00%
Other	0%	0	0	0	0	0	0.00%
Total	28.40%	3,000	3,850	4,943	6,348	8,155	28.40%

3.0 Marketing Strategy

AMT will change its focus to differentiate itself from box pushers and improve the business by satisfying the real need of the small business and high-end home office for reliable information technology including hardware, software, and all related services.

3.1 Mission

AMT is built on the assumption that the management of information technology for business is like legal advice, accounting, graphic arts, and other bodies of knowledge, in that it is not inherently a do-it-yourself prospect. Smart business people who aren't computer hobbyists need to find quality vendors of reliable hardware, software, service, and support. They need to use these quality vendors as they use their other professional service suppliers, as trusted allies.

AMT is such a vendor. It serves its clients as a trusted ally, providing them with the loyalty of a business partner and the economics of an outside vendor. We make sure that our clients have what they need to run their businesses as well as possible, with maximum efficiency and reliability. Many of our information applications are mission critical, so we give our clients the assurance that we will be there when they need us.

3.2 Marketing Objectives

We need to focus our offerings on small business as the key market segment we should own. This means the 5 to 20-unit system, tied together in a local area network, in a company with 5 to 50 employees. Our values — training, installation, service, support, knowledge — are more clearly differentiated in this segment.

13

As a corollary, the high end of the home office market is also appropriate. We do not want to compete for the buyers who go to the chain stores or mail order, but we definitely want to be able to sell individual systems to the smart HO buyers who want a reliable full-service vendor.

3.3 Financial Objectives

1. Increase sales by 20%.
2. Increase gross margin to more than 25%.
3. Increase our non-hardware sales to 65% of the total.

3.4 Target Markets

We cannot survive just waiting for the customer to come to us. Instead, we must get better at attracting the specific market segments whose needs match what we have to offer. Focusing on targeted segments is the key to our future.

Therefore, we need to finely craft our marketing message and our product offerings. We need to develop our message, communicate it, and make good on it.

3.5 Positioning

For local businesses who need reliable systems and can't afford their own full-time support employees, AMT is their strategic computer and networking ally. Unlike the major retail stores that sell low-cost PCs as appliances in boxes, AMT is an ally to our clients' businesses, and offers them a full range of services from installation to maintenance, support, and training.

3.6 Marketing Strategy Pyramid

We must differentiate ourselves from the box pushers. We need to establish our business as a clear and viable alternative for our target market, to the price-only kind of buying. We do this by promoting our value added resources.

We've developed two strategy pyramids, each based on one main fundamental strategy. The first strategy is about focusing on service and support, and the second strategy is about focusing on customer relationships instead of products. Each is explained in greater detail.

14

We've also split both our sales forecast and our expense budget into divisions based on the pyramid tactics. Sales by tactic is broken down in detail in Topic 4.2.2. You can see that the bulk of our sales doesn't track directly into specific marketing tactics, despite the pyramid. Expenses, however, do break down easily into tactics and the programs associated with the tactics. That detail is shown in Topic 4.3.2.

3.6.1 Focus on Service and Support

Our first pyramid, shown in the following illustration, is under the main strategy point of focusing on service and support instead of brand names and computers.

As the illustration shows, our first tactic under that strategy is related to networking expertise. The Internet is booming and LANs are everywhere in our target market. Major retailers simply can't match us for going to our customers' locations and solving their networking problems. This is an excellent example of something we can give that our competitors can't, and our customers want. Our specific programs for this tactic include our service training, regular mailers to our customers, and our revised price list.

Our second tactic is to develop training as a line of business. Programs include train-the-trainer and developing sales and marketing programs intended to sell this type of instruction as a line of business. This includes more mailers, a new training price list, program outlines and materials, and special sales promotions.

Finally, the third tactic is providing custom solutions. This generally links to our growing experience with databases and SQL (Structured Query Language) server applications. Our only specific sales and marketing program for this is the VAR re-marketing program, but we do have an active product development budget related to custom solutions.

15

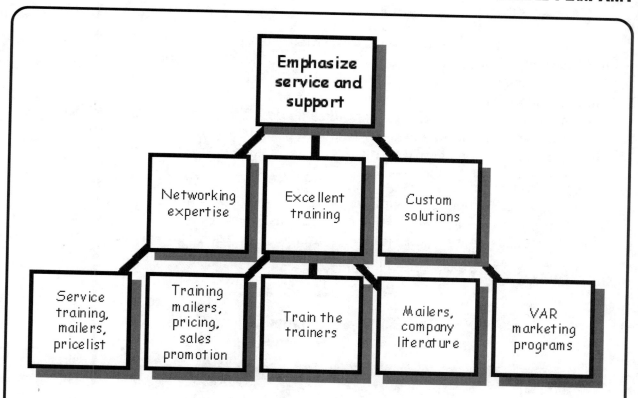

3.6.2 Focus on Relationships

Our second pyramid, shown in the following illustration, is under the main strategy point of focusing on customer relationships. We need to be strategic allies to our customers and be their experts in computing and networking systems, in a way that none of our retail-oriented competitors can ever hope to match.

This second pyramid has three main tactics:

The first tactic shown is about marketing the company, not the product. We all know what that means, that we should be emphasizing the relationship with us as AMT, instead of the brand-name on the packages such as Hewlett-Packard or Compaq. We can't sell the brand names better than the others, but we can sell ourselves and the important differences we offer. Related programs include the complete re-creation of our company literature, additional sales training, and special mailers to our customers.

16

The second tactic is to make sure we have more customer contact. We can't afford to sit back like a large retail store and wait for our customers to come to us. We need to send mailings, or emails, and even telephone calls to make sure things are going right for them. Do they need more memory or additional hard disk space? A lot of customers do, and they're grateful for our reminders. Programs for this tactic include regular mailings about upgrades, seminars, and training. Eventually we'll have an email program too. Being proactive will give us an edge over our competitors.

The third and final tactic is increased sales per customer. We work hard to find and keep our customers, and our financial analysis shows that the most economic way to increase sales is by increasing sales per customer instead of finding new customers. That's new systems, upgrades, training, and additional services. Planned programs for this tactic include upgrade mailings, service contract mailings, and Internet services.

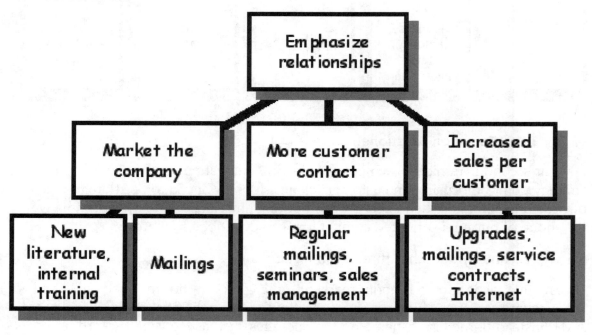

17

3.7 Marketing Mix

A core element of our marketing strategy is a change in the marketing mix. In terms of promotion, we need to sell our company as a differentiated strategic ally, not just our products. In price, we need to remain higher than the competition and we need to be able to defend that. Our product marketing has to recognize more that our service and our relationship is the key to our future product marketing. We sell a relationship more than products.

3.7.1 Product Marketing

AMT provides both computer products and services which make them useful to small businesses. We are especially focused on providing network systems and services to small and medium businesses. The systems include both PC-based LAN systems and minicomputer server-based systems. Our services include design and installation of network systems, training, and support.

In personal computers, we support three main lines:

The Super Home is our smallest and least expensive line, initially positioned by its manufacturer as a home computer. We use it mainly as a cheap workstation for small business installations. Its specifications include ...[additional specifics omitted].

The Power User is our main up-scale line. It is our most important system for high-end home and small business main workstations, because of .... Its key strengths are .... Its specifications include ....[additional specifics omitted].

The Business Special is an intermediate system, used to fill the gap in the positioning. Its specifications include ... [additional specifics omitted].

In peripherals, accessories and other hardware, we carry a complete line of necessary items from cables to forms to mousepads ... [additional specifics omitted].

In service and support, we offer a range of walk-in or depot service, maintenance contracts, and on-site guarantees. We have not had much success selling service contracts. Our networking capabilities ...[additional specifics omitted].

In software, we sell a complete line of ... [additional specifics omitted].

In training, we offer ... [additional specifics omitted].

18

3.7.2 Pricing

We must charge appropriately for the high-end, high-quality service and support that we provide our customers. Our revenue structure has to match our cost structure, so the salaries we pay to assure good service and support can be balanced by the revenue we charge.

We cannot build the service and support revenue into the price of products. The market can't bear the higher prices and the buyer feels ill-used when they see the same product priced lower at the chains. Despite the logic behind this, the market doesn't support this concept.

Therefore, we must make sure that we deliver and charge for service and support. Training, service, installation, networking support—all of this must be readily available and priced to sell and deliver revenue.

3.7.3 Promotion

One of the best places to reach the target SB is the local newspaper. Unfortunately, that medium is saturated with pure-price-only messages, and we'll have to make sure that our message is excellently stated.

Radio is potentially a good opportunity. Our SB target buyers listen to local news, talk shows, and sports. Sponsoring a technology discussion/call-in talk show is a possibility.

Seminars are a good marketing opportunity with SBs. Employees are often happy to leave their normal routines for a day to learn something new.

3.7.4 Service

Our strategy hinges on providing excellent service and support. This is critical. We are marketing our service and support; therefore, we must be prepared to deliver.

1. Training: [Details are essential in a marketing plan. Proprietary information has been removed from this sample plan.]
2. Upgrade offers: [Details are essential in a marketing plan. Proprietary information has been removed from this sample plan.]
3. Our own internal training: [Details are essential in a marketing plan. Proprietary information has been removed from this sample plan.]

19

4. <u>Installation services</u>: [Details are essential in a marketing plan. Proprietary information has been removed from this sample plan.]
5. <u>Custom software services</u>: [Details are essential in a marketing plan. Proprietary information has been removed from this sample plan.]
6. <u>Network configuration services</u>: [Details are essential in a marketing plan. Proprietary information has been removed from this sample plan.]

3.7.5 Channels of Distribution

Our strategy gives us room to promote more of our value-added sales through our existing channels, and to develop more channel points for both:

1. <u>Our sales agents</u>: At present, the agents account for roughly 10% of our sales. We can increase this amount by offering them more attention. The agents are generally as hard-pressed as we are to maintain their business through the increasing price pressure, and together we can offer a better way to compete. They can help us focus on real value, and we can help them do the same.
2. <u>VARs</u>: We should be able to add two more VARs to the two we already have. The potential customers in outlying areas also need the kinds of values we offer, and through the VARs we can give them a much better option than mail order or Internet delivery.

Channel Analysis

Channel	Maintenance	Value	Growth	Readiness	Location
Sales Reps	High	High	+	Open	East Coast
VARs	Low	High	+	Closed	West Coast
Other	0	0	0	0	0

3.8 Marketing Research

Research is an integral step in developing any marketing plan. We definitely need to know more about our customers. In the past we've been too distant, and perhaps too quick, to just guess about our customers, rather than conducting real research. For this plan we need to develop two new lines of market research:

1. <u>Primary research on our own customer base</u>. This doesn't have to be elaborate, but we do need to know more about our existing customers. Random telephone calls, through-the-mail surveys, and website surveys may be appropriate. What do our customers think about us? How do they grade our services?

2. <u>Secondary research on the Internet and in published magazines, etc</u>. We think it's time to establish a process for going through published research to find out what's available about buying patterns and demographics, business needs, etc., for our main target users. We think there is a lot of information already available on these types, and much of it is readily available for the price of a little bit of research.

4.0 Financials

As the following details show, we need to improve our gross margin and contribution margins. The business has been trending towards less profitability because we've been caught in price competition. We need to reverse that trend.

4.1 Break-even Analysis

For our break-even analysis, we assume running costs of approximately $120,000 per month, which includes our full payroll, rent, utilities, and an estimation of other running costs. Payroll alone, at our present run rate, is only about $55,000.

Margins are harder to assume. Our overall average is based on past sales. We hope to attain a higher margin in the future.

The chart shows that we need to sell about $400,000 per month (8,000 units) to break even, according to these assumptions. This is about half of our planned 1997 sales level, and significantly below our last year's sales level, so we believe we can maintain it.

Break-even Analysis

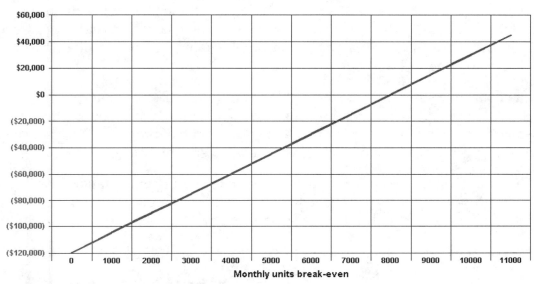

Units break-even point = where line intersects with $0

Break-even Analysis
Assumptions:

Average Per-Unit Revenue	$50.00
Average Per-Unit Variable Cost	$35.00
Estimated Fixed costs	$120,000
Monthly Units Break-even	**8,000**
Monthly Sales Break-even	**$400,000**

22

4.2 Sales Forecast

The $6 million sales forecast is shown in detail in the tables and charts below. This represents a 20% increase over the present year. We believe it is a conservative forecast, and we are sure we can make our numbers this year as a result of more effective marketing.

The data shows that we are still unable to attribute our sales in any significant way to our sales and marketing program. The "Other Sales" type shown here is the general sales coming in that is not tied to a specific type of program. This is obviously by far the largest portion of our projected sales. Advertising comes second.

This doesn't indicate a problem with the plan or our implementation; it is just a fact of life. Much of our marketing activity generates sales in ways that don't allow us the luxury of tying it back directly to a specific program.

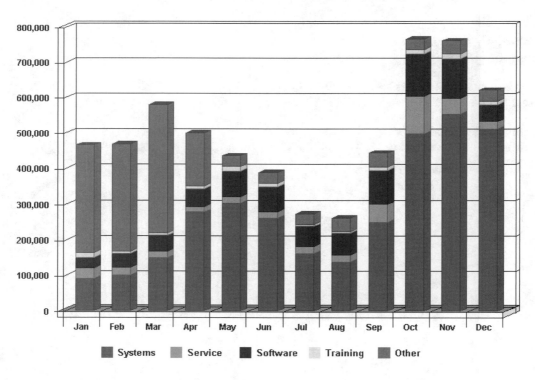

Monthly Sales Forecast

Systems ■ Service ■ Software ■ Training ■ Other

23

Sales Forecast

Unit Sales	2000	2001	2002	2003	2004
Systems	1,666	1,833	2,016	2,217	2,439
Service	4,975	5,473	6,020	6,622	7,284
Software	3,725	4,098	4,507	4,958	5,454
Training	2,230	2,453	2,698	2,968	3,265
Other	4,575	5,033	5,536	6,089	6,698
Total Unit Sales	**17,171**	**18,890**	**20,777**	**22,854**	**25,140**

Unit Prices	2000	2001	2002	2003	2004
Systems	$1,976.89	$1,976.89	$1,976.89	$1,976.89	$1,976.89
Service	$76.38	$76.38	$76.38	$76.38	$76.38
Software	$214.56	$214.56	$214.56	$214.56	$214.56
Training	$50.67	$50.67	$50.67	$50.67	$50.67
Other	$300.00	$300.00	$300.00	$300.00	$300.00

Sales	2000	2001	2002	2003	2004
Systems	$3,293,502	$3,623,639	$3,985,410	$4,382,765	$4,821,635
Service	$380,001	$418,028	$459,808	$505,788	$556,352
Software	$799,253	$879,267	$967,022	$1,063,788	$1,170,210
Training	$113,000	$124,294	$136,708	$150,389	$165,438
Other	$1,372,500	$1,509,900	$1,660,800	$1,826,700	$2,009,400
Total Sales	**$5,958,256**	**$6,555,128**	**$7,209,7478**	**$7,929,430**	**$8,723,035**

Direct Unit Costs	2000	2001	2002	2003	2004
Systems	$1,680.36	$1,686.83	$1,686.83	$1,686.83	$1,686.83
Service	$45.83	$40.00	$40.00	$40.00	$40.00
Software	$160.92	$154.89	$154.89	$154.89	$154.89
Training	$10.14	$10.00	$10.00	$10.00	$10.00
Other	$150.00	$150.00	$150.00	$150.00	$150.00

Direct Cost of Sales	2000	2001	2002	2003	2004
Systems	$2,799,479	$3,091,959	$3,400,649	$3,739,702	$4,114,178
Service	$228,004	$218,920	$240,800	$264,880	$291,360
Software	$599,443	$634,739	$698,089	$767,945	$844,770
Training	$22,602	$24,530	$26,980	$29,680	$32,650
Other	$686,250	$754,950	$830,400	$913,350	$1,004,700
Subtotal Cost of Sales	**$4,335,778**	**$4,725,098**	**$5,196,918**	**$5,715,557**	**$6,287,658**

24

4.2.1 Sales Breakdown by Manager

Sales by Manager: As might be expected, Leslie has by far the largest sales quota to manage. This is suited to our strategy of putting Leslie in charge of the sales force, and tracking sales through the sales force. Details follow.

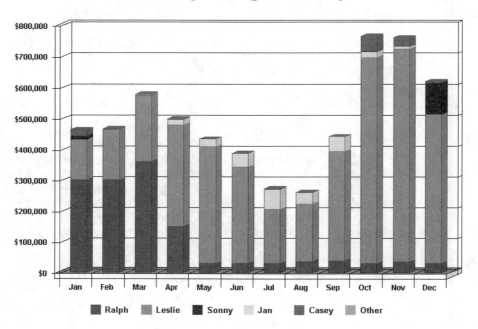

Sales by Manager Monthly

Sales by Manager

Sales	2000	2001	2002	2003	2004
Ralph	$1,372,500	$1,509,750	$1,660,725	$1,826,798	$2,009,477
Leslie	$4,089,250	$4,510,825	$4,961,908	$5,458,098	$6,003,908
Sonny	$110,000	$121,000	$133,100	$146,410	$161,051
Jan	$272,500	$299,750	$329,725	$362,698	$398,967
Casey	$102,500	$112,750	$124,025	$136,428	$150,070
Other	$11,507	$1,053	$264	($1,001)	($439)
Total	**$5,958,257**	**$6,555,128**	**$7,209,747**	**$7,929,431**	**$8,723,034**
Average	**$993,043**	**$1,092,521**	**$1,201,625**	**$1,321,572**	**$1,453,839**

25

4.2.2 Sales Breakdown by Tactic

Our sales don't really breakdown well into marketing tactics because we are still selling the same main products and services: systems, installation, and so on. However, we can still make this breakdown to at least show how we expect to see increasing sales of training, network services, and sales directly related to customer contacts and upgrades.

Sales by Tactic Monthly

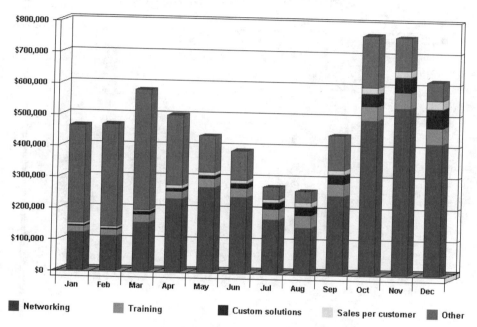

Legend: Networking | Training | Custom solutions | Sales per customer | Other

Sales by Tactic

Sales		2000	2001	2002	2003	2004
Networking	10%	$3,133,750	$3,450,000	$3,800,000	$4,180,000	$4,600,000
Training	12%	$415,000	$460,000	$520,000	$580,000	$650,000
Custom solutions	15%	$280,000	$320,000	$370,000	$430,000	$490,000
Sales per customer	25%	$150,000	$190,000	$240,000	$300,000	$380,000
Other		$1,979,507	$2,135,128	$2,279,747	$2,439,431	$2,603,034
Total		**$5,958,257**	**$6,555,128**	**$7,209,747**	**$7,929,431**	**$8,723,034**
Average		**$1,191,651**	**$1,311,026**	**$1,441,949**	**$1,585,886**	**$1,744,607**

26

4.2.3 Sales Breakdown by Product

Sales by Product: The $6 million sales forecast is shown in the following table and chart. As always, our largest single sales item is the sales of systems. The next largest item is the general, non-specific sales, which of course will also be mostly systems. The details follow.

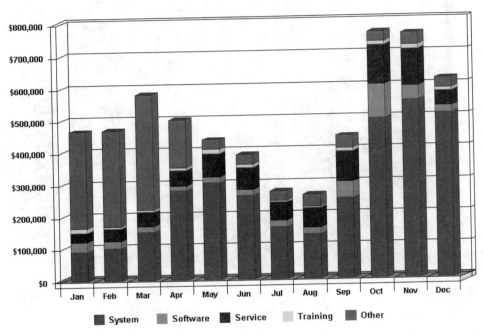

Sales by Product Monthly

Sales by Product Sales	2000	2001	2002	2003	2004
System	$3,293,500	$3,622,850	$3,985,135	$4,383,649	$4,822,013
Software	$380,000	$418,000	$459,800	$505,780	$556,358
Service	$799,250	$879,175	$967,093	$1,063,802	$1,170,182
Training	$113,000	$124,300	$136,730	$150,403	$165,443
Other	$1,372,507	$1,510,803	$1,660,990	$1,825,797	$2,009,038
Total	**$5,958,257**	**$6,555,128**	**$7,209,748**	**$7,929,431**	**$8,723,034**
Average	**$1,191,651**	**$1,311,026**	**$1,441,949**	**$1,585,886**	**$1,744,607**

27

4.3 Expense Forecast

The following marketing budget comes to a total of less than $450 thousand. This is actually a decrease over the $485 thousand we spent this year on the marketing budget. We believe we can get more effective marketing with less money, because we are managing the marketing better.

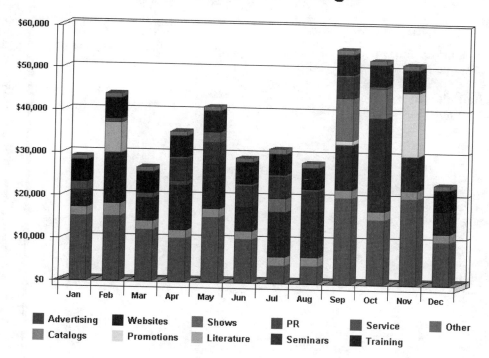

Monthly Expense Budget

Legend:
- Advertising
- Websites
- Shows
- PR
- Service
- Other
- Catalogs
- Promotions
- Literature
- Seminars
- Training

Marketing Expense Budget

Marketing Expense	2000	2001	2002	2003	2004
Advertising	$150,000	$250,000	$225,000	$200,000	$200,000
Catalogs	$25,000	$28,000	$31,000	$34,000	$37,000
Websites	$113,300	$125,000	$138,000	$152,000	$167,000
Promotions	$16,000	$18,000	$20,000	$22,000	$24,000
Shows	$20,200	$22,000	$24,000	$26,000	$29,000
Literature	$7,000	$8,000	$9,000	$10,000	$11,000
PR	$1,000	$1,000	$1,000	$1,000	$1,000
Seminars	$31,000	$34,000	$37,000	$41,000	$45,000
Service	$10,250	$11,000	$12,000	$13,000	$14,000
Training	$60,000	$66,000	$73,000	$80,000	$88,000
Other	$12,000	$15,000	$20,000	$25,000	$30,000
Total Sales/Marktg. Expen.	$445,750	$578,000	$590,000	$604,000	$646,000
Percent of Sales	7.48%	8.82%	8.18%	7.62%	7.41%
Contribution Margin	$913,563	$1,108,926	$1,266,634	$1,455,537	$1,620,792
Contribution Margin/Sales	15.33%	16.92%	17.57%	18.36%	18.58%

29

4.3.1 Expense Breakdown by Manager

Budget by Manager: As the following table and chart show, the largest budget piece is the $151 thousand (almost entirely advertising budget) managed by Ralph.

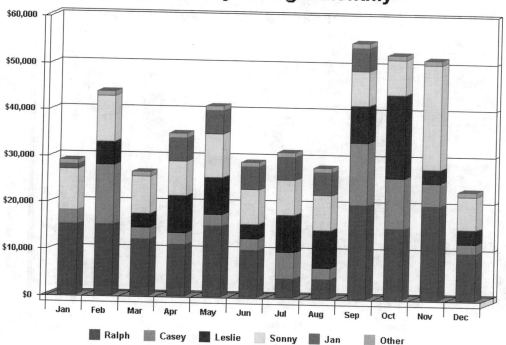

Expenses by Manager Monthly

Legend: Ralph, Casey, Leslie, Sonny, Jan, Other

Expenses by Manager

Expenses	2000	2001	2002	2003	2004
Ralph	$151,000	$163,080	$176,126	$190,217	$205,434
Casey	$65,700	$70,956	$76,632	$82,763	$89,384
Leslie	$75,000	$81,000	$87,480	$94,478	$102,037
Sonny	$111,050	$119,934	$129,529	$139,891	$151,082
Jan	$31,000	$33,480	$36,158	$139,891...	$151,082
Other	$12,000	$109,550	$84,074	$57,600	$55,888
Total	**$445,750**	**$578,000**	**$589,999**	**$604,000**	**$646,000**
Average	**$74,292**	**$96,333**	**$98,333**	**$100,667**	**$107,667**

30

4.3.2 Expense Breakdown by Tactic

Expenses by Tactic: As our budget in detail shows, we are following our priorities with our marketing expenditures. Most of our expenses follow the main priorities as assigned in the strategy pyramid. For this year, we plan to spend 80% of our sales and marketing budget on the priority areas related to tactics. That percentage will increase to more than 90% during the fifth year of our marketing plan.

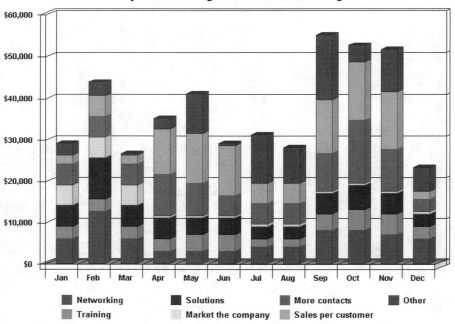

Expenses by Tactic Monthly

Expenses by Tactic

Expenses		2000	2001	2002	2003	2004
Networking	20%	$70,500	$80,000	$100,000	$120,000	$140,000
Training	10%	$41,000	$50,000	$60,000	$70,000	$80,000
Solutions	15%	$58,000	$70,000	$80,000	$90,000	$100,000
Market the company	5%	$19,500	$20,000	$20,000	$20,000	$20,000
More contacts	10%	$85,000	$90,000	$100,000	$110,000	$120,000
Sales per customer	10%	$97,000	$110,000	$120,000	$130,000	$140,000
Other		$74,750	$158,000	$110,000	$64,000	$46,000
Total		**$445,750**	**$578,000**	**$590,000**	**$604,000**	**$646,000**
Average		**$63,679**	**$82,571**	**$84,286**	**$86,286**	**$92,286**

31

4.3.3 Expense Breakdown Product

Budget by Type: The largest single expenditure program is advertising, at $150 thousand. This is actually $30 thousand less than we will have spent this year. The second largest is mailing, which is a priority because of its importance to our database marketing strategy.

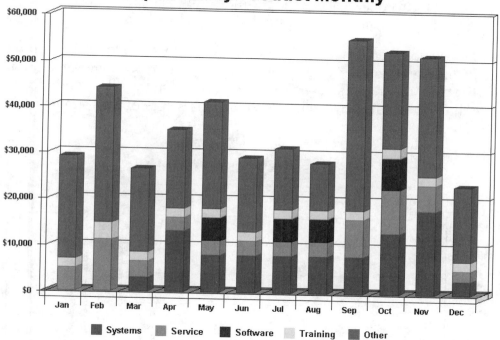

Expenses by Product Monthly

Expenses by Product

Expenses	2000	2001	2002	2003	2004
Systems	$90,000	$97,200	$104,976	$113,374	$122,444
Service	$59,750	$64,530	$69,692	$75,268	$81,289
Software	$22,000	$23,760	$25,661	$27,714	$29,931
Training	$25,800	$27,864	$30,093	$32,501	$35,101
Other	$248,200	$364,646	$359,578	$355,144	$377,235
Total	**$445,750**	**$578,000**	**$590,000**	**$604,001**	**$646,000**
Average	**$89,150**	**$115,600**	**$118,000**	**$120,800**	**$129,200**

32

4.4 Linking Expenses to Strategy and Tactics

We plan to spend about 7-8% of sales on sales and marketing expenses. As we look at specific breakdowns of sales and expenses by target market segment, of those sales that can be identified by segment the vast majority are small business, and our expenses that are tied to segments are also a ratio of 3 to 1 small business, so that matches.

Less than half of our sales and marketing expenses actually tie into the specific market segments. This makes sense for our marketing plan, since the benefits offered to both segments are frequently quite similar.

Our breakdown of expenses by product shows that we are following through on our strategy of migrating sales to the higher-margin and more-defensible product areas, particularly training and service. Although our systems sales continue to contribute the bulk of sales, the transition in expenses support our strategy.

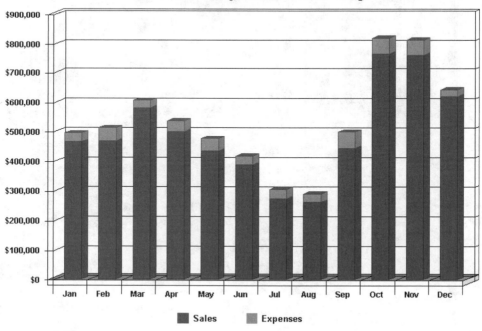

Sales vs. Expenses Monthly

33

4.5 Contribution Margins

Unfortunately, as the table shows, our contribution margin is an unimpressive 7% this year and that's the best we can do. Our gross margin has fallen significantly and we need to take steps to repair it, and, furthermore, we need to do some extra marketing to reposition ourselves with the new strategy.

The point is, however, that we are going to improve this margin over time. We expect the gross margin to go up to 25%, and the contribution margin to go up to 18% as we implement our new strategy. That's one of the main points of this plan.

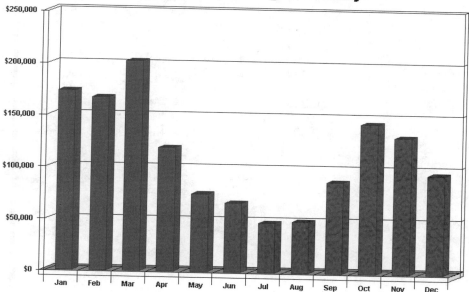

Contribution Margin Monthly

Contribution Margin

	2000	2001	2002	2003	2004
Sales	$5,958,257	$6,555,128	$7,209,747	$7,929,431	$8,723,034
Direct Cost of Sales	$4,335,779	$4,725,099	$5,196,919	$5,715,557	$6,287,658
Other Variable Costs of Sales	$263,165	$143,103	$156,195	$154,337	$168,584
Total Cost of Sales	$4,598,944	$4,868,202	$5,353,114	$5,869,894	$6,456,242
Gross Margin	**$1,359,313**	**$1,686,926**	**$1,856,633**	**$2,059,537**	**$2,266,792**
Gross Margin %	**22.81%**	**25.73%**	**25.75%**	**25.97%**	**25.99%**

Marketing Expense Budget

	2000	2001	2002	2003	2004
Advertising	$150,000	$250,000	$225,000	$200,000	$200,000
Catalogs	$25,000	$28,000	$31,000	$34,000	$37,000
Websites	$113,300	$125,000	$138,000	$152,000	$167,000
Promotions	$16,000	$18,000	$20,000	$22,000	$24,000
Shows	$20,200	$22,000	$24,000	$26,000	$29,000
Literature	$7,000	$8,000	$9,000	$10,000	$11,000
PR	$1,000	$1,000	$1,000	$1,000	$1,000
Seminars	$31,000	$34,000	$37,000	$41,000	$45,000
Service	$10,250	$11,000	$12,000	$13,000	$14,000
Training	$60,000	$66,000	$73,000	$80,000	$88,000
Other	$12,000	$15,000	$20,000	$25,000	$30,000
Total Sales and Marketing Expenses	$445,750	$578,000	$590,000	$604,000	$646,000
Percent of Sales	7.48%	8.82%	8.18%	7.62%	7.41%
Contribution Margin	**$913,563**	**$1,108,926**	**$1,266,634**	**$1,455,537**	**$1,620,792**
Contribution Margin / Sales	**15.33%**	**16.92%**	**17.57%**	**18.36%**	**18.58%**

35

5.0 Controls

1. <u>Tracking and follow-up</u>: Will we have the discipline, as an organization, to track results of the marketing plan and make sure that we implement?

2. <u>Market segment focus</u>: How can we be sure we have the discipline to maintain the focus?

3. <u>Saying no</u>: Can we say no to special deals that take us away from the target focus? Can we say no to unprofitable deals? Should we say no to profitable deals?

5.1 Implementation

- The milestones as shown are the key items in our repositioning.
- Ralph is in charge of advertising, which includes the new corporate brochure. This is an all-year project so we don't list specific dates, just starting in January and ending at the end of November. Ralph is also responsible for approving a new VP marketing, and managing the marketing plan.
- Leslie, as sales manager, has some specific programs as well as the sales goals. We expect to see six presentations by the end of February, and at least three new accounts by the end of the following month. Leslie will also be managing our mailing programs, with several specific milestones included.
- Jan will be managing the seminar programs.
- Sonny will be managing the purchase of the new vans for installation purposes, and, of course, the software engineering programs.

36

Milestones

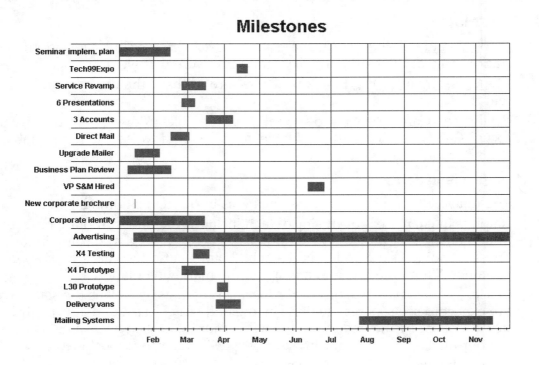

Milestones Plan

Milestone	Start Date	End Date	Budget	Manager	Department
Seminar Implementation Plan	1/3/00	2/15/00	$1,000	Jan	Sales
Tech99Expo	4/12/00	4/21/00	$15,000	Jan	GM
Service Revamp	2/25/00	3/16/00	$2,500	Kelly	Product
6 Presentations	2/25/00	3/7/00	$0	Leslie	Sales
3 Accounts	3/17/00	4/8/00	$0	Leslie	Sales
Direct Mail	2/16/00	3/2/00	$3,500	Leslie	Marketing
Upgrade Mailer	1/16/00	2/6/00	$5,000	Leslie	Sales
Business Plan Review	1/10/00	2/16/00	$0	Ralph	GM
VP Marketing Hired	6/11/00	6/25/00	$1,000	Ralph	Sales
New Corporate Brochure	1/16/00	1/16/00	$5,000	Ralph	Marketing
Corporate Identity	1/3/00	3/15/00	$10,000	Ralph	Marketing
Advertising	1/15/00	11/30/00	$150,000	Ralph	GM
X4 Testing	3/6/00	3/19/00	$1,000	Sonny	Product
X4 Prototype	2/25/00	3/15/00	$2,500	Sonny	Product
L30 Prototype	3/26/00	4/4/00	$2,500	Sonny	Product
Delivery Vans	3/25/00	4/15/00	$22,500	Sonny	Service
Mailing Systems	7/25/00	11/15/00	$10,000	Leslie	Sales

Totals   **$231,500**

37

5.2 Marketing Organization

AMT is still a small company, despite our recent growth.

Ralph, president, is responsible for general management. He specifically manages the advertising budget, but otherwise is responsible for sales and marketing as the head of the organization.

Leslie, our sales manager, is responsible for managing the in-house and the outbound sales forces. We have also put the mailing programs under Leslie because they must be carefully coordinated with the follow-up of the sales force.

Casey, our marketing manager, is responsible for marketing programs including sales literature, trade shows, the catalog, etc.

Jan, who reports to Casey, will take the key role in the seminar marketing programs.

Sonny, who is service manager, will also manage the marketing programs related to service.

5.3 Contingency Planning

1. We need to watch our results very carefully. We may need to drop sales of CPUs entirely, if we can't get the margin up. It isn't a bad option, to think that we might be able to avoid the straight competition with the major chains by focusing more on our true value.
2. If we do that, we might reposition ourselves as a networking company that also provides training and service.
3. It's possible that the value-added position without hardware sales could be a better way to go. We have to watch how the margins in the mainline sales decline.

This page intentionally blank.

39

Table 4.2: Sales Forecast

Unit Sales	Jan	Feb	Mar	Apr	May	Jun	Jul	Aug	Sep	Oct	Nov	Dec
Systems	45	50	75	152	160	133	76	65	120	253	279	258
Service	200	325	300	325	350	375	400	400	550	850	600	300
Software	150	200	225	250	325	318	233	243	428	575	548	300
Training	145	155	165	170	225	200	150	150	200	220	250	230
Other	1,000	1,000	1,200	500	100	100	100	125	130	100	120	100
Total Unit Sales	**1,540**	**1,730**	**1,965**	**1,397**	**1,160**	**1,126**	**959**	**983**	**1,428**	**1,998**	**1,797**	**1,088**

Unit Prices	Jan	Feb	Mar	Apr	May	Jun	Jul	Aug	Sep	Oct	Nov	Dec
Systems	$2,000.00	$2,000.00	$2,000.00	$1,828.95	$1,890.63	$1,966.17	$2,131.58	$2,115.38	$2,083.33	$1,966.40	$1,980.29	$1,984.50
Service	$150.00	$69.23	$58.33	$46.15	$50.00	$46.67	$50.00	$50.00	$90.91	$123.53	$75.00	$66.67
Software	$200.00	$200.00	$200.00	$200.00	$223.08	$216.98	$242.49	$253.09	$219.63	$210.87	$204.38	$206.52
Training	$100.00	$35.48	$39.39	$41.18	$55.56	$50.00	$33.33	$33.33	$50.00	$54.55	$60.00	$50.00
Other	$300.00	$300.00	$300.00	$300.00	$300.00	$300.00	$300.00	$300.00	$300.00	$300.00	$300.00	$300.00

Sales	Jan	Feb	Mar	Apr	May	Jun	Jul	Aug	Sep	Oct	Nov	Dec
Systems	$90,000	$100,000	$150,000	$278,000	$302,501	$261,501	$162,000	$137,500	$250,000	$497,499	$552,501	$512,001
Service	$30,000	$22,500	$17,499	$14,999	$17,501	$17,501	$20,000	$20,000	$50,001	$105,001	$45,000	$20,001
Software	$30,000	$40,000	$45,000	$50,000	$72,501	$69,000	$56,500	$61,501	$94,002	$121,250	$112,000	$47,500
Training	$14,500	$5,499	$6,499	$7,001	$12,501	$10,000	$5,000	$5,000	$10,000	$12,001	$15,000	$10,000
Other	$300,000	$300,000	$360,000	$150,000	$30,000	$30,000	$30,000	$37,500	$39,000	$30,000	$36,000	$30,000
Total Sales	**$464,500**	**$467,999**	**$578,998**	**$500,000**	**$435,003**	**$388,002**	**$273,500**	**$261,501**	**$443,003**	**$765,751**	**$760,501**	**$619,502**

Direct Unit Costs	Jan	Feb	Mar	Apr	May	Jun	Jul	Aug	Sep	Oct	Nov	Dec
Systems	$1,700.00	$1,700.00	$1,700.00	$1,554.61	$1,607.04	$1,671.24	$1,811.84	$1,798.07	$1,770.83	$1,671.44	$1,683.25	$1,686.83
Service	$90.00	$41.54	$35.00	$27.69	$30.00	$28.00	$30.00	$30.00	$54.55	$74.12	$45.00	$40.00
Software	$150.00	$150.00	$150.00	$150.00	$167.31	$162.74	$181.87	$189.82	$164.72	$158.15	$153.29	$154.89
Training	$20.00	$7.10	$7.88	$8.24	$11.11	$10.00	$6.67	$6.67	$10.00	$10.91	$12.00	$10.00
Other	$150.00	$150.00	$150.00	$150.00	$150.00	$150.00	$150.00	$150.00	$150.00	$150.00	$150.00	$150.00

Direct Cost of Sales	Jan	Feb	Mar	Apr	May	Jun	Jul	Aug	Sep	Oct	Nov	Dec
Systems	$76,500	$85,000	$127,500	$236,301	$257,126	$222,275	$137,700	$116,875	$212,500	$422,874	$469,627	$435,202
Service	$18,000	$13,501	$10,500	$8,999	$10,500	$10,500	$12,000	$12,000	$30,003	$63,002	$27,000	$12,000
Software	$22,500	$30,000	$33,750	$37,500	$54,376	$51,751	$42,376	$46,126	$70,500	$90,936	$84,003	$35,625
Training	$2,900	$1,101	$1,300	$1,401	$2,500	$2,000	$1,001	$1,001	$2,000	$2,400	$3,000	$2,000
Other	$150,000	$150,000	$180,000	$75,000	$15,000	$15,000	$15,000	$18,750	$19,500	$15,000	$18,000	$15,000
Subtotal												
Cost of Sales	**$269,900**	**$279,602**	**$353,050**	**$359,201**	**$339,502**	**$301,526**	**$208,077**	**$194,752**	**$334,503**	**$594,212**	**$601,630**	**$499,827**

Table 4.2.1: Sales by Manager

Sales	Jan	Feb	Mar	Apr	May	Jun	Jul	Aug	Sep	Oct	Nov	Dec
Ralph	$300,000	$300,000	$360,000	$150,000	$30,000	$30,000	$30,000	$37,500	$39,000	$30,000	$36,000	$30,000
Leslie	$134,500	$165,000	$215,000	$330,000	$380,500	$311,500	$175,000	$186,500	$354,000	$665,750	$687,000	$484,500
Sonny	$10,000	$0	$0	$0	$0	$0	$66,000	$0	$50,000	$0	$0	$100,000
Jan	$20,000	$0	$0	$18,000	$24,500	$46,500	$0	$37,500	$0	$20,000	$10,000	$0
Casey	$0	$0	$0	$0	$0	$0	$0	$0	$0	$50,000	$27,500	$5,000
Other	$0	$2,999	$3,998	$2,000	$3	$2	$2,500	$0	$2	$1	$1	$2
Total	$464,500	$467,999	$578,998	$500,000	$435,003	$388,002	$273,500	$261,500	$443,002	$765,751	$760,501	$619,502
Average	$77,417	$78,000	$96,500	$83,333	$72,500	$64,667	$45,583	$43,583	$73,834	$127,625	$126,750	$103,250

Table 4.2.2: Sales by Tactic

Sales	Jan	Feb	Mar	Apr	May	Jun	Jul	Aug	Sep	Oct	Nov	Dec
Networking	$120,000	$110,000	$155,000	$230,000	$268,000	$239,000	$170,000	$146,500	$247,500	$493,750	$534,500	$419,500
Training	$20,000	$20,000	$25,000	$25,000	$30,000	$30,000	$35,000	$40,000	$40,000	$45,000	$50,000	$55,000
Custom solutions	$5,000	$5,000	$10,000	$10,000	$10,000	$15,000	$20,000	$25,000	$30,000	$40,000	$50,000	$60,000
Sales per customer	$5,000	$5,000	$5,000	$10,000	$10,000	$10,000	$10,000	$15,000	$15,000	$20,000	$20,000	$25,000
Other	$314,500	$327,999	$383,998	$225,000	$117,003	$94,002	$38,500	$35,000	$110,502	$167,001	$106,001	$60,002
Total	$464,500	$467,999	$578,998	$500,000	$435,003	$388,002	$273,500	$261,500	$443,002	$765,751	$760,501	$619,502
Average	$92,900	$93,600	$115,800	$100,000	$87,001	$77,600	$54,700	$52,300	$88,600	$153,150	$152,100	$123,900

Table 4.2.3: Sales by Product

Sales	Jan	Feb	Mar	Apr	May	Jun	Jul	Aug	Sep	Oct	Nov	Dec
System	$90,000	$100,000	$150,000	$278,000	$302,500	$261,500	$162,000	$137,500	$250,000	$497,500	$552,500	$512,000
Software	$30,000	$22,500	$17,500	$15,000	$17,500	$17,500	$20,000	$20,000	$50,000	$105,000	$45,000	$20,000
Service	$30,000	$40,000	$45,000	$50,000	$72,500	$69,000	$56,500	$61,500	$94,000	$121,250	$112,000	$47,500
Training	$14,500	$5,500	$6,500	$7,000	$12,500	$10,000	$5,000	$5,000	$10,000	$12,000	$15,000	$10,000
Other	$300,000	$299,999	$359,998	$150,000	$30,003	$30,002	$30,000	$37,500	$39,002	$30,001	$36,001	$30,002
Total	$464,500	$467,999	$578,998	$500,000	$435,003	$388,002	$273,500	$261,500	$443,002	$765,751	$760,501	$619,502
Average	$92,900	$93,600	$115,800	$100,000	$87,001	$77,600	$54,700	$52,300	$88,600	$153,150	$152,100	$123,900

Table 4.3: Marketing Expense Budget

Marketing Expense Budget	Jan	Feb	Mar	Apr	May	Jun	Jul	Aug	Sep	Oct	Nov	Dec
Advertising	$15,000	$15,000	$12,000	$10,000	$15,000	$10,000	$4,000	$4,000	$20,000	$15,000	$20,000	$10,000
Catalogs	$2,000	$3,000	$2,000	$2,000	$2,000	$2,000	$2,000	$2,000	$2,000	$2,000	$2,000	$2,000
Websites	$3,000	$11,800	$5,500	$10,500	$10,500	$5,500	$10,500	$10,500	$10,500	$22,000	$8,000	$5,000
Promotions	$0	$0	$0	$0	$0	$0	$0	$0	$1,000	$0	$15,000	$0
Shows	$0	$7,000	$0	$0	$0	$0	$3,200	$0	$10,000	$7,000	$0	$0
Literature	$0	$0	$0	$0	$0	$0	$0	$0	$0	$0	$0	$0
PR	$0	$0	$0	$1,000	$0	$0	$0	$0	$0	$0	$0	$0
Seminars	$1,000	$0	$0	$5,000	$5,000	$5,000	$5,000	$5,000	$5,000	$0	$0	$0
Service	$2,000	$1,000	$1,000	$500	$2,500	$500	$500	$500	$500	$500	$500	$250
Training	$5,000	$5,000	$5,000	$5,000	$5,000	$5,000	$5,000	$5,000	$5,000	$5,000	$5,000	$5,000
Other	$1,000	$1,000	$1,000	$1,000	$1,000	$1,000	$1,000	$1,000	$1,000	$1,000	$1,000	$1,000
Total Sales/Marketing Expenses	$29,000	$43,800	$26,500	$35,000	$41,000	$29,000	$31,200	$28,000	$55,000	$52,500	$51,500	$23,250
Percent of Sales	6.24%	9.36%	4.58%	7.00%	9.43%	7.47%	11.41%	10.71%	12.42%	6.86%	6.77%	3.75%
Contribution Margin	$144,310	$123,238	$175,868	$83,799	$33,801	$37,715	$16,754	$21,519	$32,639	$91,723	$80,161	$72,035
Contribution Margin/Sales	31.07%	26.33%	30.37%	16.76%	7.77%	9.72%	6.13%	8.23%	7.37%	11.98%	10.54%	11.63%

Table 4.3.1: Expenses by Manager

Expenses	Jan	Feb	Mar	Apr	May	Jun	Jul	Aug	Sep	Oct	Nov	Dec
Ralph	$15,000	$15,000	$12,000	$11,000	$15,000	$10,000	$4,000	$4,000	$20,000	$15,000	$20,000	$10,000
Casey	$3,000	$13,000	$2,500	$2,500	$2,500	$2,500	$5,700	$2,500	$13,500	$11,000	$5,000	$2,000
Leslie	$0	$5,000	$3,000	$8,000	$8,000	$3,000	$8,000	$8,000	$7,500	$18,000	$3,000	$3,000
Sonny	$9,000	$9,800	$8,000	$7,500	$9,500	$7,500	$7,500	$7,500	$7,500	$7,500	$22,500	$7,250
Jan	$1,000	$0	$0	$5,000	$5,000	$5,000	$5,000	$5,000	$5,000	$0	$0	$0
Other	$1,000	$1,000	$1,000	$1,000	$1,000	$1,000	$1,000	$1,000	$1,000	$1,000	$1,000	$1,000
Total	**$29,000**	**$43,800**	**$26,500**	**$35,000**	**$41,000**	**$29,000**	**$31,200**	**$28,000**	**$55,000**	**$52,500**	**$51,500**	**$23,250**
Average	**$4,833**	**$7,300**	**$4,417**	**$5,833**	**$6,833**	**$4,833**	**$5,200**	**$4,667**	**$9,167**	**$8,750**	**$8,583**	**$3,875**

Table 4.3.2: Expenses by Tactic

Expenses	Jan	Feb	Mar	Apr	May	Jun	Jul	Aug	Sep	Oct	Nov	Dec
Networking	$6,000	$12,500	$6,000	$3,000	$3,000	$3,000	$4,000	$4,000	$8,000	$8,000	$7,000	$6,000
Training	$3,000	$3,000	$3,000	$3,000	$4,000	$4,000	$2,000	$2,000	$4,000	$5,000	$5,000	$3,000
Solutions	$5,000	$10,000	$5,000	$5,000	$4,000	$4,000	$3,000	$3,000	$5,000	$6,000	$5,000	$3,000
Market the company	$5,000	$5,000	$5,000	$500	$500	$500	$500	$500	$500	$500	$500	$500
More contacts	$5,000	$5,000	$5,000	$10,000	$8,000	$5,000	$5,000	$5,000	$9,000	$15,000	$10,000	$3,000
Sales per customer	$2,000	$5,000	$2,000	$11,000	$12,000	$12,000	$5,000	$5,000	$13,000	$14,000	$14,000	$2,000
Other	$3,000	$3,300	$500	$2,500	$9,500	$500	$11,700	$8,500	$15,500	$4,000	$10,000	$5,750
Total	**$29,000**	**$43,800**	**$26,500**	**$35,000**	**$41,000**	**$29,000**	**$31,200**	**$28,000**	**$55,000**	**$52,500**	**$51,500**	**$23,250**
Average	**$4,143**	**$6,257**	**$3,786**	**$5,000**	**$5,857**	**$4,143**	**$4,457**	**$4,000**	**$7,857**	**$7,500**	**$7,357**	**$3,321**

Table 4.3.3: Expenses by Product

Expenses	Jan	Feb	Mar	Apr	May	Jun	Jul	Aug	Sep	Oct	Nov	Dec
Systems	$0	$0	$3,000	$13,000	$8,000	$8,000	$8,000	$8,000	$8,000	$13,000	$18,000	$3,000
Service	$5,000	$11,000	$3,500	$3,000	$3,000	$3,000	$3,000	$3,000	$8,000	$9,500	$5,500	$2,250
Software	$0	$0	$0	$0	$5,000	$0	$5,000	$5,000	$0	$7,000	$0	$0
Training	$2,000	$3,800	$2,000	$2,000	$2,000	$2,000	$2,000	$2,000	$2,000	$2,000	$2,000	$2,000
Other	$22,000	$29,000	$18,000	$17,000	$23,000	$16,000	$13,200	$10,000	$37,000	$21,000	$26,000	$16,000
Total	**$29,000**	**$43,800**	**$26,500**	**$35,000**	**$41,000**	**$29,000**	**$31,200**	**$28,000**	**$55,000**	**$52,500**	**$51,500**	**$23,250**
Average	**$5,800**	**$8,760**	**$5,300**	**$7,000**	**$8,200**	**$5,800**	**$6,240**	**$5,600**	**$11,000**	**$10,500**	**$10,300**	**$4,650**

Table 4.5: Contribution Margin

	Jan	Feb	Mar	Apr	May	Jun	Jul	Aug	Sep	Oct	Nov	Dec
Sales	$464,500	$467,999	$578,998	$500,000	$435,003	$388,002	$273,500	$261,500	$443,002	$765,751	$760,501	$619,502
Direct Cost of Sales	$269,900	$279,601	$353,050	$359,201	$339,502	$301,526	$208,076	$194,751	$334,502	$594,213	$601,630	$499,827
Other Variable Costs of Sales	$21,290	$21,360	$23,580	$22,000	$20,700	$19,760	$17,470	$17,230	$20,860	$27,315	$27,210	$24,390
Total Cost of Sales	**$291,190**	**$300,961**	**$376,630**	**$381,201**	**$360,202**	**$321,286**	**$225,546**	**$211,981**	**$355,362**	**$621,528**	**$628,840**	**$524,217**
Gross Margin	**$173,310**	**$167,038**	**$202,368**	**$118,799**	**$74,801**	**$66,716**	**$47,954**	**$49,519**	**$87,640**	**$144,223**	**$131,661**	**$95,285**
Gross Margin %	37.31%	35.69%	34.95%	23.76%	17.20%	17.19%	17.53%	18.94%	19.78%	18.83%	17.31%	15.38%
Marketing Expense Budget												
Advertising	$15,000	$15,000	$12,000	$10,000	$15,000	$10,000	$4,000	$4,000	$20,000	$15,000	$20,000	$10,000
Catalogs	$2,000	$3,000	$2,000	$2,000	$2,000	$2,000	$2,000	$2,000	$2,000	$2,000	$2,000	$2,000
Websites	$3,000	$11,800	$5,500	$10,500	$10,500	$5,500	$10,500	$10,500	$10,500	$22,000	$8,000	$5,000
Promotions	$0	$0	$0	$0	$0	$0	$0	$0	$1,000	$0	$15,000	$0
Shows	$0	$0	$0	$0	$0	$0	$0	$0	$0	$7,000	$0	$0
Literature	$0	$7,000	$0	$0	$0	$0	$3,200	$0	$10,000	$0	$0	$0
PR	$0	$0	$0	$1,000	$0	$0	$0	$0	$0	$0	$0	$0
Seminars	$1,000	$0	$0	$5,000	$5,000	$5,000	$5,000	$5,000	$5,000	$0	$0	$0
Service	$2,000	$1,000	$1,000	$500	$2,500	$500	$500	$500	$500	$500	$500	$250
Training	$5,000	$5,000	$5,000	$5,000	$5,000	$5,000	$5,000	$5,000	$5,000	$5,000	$5,000	$5,000
Other	$1,000	$1,000	$1,000	$1,000	$1,000	$1,000	$1,000	$1,000	$1,000	$1,000	$1,000	$1,000
Total Sales/Marketing Expenses	**$29,000**	**$43,800**	**$26,500**	**$35,000**	**$41,000**	**$29,000**	**$31,200**	**$28,000**	**$55,000**	**$52,500**	**$51,500**	**$23,250**
Percent of Sales	6.24%	9.36%	4.58%	7.00%	9.43%	7.47%	11.41%	10.71%	12.42%	6.86%	6.77%	3.75%
Contribution Margin	**$144,310**	**$123,238**	**$175,868**	**$83,799**	**$33,801**	**$37,716**	**$16,754**	**$21,519**	**$32,640**	**$91,723**	**$80,161**	**$72,035**
Contribution Margin/Sales	31.07%	26.33%	30.37%	16.76%	7.77%	9.72%	6.13%	8.23%	7.37%	11.98%	10.54%	11.63%

This page intentionally blank.

SAMPLE PLAN: Franklin & Moore LLC

This sample marketing plan has been made available to users of *Marketing Plan Pro*™, marketing plan software published by Palo Alto Software. It is based on a real marketing plan of an existing company. Names and numbers have been changed, and substantial portions of text may have been omitted to preserve confidential information.

You are welcome to use this plan as a starting point to create your own, but you do not have permission to reproduce, publish, distribute, or even copy this plan as it exists here.

Requests for reprints, academic use, and other dissemination of this sample plan should be addressed to the marketing department of Palo Alto Software.

Table of Contents

1.0 Executive Summary

Franklin & Moore LLC is an accounting firm offering traditional accounting services and business consulting. The firm's reputation is impeccable and is known throughout the San Clemente, California area as one of the top three accounting firms. Franklin & Moore LLC serves the accounting and financial needs of businesses and individuals to enable them to realize their financial goals.

Our target markets include the following.

- Businesses of more that 50 employees and/or $5 million in annual sales, particularly those in the medical/health, dental and lodging industries.
- Growth oriented businesses that will benefit from our areas of pension and retirement planning specialization.
- Individuals with a net worth of greater than $1.2 million.

Diversifying our revenue streams and leveraging our core strengths will optimize our position for the future. We will also implement marketing tactics to better leverage the firm's total capacity throughout the year, versus a heavy concentration.

2.0 Situation Analysis

Franklin & Moore LLC offers expertise in all areas of accounting, bookkeeping, and financial-based planning. The firm has a solid and loyal customer base in a market that has experienced constant but slowing growth in recent years. We have increasing competition from a variety of sources. The firm is highly dependant on revenues from tax planning and preparation for businesses and individuals. These areas account for more than 75% of total revenues. This presents a long-term threat to the firm due to competition and changes in our market. We must diversify our revenue base to realize ongoing growth and stability in a changing industry.

2.1 Market Summary

Franklin & Moore LLC is a full-service accounting firm, serving the personal and business needs for the community of San Clemente, California and beyond. Our most important clients are mid to large-size organizations that rely on our services for their accounting needs. Tax preparation and planning is just the beginning as we strive to become an integral part of their financial management and planning process. Our best clients value their time and resources, and seek to minimize their tax obligations. They do not like negative surprises. They realize and appreciate the value in the services we offer, along with the lost opportunity costs of not benefiting from our services.

1

Target Market Forecast

Potential Customers	Growth	2000	2001	2002	2003	2004	CAGR
Large Business	8%	435,000	469,800	507,384	547,975	591,813	8.00%
Growth Business	11%	342,000	379,620	421,378	467,730	519,180	11.00%
Select Individual Accts.	6%	380,000	402,800	426,968	452,586	479,741	6.00%
Total	8.28%	1,157,000	1,252,220	1,355,730	1,468,291	1,590,734	8.28%

Target Markets

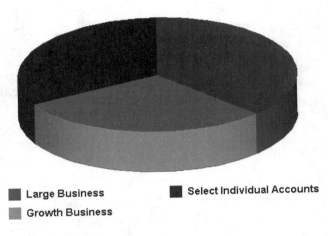

■ Large Business ■ Select Individual Accounts
■ Growth Business

2.1.1 Market Demographics

Individual Accounts - The base of individual accounts serves to offer consistent revenues for the firm. Approximately 20% of these accounts also depend on the firm for ongoing financial planning of their investment portfolios. The balance of the clients primarily look to the firm for tax planning and preparation.

Organizations of Over 50 Employees - Our most profitable business clients fall into the "over 50 employees" category. These corporate accounts generate the highest revenues on a per-hour basis and also generate revenues on the most consistent basis throughout the year. Many of these accounts are in the medical/health, dental, and lodging industries. These clients are also more likely to look to Franklin & Moore LLC for the widest range of services the firm offers, such as assisting with pension planning and investment management services. Target clients in this category have annual sales over $3 million, operate more than one location, serve a national customer base, and are publicly owned.

2

Organizations Under 50 Employees - Organizations under 50 employees represent some of the fastest growing clients within the firm. Franklin & Moore LLC offers attractive services that understand and meet the needs of these clients. Again, many of these clients are in select vertical markets, including medical/health, dental, and lodging industries. The key clients in this category have annual sales between $250,000 and $3,000,000, serve customers in the Southern California market, have a local or statewide customer base, and are privately owned. The long-term strategy is to grow with these clients as their needs for our services increase.

2.1.2 Market Needs

Franklin & Moore LLC provides tangible and intangible value. Our objective is to minimize the tax exposure of our clients and adhere to all state and federal tax laws. The bigger picture means that we are providing peace of mind for our clients—they are legally using their financial resources in the most productive manner possible. We work to make the complex understandable. We act in an advisory role to our clients that will enable them to better influence and optimize their personal and/or corporate wealth. We desire to make them more money and give them a better night's sleep.

2.1.3 Market Trends

Market trends fall into three general categories: static tax laws, increasing use of software, and key client growth.

Static tax laws—Although minor revisions have been made in past years, tax laws have not changed dramatically since 1988. This enables greater efficiencies within our firm, but reduces involvement with our clients and can result in a decrease of billable hours.

Increasing use of software—Tax software is one of our major competitors and continues to erode revenue from individual clients with simple returns. This includes products produced by Intuit with their "Turbo Tax" line and Block Financial with their "Kiplinger Tax Cut" products. Software has also been a resource to increase efficiencies within the firm. For example, we are producing in excess of 50% more work, and therefore billable hours, with the same resources we did in 1995 due to the computer systems now in place.

Key client growth—A cluster of our premier clients have experienced substantial success and growth. Meeting these client's needs will "bring us along" to offer addi-

3

tional services and provide an opportunity for us to strategically expand the services we offer. As we gain expertise and establish our reputation in these areas, we market those to other clients and use them as a point of interest to attract new clients. Pension planning services are one example of this phenomenon.

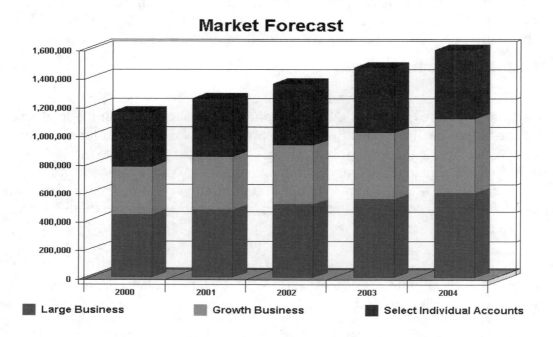

2.1.4 Market Growth

The growth rate of our combined target markets has averaged approximately 8.6%. This is due to the growth of established businesses as well as movement into the San Clemente area. This growth rate has plateaued in the past years and is expected to remain constant for the foreseeable future.

2.2 SWOT Analysis

The SWOT analysis addresses the strengths and weakness within Franklin & Moore LLC and the opportunities and threats that exist in our environment. This analysis highlights areas to be leveraged and points out where we must improve within the firm and within our industry and market.

4

2.2.1 Strengths

Franklin & Moore's strengths include:

- A core of CPAs that have established solid reputations within our market
- Highly experienced staff with an increase in total billable hours.
- A state-of-the-art computer system, utilizing the latest software that continues to enhance our productivity and expand our capacity.
- High client retention, providing consistent referrals to the firm.
- Expertise in specific vertical markets of medical/health, dental, and lodging industries.
- Three CPAs, our "rainmakers," who bring in an estimated 65% of the new client work.

2.2.2 Weaknesses

Franklin & Moore's weaknesses include:

- Over dependence on tax preparation work for individual and business clients and, therefore, a lack of diversification in our revenue sources.
- Inability to generate sufficient billable hours in the off-season, based on the current capacity of our systems and full-time staff.
- Difficulty in retaining aggressive non-partner CPAs, as they move to smaller firms that will make them partners sooner.
- Being perceived as a non-progressive, "too traditional" firm and maybe overlooked as a viable option for new clients.
- Some individuals within the professional staff do not have an understanding of or a commitment to the marketing activities of the firm.

2.2.3 Opportunities

Opportunities available to Franklin & Moore LLC include:

- Benefiting from the ongoing increase in population to the San Clemente area, particularly for the retirement segment.
- Increasing income levels of the population over the age of 60 that have aggressively saved for retirement and have increasingly complex tax planning, tax preparation, and estate planning needs.
- Leveraging the positive perception business has about locating in this section of Orange County.
- Growth that is occurring in three industries where we possess expertise; health/medical, dental, and lodging.

5

2.2.4 Threats

Threats include:

- Increased competition from sole practitioners and new firms.
- Continued sophistication and affordability of software that replaces or minimizes the role of a CPA for tax preparation, accounting, and book-keeping services.
- General perceptions that accounting firms are only used for tax-related aspects of business rather than as a valuable resource for broader business consulting issues.
- Some organizations planning for an Initial Public Offering (IPO) perceive they must use a national accounting firm.
- State and/or federal tax laws that lead to gross simplification, such as legislation leading to a flat income tax, which would result in reducing billable hours for business and individual taxes.

2.3 Competition

Competitors fall into four primary categories; other firms, sole practitioners, licensed tax consultants and bookkeeping services, and software.

Other CPA firms - A total of five firms conduct business in our area that are comparable to Franklin & Moore LLC in size and capabilities, including one that is a national firm. These firms have staff and technology resources similar to ours, although their focus and areas of specialization vary.

Sole practitioners - An estimated 23 sole practitioners exist in the immediate area. This ranges from individuals that have been in business for over 20 years to those that are in their sixth month. Their resources are limited in terms of staff and technology.

Licensed tax consultants and bookkeeping services - The "Type I" individual client, with straightforward and uncomplicated needs, often looks to licensed tax consultants and bookkeeping services in lieu of the services we offer. This client type may consider these preparers on the basis of "self preparation avoidance" rather than from seeking proactive advice and council.

Software - Increasing competition from individual software, particularly Intuit's "Turbo Tax" and Block Financials'"Kiplinger Tax Cut."

6

Growth and Share

Competitor	Price	Growth Rate	Market Share
Huber & Huber PC	$150	10%	9%
Lang Pauls & Rowe	$145	7%	14%
Wright & Ellison	$155	6%	11%
Insight	$125	16%	6%
Franklin & Moore LLC	$160	9%	15%
Average	**$147.00**	**9.60%**	**11.00%**
Total	**$735.00**	**48.00%**	**55.00%**

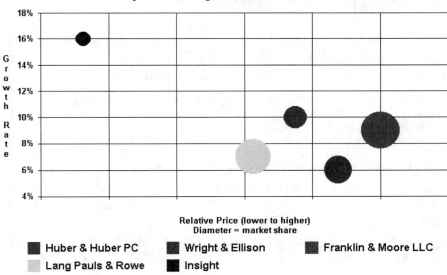

Competitor by Growth and Share

Relative Price (lower to higher)
Diameter = market share

■ Huber & Huber PC   ■ Wright & Ellison   ■ Franklin & Moore LLC
■ Lang Pauls & Rowe   ■ Insight

2.4 Services

Our services offer expertise to enable our clients to better realize their financial objectives. Accomplishing this for our clients falls into these basic service areas:

Business Clients

- · Tax advising, planning, and preparation
- · Consulting services, including;
    - Industry-specific consulting
    - At-risk business consulting
    - Corporate-pension consulting

7

Individual Clients

- Tax advising, planning, and preparation for individuals
- Consulting services, including;
  - Personal financial planning (general)
  - Pension planning
  - Retirement planning

Providing quality service is also critical. Our business and individual clients judge our competence based on how we treat them. This is their primary—and in many cases their only—measurement of our capabilities. They ask themselves the following about our firm:

- Do they act in a professional manner?
- Do they know who I am?
- Do they remember my name?
- Are they genuinely concerned about my best interest?
- Will they actively support and defend their advice and council if needed?

We must have each of our clients answer positively to these questions.

2.5 Keys to Success

- Continuing to leverage the in-house computer system to keep efficiencies high and costs, specifically payroll, to a minimum.
- Further develop areas of specialization to attract and retain key clients.
- Continued development of client referrals from individuals and business contacts.
- Marketing training to develop networking and other marketing skills within the professional staff.

2.6 Critical Issues

The firm appears to be approaching a "mature" category. We have relatively low major opportunities, fairly low threats, limited growth potential, and relatively low risk.

Critical issues for Franklin & Moore LLC include:

- Retaining clients is essential and will be determined by maintaining our reputation built upon professionalism, trust, accuracy, and timeliness.
- Continuing to leverage our computer-based capabilities within the firm on a cost-effective basis.

8

- Tracking results to better understand which activities offer the best return.
- Focusing on key market segments that will produce the greatest return.
- Educating our staff so everyone takes a role in marketing the firm and not leaving this responsibility to the few "rainmakers" that now account for a large percentage of new business.

2.7 Historical Results

Our past marketing activities have produced mixed results. The following is a summary of those activities and categorizes them in terms of "successful" and "unsuccessful." A successful marketing activity produced billable hours that were equal to or greater than the total investment into the activity, excluding time. An unsuccessful activity generated traceable revenue but was less than the cost of the effort.

Successful—

- Referral-based activities; Professional referrals, individual referrals.
- Selective sponsorships: Southern California Opera, Youth Sports.
- Yellow Pages: Competitive size ads for our area.
- Board member participation: Lodging Association of Southern California, San Clemente City Commission on Land Use, California Opera, Youth Sports.

Unsuccessful—

- Advertising (non-sponsorship based).
- Service club participation; Rotary, Lions, Sierra Club, Boy Scouts of America.

Additional work is required to better track revenues resulting from each of our marketing activities.

Historical Data

Variable	1997	1998	1999
Industry Revenue	$10,006,800.00	$10,905,600.00	$11,692,000.00
Company Market Share	12%	13%	13%
Company Revenue	**$1,200,816**	**$1,417,728**	**$1,519,960**
Industry Variable Costs	$1,318,100.00	$1,448,400.00	$1,539,200.00
Company Variable Costs	$120,081.60	$136,320.00	$151,996.00
Industry Gross Contribution Margin	**$8,688,700.00**	**$9,457,200.00**	**$10,152,800.00**
Company Gross Contribution Margin	**$1,080,734.40**	**$1,226,880.00**	**$1,367,964.00**
Marketing Expenses	$4,000.00	$4,400.00	$4,840.00
Company Net Contribution Margin	**$1,076,734.40**	**$1,222,480.00**	**$1,363,124.00**

9

2.8 Macroenvironment

Consumer trends - Those clients that are PC literate are more likely to consider tax preparation software as a viable alternative to using our services.

Economic changes - Two economic changes are taking place, due to the increasing assets of the over-60 "depression generation" and their saving behavior. First, they have proportionately greater assets than their predecessors, particularly individuals with assets in excess of $1.2 million. This group and their heirs may realize increased benefits from tax and estate planning. There is also a phenomenon where the children of this aging population are more likely to inherit assets and need to integrate these newly acquired assets with their own. Both present opportunities for tax and estate planning activities.

Technology advancements - Franklin & Moore LLC has benefited from firm-based software that is enabling us to become increasingly more productive with our existing resources. Unfortunately, technological advancements are also creating greater challenges in the competitive environment.

Competitive activity - Competition has increased on all fronts. In addition to the impact end-user software is having on the industry, firms of similar size have grown and expanded and there are more sole proprietors and licensed tax consultants and bookkeeping services. We consider the market to be at or near saturation.

Political and legal environment - Our business activity is directly related to changes in state and federal tax laws. Other than capital gain laws, this has been relatively static for the past 10 years. We do not anticipate significant changes in the near future. The most negative activity in this area would be tax laws that lead to significant simplification of tax laws.

3.0 Marketing Strategy

Our marketing strategies are based on meeting the needs of existing and future clients. We will do this through leveraging internal and external business strengths and understanding the competitive environment. All marketing strategies work toward supporting our mission statement and realizing our stated goals.

Our marketing strategies fall into these three categories:

1. Revenue diversification including service and industry specialization.
2. Fixed fee structure focus.
3. Marketing awareness training.

3.1 Mission

Franklin & Moore LLC is to be a profitable firm that continues to meet the financial objectives of the shareholders and provides a successful environment for its employees. Our firm will maintain strong growth as a provider of high quality professional services to our clients. We will strive to consistently be perceived as a firm that is professional, trustworthy, accurate, and timely. Franklin & Moore LLC will offer the innovative approach clients need to reach their business and personal financial goals. Wealth is good.

3.2 Marketing Objectives

1. To realize an annual growth rate of 8.25% greater than the previous year.
2. To diversify our revenue stream through increased business consulting (non-tax related) activities to account for 26% or more of total revenues.
3. To create a visible profile through establishing reciprocal referral sources with the following:
   · (3) major banks
   · (1) credit union
   · (2) major law firms
   · (2) brokerage firms
4. Train the entire staff to understand, appreciate, and reinforce their role in marketing the firm.

3.3 Financial Objectives

1. Revenues of $1.6 million by year-end to realize a growth rate of 8.25% compared to the previous year.
2. Non-tax preparation revenues greater than 25% of total billing.
3. Payroll expenses to increase no more than 8% compared to the previous year.

3.4 Target Marketing

Our primary target markets include these three areas:

1. Established businesses of more than 50 employees that value an accounting firm that offers comprehensive business planning services, particularly those in the medical/health, dental, and lodging industries.
2. Growing businesses of less than 50 employees that need our services now and will rely on them to a greater extent as their businesses and requirements grow, particularly those that will benefit from areas of specialization, such as pension and retirement program planning.
3. Individual clients with a net worth in excess of $1.2 million that are concerned about the current earning capabilities of their assets and what will happen to those assets when they are passed to their heirs.

Target Market Analysis

Market Segments	Region	Benefits	Product Attitude	Loyalty Status	Buyer-readiness
Large Business	So. Calif.	Quality	Questioning	Volatile	Informed
Growth Business	Orange Cty	Future Plans	Interested	Medium	Unaware
Individual Accts	San Clemente	Reduce Taxes	Positive	High	Ready-to-buy

3.5 Positioning

Franklin & Moore LLC offers a unique team of CPAs and a professional accounting and bookkeeping staff with proven expertise as business consultants. We do more than prepare taxes. We also provide a variety of valuable services that enable a business to optimize their profitability and minimize their tax exposure. We will work to offer our services in an innovative manner to create a source for business planning solutions that will be difficult to emulate. We offer a premium level of service and expect to receive premium compensation for those services.

3.6 Strategy Pyramids

Franklin & Moore's strategy is focused on leveraging our existing strengths. We will strive to emphasize those strengths that cannot be duplicated by our competitors or through the use of software. This is an important factor in differentiating the firm. All tactics to implement this strategy include leveraging the quality of our work and our in-house computer capabilities.

12

STRATEGY #1

Revenue Diversification

Tactic #1 Industry specialization through expanding in medical/health, dental, and lodging clients.
- Program 1-A   Identify potential new clients
- Program 1-B   Additional involvement in industry associations

Tactic #2 Service specialization and building on proven skills.
- Program 2-A   Promotion of areas of specialization
- Program 2-B   Leveraging contacts in vertical markets
- Program 2-C   Utilize our website to communicate and demonstrate these skills

Tactic #3 Expertise-based marketing.
- Program 3-A   Articles in industry publications
- Program 3-B   Presentations at regional or national industry conferences
- Program 3-C   Utilize our website to communicate and demonstrate this expertise

STRATEGY #2

Fixed Fee Structure Emphasis

Tactic #4 Support System.
- Program 4-A   Identification of high potential fixed fee work
- Program 4-B   Implement tracking program

Tactic #5 Increase fixed fee billing.
- Program 5-A   Training regarding fixed fee approach
- Program 5-B   Implement incentive program

13

STRATEGY #3

Marketing Awareness Training

Tactic #6   Train all employees on the firm's marketing strategy and their role.
- Program 6-A   Initial overview of marketing plan
- Program 6-B   Define roles based on position
- Program 6-C   Individual training for all partners and staff CPAs

Tactic #7   Formalization of referral program.
- Program 7-A   Referral log automated for tracking performance
- Program 7-B   Identify high potential professional contacts for referrals
- Program 7-C   Generate monthly reports for all employees

3.7 Marketing Mix

Our experience has proven that the most significant factor in acquiring new clients is a direct result of referrals from our existing client base. In 1998, more than 80% of our new clients directly or indirectly resulted from a referral by an individual or business client. Client retention is essential. Receiving referrals from them will determine our success or failure. People ask other people they know, trust, and share a similar financial position to tell them what firm or CPA to use. It is as simple as that. Our marketing mix will consistently work to optimize the volume and quality of those referrals.

3.7.1 Services and Service Marketing

We need to fulfill the promise we make to each client—to provide them the resources they need to reach their business and personal financial goals, with unfaltering confidence in our firm throughout that process and, ultimately, throughout their lives.

3.7.2 Pricing

Franklin & Moore LLC will seek to provide a premium product at a premium price that offers the best overall value to our clients. Ultimately, our clients will realize greater wealth as a result of their ability to optimize profitability and minimize their tax obligations.

14

Client billing rates reflect the level of expertise required to perform the work. Our average hourly billing rates are as follows:

· Partner	$165
· Staff CPA	$110
· Accounting Staff	$65
· Bookkeeping Staff	$45

As mentioned in our marketing strategy, we will also work to bill more of our work on a fixed-fee basis, particularly the work that can better utilize our computerized capabilities. These fees will be based on the value offered the client, not the internal time required to complete the task.

3.7.3 Promotion

1. Leveraging referrals from professional contacts and individual clients to make this an integral part of how we conduct business.
2. Enhance our profile within our targeted industries and areas of specialization through being cited as possessing unique expertise in these areas.
3. Have the expectation that all employees will take on the task of marketing the firm as they approach their other areas of responsibility. We will track, give feedback, and acknowledge efforts, accomplishments, and results from these actions.
4. Continue to use the technology we have, including our in-house computer capabilities and our website. Both possess incredible potential for future differentiation in an increasingly competitive market.

3.7.4 Service

This topic is a reminder that, throughout the business, providing a quality service experience is also critical. Our business and individual clients judge our competence based on how we treat them. This is their primary—and in many cases their only—measurement of our capabilities. We must have each of our clients answer positively to these questions: Do they act in a professional manner? Do they know who I am? Do they remember my name? Are they genuinely concerned about my best interest? Will they defend their advice and council if needed?

15

3.8 Marketing Research

We will continue to subscribe to Southern California Research Institute to better understand demographic and psychographic data for our region. Additional research will involve tracking competitive activities, gathering data on key business clients and their industries, and watching the evolution of software and its impact on our industry.

4.0 Financials, Budgets, and Forecasts

Our marketing plan requires annual revenues of $1,600,000 for this year. We anticipate that we will have revenues of more than $2,500,000 within five years. Our marketing expenses will equate to an average of 2.5% of total sales throughout.

The marketing plan is based on these three parameters:

1. Increasing our efficiencies through better use of our facilities and expertise. Variable costs will be reduced, as we are able to make use of the capital investment we have in our systems. We will invest in these systems with the expectation that we will benefit as we have in the past from their capabilities. It provides us a competitive edge many of our competitors cannot afford.
2. We will continue to invest in marketing activities based on a percent of total revenues. As our revenues increase, so will our marketing resources.
3. We will forecast and track revenues on a detail basis to provide objective feedback regarding progress in the areas of industry expertise, specialization, and client revenue sources by type.

4.1 Break-even Analysis

Our variable costs are less than 38% of revenues. This is a result of our fixed costs including our facility, computer and technology expenses, and our salaried staff. Variable costs include temporary/seasonal hires, compensation for CPAs based on performance, and client demands that require travel and other per-job based expenditures. Variable costs are expected to continue to decrease as a percent of revenues as we strive to further benefit from technology and become less dependent on wages and salaries.

Break Even Analysis

Assumptions

Average Per-Unit Revenue	$395.00
Average Per-Unit Variable Cost	$152.00
Estimated Fixed costs	$42,250

Monthly Units Break-even	174
Monthly Sales Break-even	$68,678

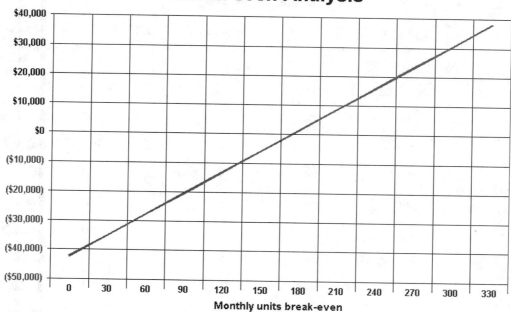

Break-even Analysis

Monthly units break-even

Units break-even point = where line intersects with $0

17

4.2 Sales Forecast

Revenues for this year are based on a 5% growth rate. This is conservative and will be more challenging as we work to diversify our revenue base.

Sales Forecast

Sales	2000	2001	2002	2003	2004
Business Clients - Tax Preparation	$448,000	$447,200	$480,000	$614,400	$787,000
Business Clients - Tax Planning	$272,000	$258,000	$260,000	$304,200	$356,000
Business Clients - Consulting	$144,000	$206,400	$300,000	$324,000	$350,000
Business Clients - Other	$112,000	$154,800	$200,000	$216,000	$233,000
Individual Clients - Tax Preparation	$352,000	$309,600	$300,000	$360,000	$432,000
Individual Clients - Tax Planning	$128,000	$137,600	$140,000	$152,600	$166,000
Individual Clients - Finance Consulting	$96,000	$154,800	$240,000	$256,800	$275,000
Individual Clients - Other	$48,000	$51,600	$80,000	$82,400	$85,000
Total Sales	**$1,600,000**	**$1,720,000**	**$2,000,000**	**$2,310,400**	**$2,684,000**

Direct Cost of Sales	2000	2001	2002	2003	2004
Business Clients - Tax Preparation	$147,839	$147,567	$148,550	$149,800	$150,500
Business Clients - Tax Planning	$89,760	$91,200	$92,800	$93,400	$94,500
Business Clients - Consulting	$47,522	$48,500	$49,500	$50,500	$52,000
Business Clients - Other	$36,960	$37,500	$38,500	$39,500	$40,000
Individual Clients - Tax Preparation	$95,039	$96,500	$97,500	$98,500	$99,500
Individual Clients - Tax Planning	$34,561	$36,000	$37,200	$38,300	$39,200
Individual Clients - Finance Consulting	$25,921	$26,500	$27,500	$28,500	$29,000
Individual Clients - Other	$12,960	$13,500	$14,500	$15,500	$16,000
Subtotal Cost of Sales	**$490,562**	**$497,267**	**$506,050**	**$514,000**	**$520,700**

19

4.2.1 Sales by Partner

As the projection shows, we track revenue by partner, but a significant amount of the total revenue comes from the billing of the staff itself. Craig Moore will be retiring in the year 2004. The detail for this table is included in the appendices.

Sales by Partner

Sales	2000	2001	2002	2003	2004
Franklin	$215,300	$223,000	$230,000	$234,000	$236,000
Moore	$191,600	$200,000	$207,000	$150,000	Retiring
Benning	$189,000	$195,000	$202,000	$210,000	$230,000
Sonnett	$175,300	$184,500	$189,000	$195,000	$200,000
Cummings	$176,100	$185,000	$190,000	$196,000	$200,000
Williams	$171,600	$178,000	$186,000	$192,000	$200,000
Other	$481,100	$554,500	$796,000	$1,133,400	$1,618,000
Total	**$1,600,000**	**$1,720,000**	**$2,000,000**	**$2,310,400**	**$2,684,000**
Average	**$228,571**	**$245,714**	**$285,714**	**$330,057**	**$447,333**

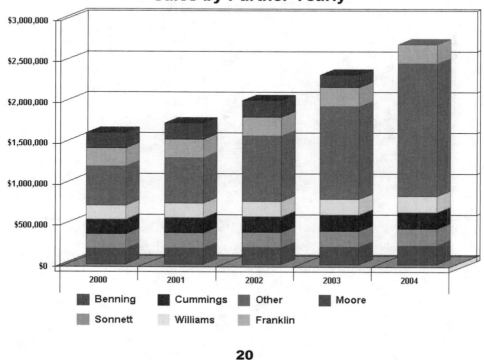

Sales by Partner Yearly

20

4.2.2 Sales by Segment

Our most important markets are our "large" and "growth" business clients. We have made strides to focus on revenues from these more profitable and faster-growing segments. This lowers the dependency on our "individual" client base, and our goal is to continue this focus for the future.

Sales by Segment

Sales	2000	2001	2002	2003	2004
Large Business	$672,850	$702,000	$815,000	$889,000	$1,000,000
Growth Business	$538,500	$516,000	$600,000	$694,000	$900,000
Individuals	$388,650	$502,000	$585,000	$727,400	$784,000
Total	$1,600,000	$1,720,000	$2,000,000	$2,310,400	$2,684,000
Average	$533,333	$573,333	$666,667	$770,133	$894,667

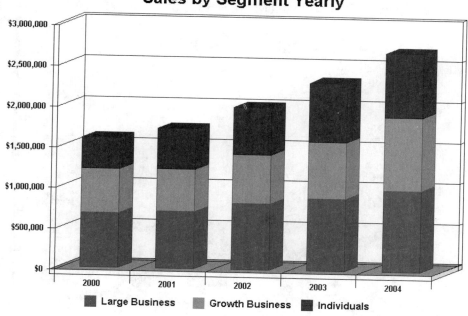

Sales by Segment Yearly

21

4.2.3 Sales by Specialization

Our three targeted areas of specialization in medical/health, dental, and lodging represent a relatively small portion of total income, but these are some of the most profitable accounts for the firm. These areas also offer the possibility of ongoing monthly billing opportunities to spread billing throughout the year, versus the heavy concentration of activity around the tax schedule. Manufacturing still represents a significant number of annual billable hours, but the low to no-growth rate no longer makes this an attractive segment.

Sales by Specialization

Sales	2000	2001	2002	2003	2004
Medical/Health	$27,200	$309,600	$380,000	$472,500	$550,000
Dental	$24,000	$275,200	$340,000	$405,000	$500,000
Lodging	$192,000	$223,600	$280,000	$337,500	$400,000
Manufacturing	$64,000	$68,800	$60,000	$67,500	$75,000
Individual Revenues	$304,000	$550,400	$620,000	$652,500	$67,500
Other	$988,800	$292,400	$320,000	$375,400	$1,091,500
Total	**$1,600,000**	**$1,720,000**	**$2,000,000**	**$2,310,400**	**$2,684,000**
Average	**$266,667**	**$286,667**	**$333,333**	**$385,067**	**$447,333**

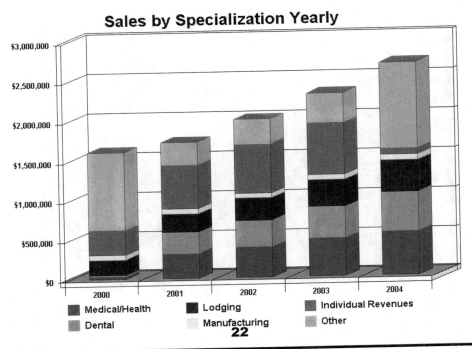

Sales by Specialization Yearly

22

4.3 Expense Forecast

Marketing expenses will correlate with firm revenues. This is based on a 2.5% factor of annual revenues. These expenses include any client development activities that promote the firm or any individual within the firm.

Each partner has an individual budget for his or her marketing activities. The combined totals for those by marketing line item are listed in the following table.

Marketing Expense Budget

Expense	2000	2001	2002	2003	2004
Advertising	$4,848	$5,000	$5,200	$5,400	$5,600
Dues	$1,940	$2,250	$2,450	$2,650	$2,800
Meals & Entertain.	$2,020	$2,400	$2,600	$2,800	$3,000
Printed Materials	$9,700	$10,800	$12,900	$14,500	$16,000
Public Relations	$5,600	$5,850	$6,350	$6,550	$7,200
Sponsorships	$6,868	$7,200	$7,650	$7,800	$8,400
Travel	$4,444	$4,600	$4,900	$5,200	$5,600
Web Support	$4,848	$5,500	$6,000	$6,800	$7,500
Other	$600	$600	$800	$1,000	$1,200
Total Sales & Marketing Exp.	$40,868	$44,200	$48,850	$52,700	$57,300
Percent of Sales	2.55%	2.57%	2.44%	2.28%	2.13%
Contrib. Margin	$1,063,715	$1,173,333	$1,439,500	$1,737,850	$2,100,000
Cont. Margin/Sales	66.48%	68.22%	71.98%	75.22%	78.24%

23

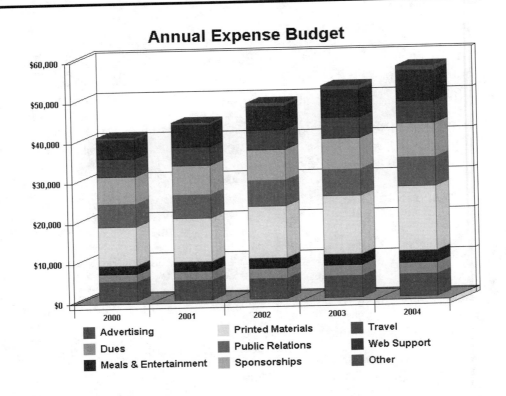

4.3.1 Expenses by Partner

As the table and chart shows, with additional information in the appendices, a majority of our expenses are managed by the seven partners, not by marketing. Each partner has an expense allocation that is overseen by marketing to deal with specific client development programs, marketing of expertise, and related projects. Marketing holds each partner accountable, although not always an easy task, to leverage these client development resources for the best return possible.

24

Expenses by Partner

Expenses	2000	2001	2002	2003	2004
Franklin	$5,850	$6,000	$6,500	$6,750	$7,000
Moore	$5,850	$6,000	$6,500	$6,750	$0
Benning	$5,300	$5,500	$6,000	$6,250	$6,600
Sonnett	$5,300	$5,500	$6,000	$6,250	$6,600
Cummings	$5,050	$5,000	$6,000	$6,250	$6,600
Williams	$4,900	$5,000	$5,500	$6,000	$6,500
Moore	$4,900	$5,000	$5,500	$6,000	$6,500
Other	$17,468	$6,200	$6,850	$8,450	$17,500
Total	**$54618**	**$44,200**	**$48,850**	**$52,700**	**$57,300**
Average	**$6,827**	**$5,525**	**$6,106**	**$6,588**	**$7,163**

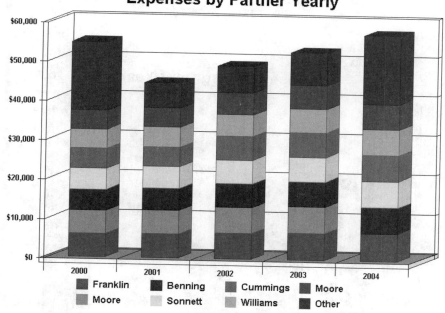

Expenses by Partner Yearly

Legend: Franklin, Moore, Benning, Sonnett, Cummings, Williams, Moore, Other

25

4.3.2 Expenses by Segment

Consistent with our growth strategy, a majority of our expenses are dedicated towards marketing to businesses rather than individuals. Our marketing expenses are targeted to communicate our expertise and how those skills will benefit business clients.

Expenses by Segment

Expenses	2000	2001	2002	2003	2004
Business	$26,900	$30,000	$34,000	$36,000	$39,000
Individual	$11,000	$12,000	$13,500	$15,400	$17,000
Other	$2,968	$2,200	$1,350	$1,300	$1,300
Total	**$40,868**	**$44,200**	**$48,850**	**$52,700**	**$57,300**
Average	**$13,623**	**$14,733**	**$16,283**	**$17,567**	**$19,100**

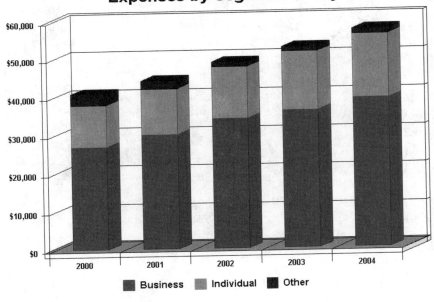

Expenses by Segment Yearly

26

4.4 Linking Sales and Expenses to Strategy

Our marketing expenses represent a small portion of total revenue generated, as illustrated on the following graph. Regardless, marketing-based efforts and our marketing expenditures must produce results. Our marketing director tracks this correlation and reports to the partners regarding our progress at our scheduled meetings. We expect to see our strategies impact the bottom line in the preferred areas. Our relatively conservative approach appears to be a good fit. An unexpected decrease in revenues will impact our marketing budget, and we will address this issue if required.

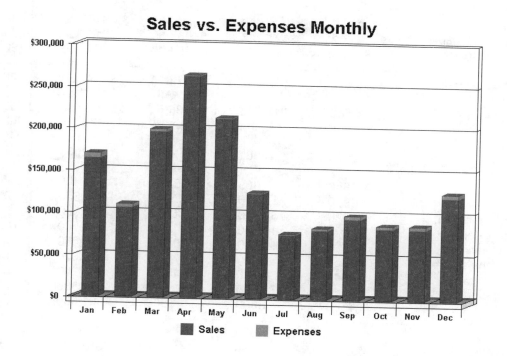

27

4.5 Contribution Margin

Contribution margins should increase as a result of these factors:

1. Increased efficiencies and revenue through specialization.
2. Increased efficiencies through use of our available technology.
3. Economies of scale from growth and better utilization of capacity.
4. More evenly spreading work out throughout the calendar year.

Contribution Margin

Sales	2000	2001	2002	2003	2004
Sales	$1,600,000	$1,720,000	$2,000,000	$2,310,400	$2,684,000
Direct Cost of Sales	$490,562	$497,267	$506,050	$514,000	$520,700
Other Variable COS	$4,855	$5,200	$5,600	$5,850	$6,000
Total Cost of Sales	$495,417	$502,467	$511,650	$519,850	$526,700
Gross Margin	$1,104,583	$1,217,533	$1,488,350	$1,790,550	$2,157,300
Gross Margin %	69.04%	70.79%	74.42%	77.50%	80.38%
Mktg. Exp. Budget	2000	2001	2002	2003	2004
Advertising	$4,848	$5,000	$5,200	$5,400	$5,600
Dues	$1,940	$2,250	$2,450	$2,650	$2,800
Meals & Entertain.	$2,020	$2,400	$2,600	$2,800	$3,000
Printed Materials	$9,700	$10,800	$12,900	$14,500	$16,000
Public Relations	$5,600	$5,850	$6,350	$6,550	$7,200
Sponsorships	$6,868	$7,200	$7,650	$7,800	$8,400
Travel	$4,444	$4,600	$4,900	$5,200	$5,600
Web Support	$4,848	$5,500	$6,000	$6,800	$7,500
Other	$600	$600	$800	$1,000	$1,200
Total Sales & Marketing Exp.	$40,868	$44,200	$48,850	$52,700	$57,300
Percent of Sales	2.55%	2.57%	2.44%	2.28%	2.13%
Contrib. Margin	$1,063,715	$1,173,333	$1,439,500	$1,737,850	$2,100,000
Cont. Margin/Sales	66.48%	68.22%	71.98%	75.22%	78.24%

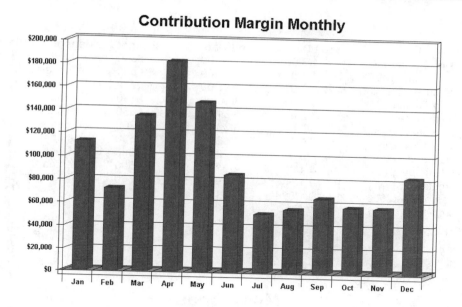

Contribution Margin Monthly

5.0 Controls

The focus of this marketing plan is to initiate action that will generate additional revenues for Franklin & Moore LLC and better position us for the future. These marketing challenges exist:

- We offer intangible "products."
- Our clients evaluate our capabilities based on things they see and hear.
- Marketing is not well understood or received within our profession.

Putting our marketing plan into action through the use of professional and credible techniques is what it is all about.

5.1 Implementation Milestones

The milestones graphic illustrates key implementation activities. Each partner understands the programs, and they have been assigned to oversee specific actions involved with each. We will track plan-vs.-actual results for each program. Status and progress will be addressed at the monthly partners meeting and reported to all of our staff in our monthly bulletin.

This will be a topic of focus at the end-of-the-year partners' meeting to evaluate annual results and validate or challenge the marketing plan for the upcoming year.

29

Milestones Plan

Milestone	Start Date	End Date	Budget	Manager	Department
Referral Tracking Program	1/3/00	1/14/00	$300	Chris	Admin.
Advertising Campaign (1999-2000)	1/1/00	4/7/00	$9,500	Lane	Marketing
Marketing Awareness Training	1/17/00	2/25/00	$1,250	Lane	Marketing
Fixed Fee Billing Training	3/6/00	3/10/00	$850	Thomas	Partner
Service Specialization-Cross Train.	5/22/00	5/31/00	$850	Pat	Staff
Review/Reprint Firm Brochure	6/5/00	6/30/00	$2,200	Lane	Marketing
Press Release "Expansion"	7/5/00	7/12/00	$1,800	Jan	PR
Mid-Year Review and Training	7/15/00	7/28/00	$850	Chris	Admin.
Client Contact Campaign	8/1/00	8/31/00	$1,500	James	Staff
Web Site Promotion	9/1/00	9/29/00	$3,500	Kim	MIS
Advertising Campaign (2000-2001)	10/1/00	12/31/00	$10,500	Lane	Marketing
Press Release "Plan Your Year"	12/11/00	12/18/00	$1,800	Jan	PR
Review Meeting	12/15/00	12/15/00	$500	Chris	Admin.

Totals $35,400

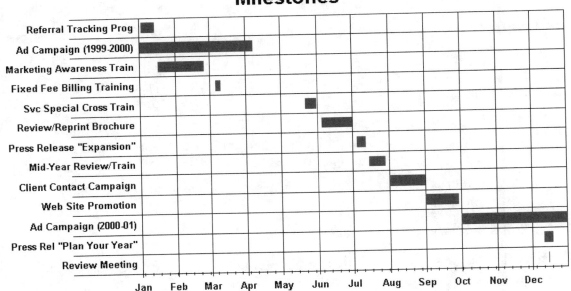

Milestones

30

5.2 Marketing Organization

Our marketing director heads our marketing efforts. This full-time position is responsible to oversee all marketing activities for the firm. Lane interfaces with each partner and staff member. This places Lane in the role of administrator and coordinator of marketing activities, but also requires training and individual development activities for each partner and CPA on our staff. We all recognize the challenge Lane faces as an employee, coach, and supervisor.

5.3 Contingency Planning

Industry or economic downturns - At this time, the targeted industries are experiencing solid growth in our area. If industry growth does not occur, we will re-examine our select industries and/or activities and change our focus and direction.

Loss of key resources - Losing key individuals in the firm could result in lost accounts or lost areas of expertise. We need to review our "Stage 2" strategy if any person in the firm should not be able to perform their function.

Online tax services - Competition from any geographic location may emerge from on-line services conducted by larger and better funded firms.

Tax law changes - Simplification of tax laws is unlikely, but will demand that we would take a "big picture" assessment of the firm's position, due to the significant overhead commitments that we have made.

31

This page intentionally blank.

Franklin & Moore - Appendix Tables

Table 4.2: Sales Forecast

Sales	Jan	Feb	Mar	Apr	May	Jun	Jul	Aug	Sep	Oct	Nov	Dec
Business - Tax Prep.	$45,640	$29,400	$54,600	$73,640	$59,360	$34,440	$21,000	$22,680	$26,600	$23,500	$23,240	$33,900
Business - Tax Plan.	$27,710	$17,850	$33,150	$44,710	$36,040	$20,910	$12,750	$13,770	$16,150	$14,280	$14,110	$20,570
Business - Gen. Consult.	$14,670	$9,450	$17,550	$23,670	$19,080	$11,070	$6,750	$7,290	$8,550	$7,560	$7,470	$10,890
Business - Other	$11,410	$7,350	$13,650	$18,410	$14,840	$8,610	$5,250	$5,670	$6,650	$5,880	$5,810	$8,470
Individual - Tax Prep.	$35,860	$23,100	$42,900	$57,860	$46,640	$27,060	$16,500	$17,820	$20,900	$18,480	$18,260	$26,620
Individual - Tax Plan.	$13,040	$8,400	$15,600	$21,040	$16,960	$9,840	$6,000	$6,480	$7,600	$6,720	$6,640	$9,680
Individual - Fin. Consult.	$9,780	$6,300	$11,700	$15,780	$12,720	$7,380	$4,500	$4,860	$5,700	$5,040	$4,980	$7,260
Individual - Other	$4,890	$3,150	$5,850	$7,890	$6,360	$3,690	$2,250	$2,430	$2,850	$2,520	$2,490	$3,630
Total Sales	$163,000	$105,000	$195,000	$263,000	$212,000	$123,000	$75,000	$81,000	$95,000	$83,980	$83,000	$121,020

Direct Cost of Sales	Jan	Feb	Mar	Apr	May	Jun	Jul	Aug	Sep	Oct	Nov	Dec
Business - Tax Prep.	$15,061	$9,702	$18,018	$24,301	$19,589	$11,365	$6,930	$7,484	$8,778	$7,762	$7,669	$11,180
Business - Tax Plan.	$9,144	$5,891	$10,940	$14,754	$11,893	$6,900	$4,208	$4,544	$5,330	$4,712	$4,656	$6,788
Business - General Consult.	$4,841	$3,119	$5,792	$7,811	$6,296	$3,653	$2,228	$2,406	$2,822	$2,495	$2,465	$3,594
Business - Other	$3,765	$2,426	$4,505	$6,075	$4,897	$2,841	$1,733	$1,871	$2,195	$1,940	$1,917	$2,795
Individual - Tax Prep.	$9,682	$6,237	$11,583	$15,622	$12,593	$7,306	$4,455	$4,811	$5,643	$4,990	$4,930	$7,187
Individual - Tax Plan.	$3,521	$2,268	$4,212	$5,681	$4,579	$2,657	$1,620	$1,750	$2,052	$1,814	$1,793	$2,614
Individual - . Fin. Consult.	$2,641	$1,701	$3,159	$4,261	$3,434	$1,993	$1,215	$1,312	$1,539	$1,361	$1,345	$1,960
Individual - Other	$1,320	$851	$1,580	$2,130	$1,717	$996	$608	$656	$770	$680	$672	$980
Subtotal Cost of Sales	$49,975	$32,195	$59,789	$80,635	$64,998	$37,711	$22,997	$24,834	$29,129	$25,754	$25,447	$37,098

Table 4.2.1: Sales by Partner

Sales	Jan	Feb	Mar	Apr	May	Jun	Jul	Aug	Sep	Oct	Nov	Dec
Franklin	$16,200	$14,500	$40,500	$71,500	$11,500	$9,500	$6,500	$6,600	$9,800	$8,800	$5,500	$14,400
Moore	$17,000	$12,800	$19,600	$70,500	$19,200	$9,200	$6,600	$6,800	$1,000	$8,800	$5,600	$14,500
Benning	$16,000	$10,200	$36,000	$66,500	$16,000	$8,000	$4,100	$4,200	$7,200	$4,800	$4,500	$11,500
Sonnett	$15,800	$9,200	$34,500	$62,500	$13,200	$7,800	$3,800	$2,600	$6,800	$4,200	$3,800	$11,100
Cummings	$14,800	$9,100	$34,000	$64,000	$12,850	$7,700	$4,200	$4,200	$6,400	$4,150	$3,700	$11,000
Williams	$14,500	$9,000	$34,200	$60,500	$13,000	$7,600	$4,000	$4,100	$6,200	$4,100	$3,600	$10,800
Other	$68,700	$40,200	($3,800)	($132,500)	$126,250	$73,200	$45,800	$52,500	$57,600	$49,130	$56,300	$47,720
Total	$163,000	$105,000	$195,000	$263,000	$212,000	$123,000	$75,000	$81,000	$95,000	$83,980	$83,000	$121,020
Average	$23,286	$15,000	$27,857	$37,571	$30,286	$17,571	$10,714	$11,571	$13,571	$11,997	$11,857	$17,289

Table 4.2.2: Sales by Segment

Sales	Jan	Feb	Mar	Apr	May	Jun	Jul	Aug	Sep	Oct	Nov	Dec
Large Business	$67,200	$46,750	$78,250	$102,400	$84,200	$53,100	$36,250	$38,400	$44,000	$39,400	$40,500	$42,400
Growth Business	$57,000	$36,750	$68,250	$92,100	$74,200	$42,500	$26,250	$26,250	$28,000	$26,000	$24,900	$36,300
Individuals	$38,800	$21,500	$48,500	$68,500	$53,600	$27,400	$12,500	$16,350	$23,000	$18,580	$17,600	$42,320
Total	$163,000	$105,000	$195,000	$263,000	$212,000	$123,000	$75,000	$81,000	$95,000	$83,980	$83,000	$121,020
Average	$54,333	$35,000	$65,000	$87,667	$70,667	$41,000	$25,000	$27,000	$31,667	$27,993	$27,667	$40,340

Table 4.2.3: Sales by Specialization

Sales	Jan	Feb	Mar	Apr	May	Jun	Jul	Aug	Sep	Oct	Nov	Dec
Medical/Health	$2,992	$1,904	$3,536	$4,624	$3,536	$2,176	$1,088	$1,224	$1,360	$1,224	$1,360	$2,176
Dental	$2,640	$1,680	$3,120	$4,080	$3,120	$1,920	$960	$1,080	$1,200	$1,080	$1,200	$1,920
Lodging	$21,120	$13,440	$24,960	$32,640	$24,960	$15,360	$7,680	$8,640	$9,600	$8,640	$9,600	$15,360
Manufacturing	$7,040	$4,480	$8,320	$10,880	$8,320	$5,120	$2,560	$2,880	$3,200	$2,880	$3,200	$5,120
Individual Revenues	$33,440	$21,280	$39,520	$51,680	$39,520	$24,320	$12,160	$13,680	$15,200	$13,680	$15,200	$24,320
Other	$95,768	$62,216	$115,544	$159,096	$132,544	$74,104	$50,552	$53,496	$64,440	$56,476	$52,440	$72,124
Total	$163,000	$105,000	$195,000	$263,000	$212,000	$123,000	$75,000	$81,000	$95,000	$83,980	$83,000	$121,020
Average	$27,167	$17,500	$32,500	$43,833	$35,333	$20,500	$12,500	$13,500	$15,833	$13,997	$13,833	$20,170

Table 4.3: Marketing Expense Budget

Expenses	Jan	Feb	Mar	Apr	May	Jun	Jul	Aug	Sep	Oct	Nov	Dec
Advertising	$624	$540	$504	$180	$204	$180	$180	$384	$432	$456	$540	$624
Dues	$1,200	$0	$0	$60	$0	$120	$0	$0	$360	$0	$0	$200
Meals & Entertainment	$260	$225	$210	$75	$85	$75	$75	$160	$180	$190	$225	$260
Printed Materials	$1,248	$1,080	$1,008	$360	$408	$360	$360	$768	$870	$910	$1,080	$1,248
Public Relations	$728	$630	$588	$210	$236	$210	$210	$450	$450	$530	$630	$728
Sponsorships	$884	$765	$714	$255	$289	$255	$255	$544	$612	$646	$765	$884
Travel	$572	$495	$462	$165	$187	$165	$165	$352	$396	$418	$495	$572
Web Support	$624	$540	$504	$180	$204	$180	$180	$384	$432	$456	$540	$572
Other	$50	$50	$50	$50	$50	$50	$50	$50	$50	$50	$50	$50
Total Sales & Mktg. Exp.	$6,190	$4,325	$4,040	$1,535	$1,663	$1,595	$1,475	$3,092	$3,782	$3,656	$4,325	$5,190
Percent of Sales	3.80%	4.12%	2.07%	0.58%	0.78%	1.30%	1.97%	3.82%	3.98%	4.35%	5.21%	4.29%
Contribution Margin	$106,285	$67,920	$130,591	$180,510	$145,119	$83,469	$50,178	$52,654	$61,639	$54,220	$52,878	$78,252
Contribution Margin / Sales	65.21%	64.69%	66.97%	68.63%	68.45%	67.86%	66.90%	65.00%	64.88%	64.56%	63.71%	64.66%

Table 4.3.1: Expenses by Partner

Expenses	Jan	Feb	Mar	Apr	May	Jun	Jul	Aug	Sep	Oct	Nov	Dec
Franklin	$750	$600	$750	$750	$150	$300	$300	$300	$300	$300	$600	$750
Moore	$750	$600	$750	$750	$150	$300	$300	$300	$300	$300	$600	$750
Benning	$650	$550	$650	$650	$300	$300	$150	$300	$300	$300	$500	$650
Sonnett	$650	$550	$650	$650	$300	$300	$150	$300	$300	$300	$500	$650
Cummings	$600	$500	$600	$600	$300	$300	$300	$300	$300	$300	$400	$550
Williams	$600	$500	$600	$600	$300	$150	$300	$300	$300	$300	$400	$550
Moore	$600	$500	$600	$600	$300	$150	$300	$300	$300	$300	$400	$550
Other	$4,040	$2,575	$1,890	($615)	$1,063	$695	$725	$2,192	$1,682	$1,556	$925	$740
Total	$8,640	$6,375	$6,490	$3,985	$2,863	$2,495	$2,525	$4,292	$3,782	$3,656	$4,325	$5,190
Average	$1,080	$797	$811	$498	$358	$312	$316	$537	$473	$457	$541	$649

Table 4.3.2: Expenses by Segment

Expenses	Jan	Feb	Mar	Apr	May	Jun	Jul	Aug	Sep	Oct	Nov	Dec
Business	$4,300	$2,900	$2,800	$1,000	$1,000	$1,000	$1,000	$2,000	$2,400	$2,400	$2,800	$3,300
Individual	$1,300	$1,200	$1,000	$500	$500	$500	$300	$800	$1,000	$1,000	$1,200	$1,700
Other	$590	$225	$240	$35	$163	$95	$175	$292	$382	$256	$325	$190
Total	$6,190	$4,325	$4,040	$1,535	$1,663	$1,595	$1,475	$3,092	$3,782	$3,656	$4,325	$5,190
Average	$2,063	$1,442	$1,347	$512	$554	$532	$492	$1,031	$1,261	$1,219	$1,442	$1,730

Table 4.5: Contribution Margin

	Jan	Feb	Mar	Apr	May	Jun	Jul	Aug	Sep	Oct	Nov	Dec
Sales	$163,000	$105,000	$195,000	$263,000	$212,000	$123,000	$75,000	$81,000	$95,000	$83,980	$83,000	$121,020
Direct Cost of Sales	$49,975	$32,195	$59,789	$80,635	$64,998	$37,711	$22,997	$24,834	$29,129	$25,754	$25,447	$37,098
Other Variable Costs of Sales	$550	$560	$580	$320	$220	$225	$350	$420	$450	$350	$350	$480
Total Cost of Sales	$50,525	$32,755	$60,369	$80,955	$65,218	$37,936	$23,347	$25,254	$29,579	$26,104	$25,797	$37,578
Gross Margin	$112,475	$72,245	$134,631	$182,045	$146,782	$85,064	$51,653	$55,746	$65,421	$57,876	$57,203	$83,442
Gross Margin %	69.00%	68.80%	69.04%	69.22%	69.24%	69.16%	68.87%	68.82%	68.86%	68.92%	68.92%	68.95%

Mktg. Exp. Budget	Jan	Feb	Mar	Apr	May	Jun	Jul	Aug	Sep	Oct	Nov	Dec
Advertising	$624	$540	$504	$180	$204	$180	$180	$384	$432	$456	$540	$624
Dues	$1,200	$0	$0	$60	$0	$120	$0	$0	$360	$0	$0	$200
Meals & Entertain.	$260	$225	$210	$75	$85	$75	$75	$160	$180	$190	$225	$260
Printed Materials	$1,248	$1,080	$1,008	$360	$408	$360	$360	$768	$870	$910	$1,080	$1,248
Public Relations	$728	$630	$588	$210	$236	$210	$210	$450	$450	$530	$630	$728
ponsorships	$884	$765	$714	$255	$289	$255	$255	$544	$612	$646	$765	$884
Travel	$572	$495	$462	$165	$187	$165	$165	$352	$396	$418	$495	$572
Web Support	$624	$540	$504	$180	$204	$180	$180	$384	$432	$456	$540	$624
Other	$50	$50	$50	$50	$50	$50	$50	$50	$50	$50	$50	$50
Total Sales & Mktg. Exp.	$6,190	$4,325	$4,040	$1,535	$1,663	$1,595	$1,475	$3,092	$3,782	$3,656	$4,325	$5,190
Percent of Sales	3.80%	4.12%	2.07%	0.58%	0.78%	1.30%	1.97%	3.82%	3.98%	4.35%	5.21%	4.29%
Contribution Margin	$106,285	$67,920	$130,591	$180,510	$145,119	$83,469	$50,178	$52,654	$61,639	$54,220	$52,878	$78,252
Contribution Margin / Sales	65.21%	64.69%	66.97%	68.63%	68.45%	67.86%	66.90%	65.00%	64.88%	64.56%	63.71%	64.66%

This page intentionally blank.

Appendix B:

ILLUSTRATION LIST

This appendix is a list of illustrations found throughout this book.

Table of Contents

Chapter 2: Marketing Plans

Chapter 4: Strategy is Focus

Chapter 5: Focus on Customer Benefits

Chapter 6: Business Forecasting

Chapter 7: Market Research

Chapter 9: Market Analysis

Chapter 10: SWOT Analysis

Chapter 12: Positioning

Chapter 13: Strategy Pyramid

Chapter 15: Segmentation

Chapter 16: Pricing

Chapter 17: Advertising

Chapter 20: Direct Marketing

Chapter 22: Sales Forecast

Chapter 23: Market Forecast

INDEX